W9-CGV-566

THE FIGURE IN THE CAVE AND OTHER ESSAYS

Richard Fallis, Series Editor

Irish Studies

Irish Studies presents a wide range of books interpreting aspects of Irish life and culture to scholarly and general audiences. Irish literature is a special concern in the series, but works from the perspectives of the fine arts, history, and the social sciences are also welcome, as are studies which take multidisciplinary approaches.

THE FIGURE
IN THE CAVE

AND OTHER ESSAYS

JOHN MONTAGUE

Editor
ANTOINETTE QUINN

Syracuse University Press

HOUSTON PUBLIC LIBRARY   R0127831579
humca

Copyright © John Montague 1989.

Syracuse University Press, Syracuse, New York 13244-5160

First published 1989
All rights reserved.
First Edition

INDEXED IN *EGLI 1990*

95 94 93 92 91 90 89   6 5 4 3 2 1

John Montague was born in Brooklyn, New York, in 1929, and grew up in County Tyrone, Northern Ireland. He studied at University College Dublin, Yale, Iowa, and Berkeley, and taught in the late 1960s in Berkeley and at the University of Paris, and at University College Cork from 1974 to 1988, taking up an appointment at SUNY Albany in the United States in 1989. He has published two works of fiction, *Death of a Chieftain* (1964) and *The Lost Notebook* (1988), as well as some nine collections of poetry, from *Forms of Exile* (1958) to *Mount Eagle* (1988). In 1974 he edited *The Faber Book of Irish Verse*, published as *The Book of Irish Verse* in 1977 in America, where his anthology *Bitter Harvest* appeared in 1989.

The paper used in this publication meets the minimum requirements of American National Standard for Information Sciences——Permanence of Paper for Printed Library Materials, ANSI Z39.48-1984.

Library of Congress Cataloging-in-Publication Data
Montague, John.
   The figure in the cave and other essays
   (Irish studies)
   Bibliography: p.
   I. Title. II. Series: Irish studies (Syracuse, N.Y.)
PR6063.05F5   1989   824'.914   89-4635
ISBN 0-8156-2478-6
ISBN 0-8156-0240-5 (pbk.)

Contents

III

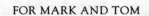
FOR MARK AND TOM

PREFACE

These essays have gone through several transformations. I always knew I would collect them; did John Jordan, that saint of McDaids, not once mischievously describe me as 'a full-time prose man'? My papers are full of little title lists but since, for me, poetry always came first, in the intervals between earning a living, reviewing and lecturing, I never had the push left to make a definitive selection. Several people came to my aid: Thomas Dillon Redshaw assembled all my reviews in a massive effort to make me more systematic. If God is good, or if Redshaw becomes God, I will end up with as many volumes as Goldsmith, or Randall Jarrell. Then Mark Waelder made a selection which ended up on the dying Liam Miller's desk, before it disappeared: all that is left of it is his chronology. Then, nearer home, Antoinette Quinn made her own rigorous but sensitive selection which you hold in your hands.

There is one general factor that colours these essays. Because of what Derek Mahon calls my mythical stammer there are few full-scale lectures here. I admire that discipline, the leap of the mind over the hurdles of a predetermined course, and have sat delighted as a Deane or Donoghue, an O'Brien or Brown, made the lecture rooms of UCD or TCD, or some Summer School, sparkle with ideas. But as the play of the mind, that Berkeleyan fountain, sank, I wondered often what was left, even for the lecturer. The fluency of the professional is shadowed by the anguished reticence of a Beckett or Wittgenstein, leaving the lecture room because they could not teach what they could not fully understand. In the myriad-minded Coleridge, the critic I most admire, confusion and coherence co-exist: no word is final except the always renewed text, which the critic should serve as enthusiastic mediator.

As for method, I cling to the old-fashioned notion that most of the best criticism is by writers, from Samuel Johnson to John Berryman: they know by training what they are talking about. Writers who are sure of their own gift can often show a warming generosity towards fellow craftsmen; what is regarded as envy is often dismay at disproportionate success, which fuels still further the paranoia of the neglected. It may be hard to realize it now, but when I was starting out all Irish poets were in a state of stunned isolation, except for Louis MacNeice.

So many of my earlier essays were strategic, attempts to get respected elders back into print, to recreate a fertile context. My publisher in the sixties was Timothy O'Keeffe, then with MacGibbon & Kee, and he accepted my case for a collected Hewitt, as well as embarking on a fraught attempt to assist the ageing Kavanagh. But not only Irish writers were invisible to the then British establishment: Tim also shared my admiration for another neglected elder genius, whom he affectionately nicknamed Red Hugh MacDiarmid. O'Keeffe was also aware of the transatlantic time-lag: 'American Pegasus' may seem obvious now, but despite the polemical anthology of Alvarez there was, and still is, little appreciation of the complexity of the American poetic adventure in this century. This, and other promptings, led him to remedy one great omission by publishing William Carlos Williams for the first time in England: another master of the idiom of the ordinary.

I am proud to be associated with the publication of these writers and salute the practical generosity of my English publisher. Meanwhile, back in Ireland, Liam Miller was working to make the later Clarke more widely known, also partly against his will. And he would assemble faulty but useful editions of Devlin and Fallon. I am glad that Irish poetry is now better understood, and given the grace of more leisure I would like to examine some of the themes that concern me most deeply, like the implications for the tradition of courtly love of our modern dispute between the sexes. What happens to the love poetry of Yeats and Graves when the Muse, the White Goddess, disdains her role? What can poetry say when history and politics are stained with violence, those ultra-modern techniques of disintegration and sudden death now so commonplace in Ulster? And I have still to do justice to that gentle prophet Oliver Goldsmith, who has become for me what Henry Adams was for R. P. Blackmur, an example and an albatross. I have already started a mosaic of praise to the fellow writers I have admired, amused glimpses of whom emerge through these pages; another *Lives of the Poets?*

THE FIGURE IN THE CAVE

Young men (young women) ask about my 'roots'
As if I were a *plant* . . .

I can't see it. Many are wanderers,
both Lawrences, Byron, & the better for it.
Many stay home forever: Hardy: fine.
Bother these bastards with their preconceptions. . .

I'd rather live in Venice or Kyoto,
except for the languages. . .
                              (John Berryman, 'Roots')

'With all my circling a failure to return': but to where? I was born in
Brooklyn, St Catherine's Hospital, Bushwick Avenue, in 1929, the
year of the Depression. I returned there in the mid-1980s at the
insistence of a journalist from *Newsday* ; I feared to find the usual
run-down brownstone. To my astonishment there was more left of
the neighbourhood than of Garvaghey. Yes, there was the local
cinema with its matinée of monsters and Mickey Mouse. The
wooden Indian was gone but one cannot expect one's childhood to
be preserved, like a doll's house; or a Montague museum. And yes,
there was the library, steps upward to a wide room full of books
with, wonder of wonders, some of my own! And when I climbed the
steps to the platform of the old El, I instinctively reached for a
larger, taller hand. The trains must have been more sedate in my
day, not scrawled with graffiti like action paintings, but, as a
sympathetic critic has suggested, 'All Legendary Obstacles' could
only have been written by someone whose infancy was full of the

1

rumble of trains; likewise 'The Cage' and 'Last Journey'.

And my first church was not Garvaghey chapel, where most of the Montagues lie buried, but a big Brooklyn church built by the dimes of Irish emigrants at the turn of the century. In its font I was baptized, fidgeted through mass with my family, until the funeral of my godfather, John Montague, bootlegger and quondam bush-league gangster. My Aunt Freda declares I got it all wrong in 'The Country Fiddler' and that he would not be let off the boat in New York until he played a jig on the gang plank for the waiting crowd. I remember him as large-hatted, cheerful and kind, but I hear no music in the background. Instead the sound of many voices, sometimes quarrelling, the clink of glasses. And then the sounds die away because, without his help, we could not survive as a family. So my two elder brothers were sent home to the small town where they had been born, resuming their Fintona lives after only a five-year break in America. In Derry the children were shared out, and I went home with my aunt to become the last Montague, in the male line, to live in Garvaghey.

Garvaghey! I suppose that name is associated with mine, forever or nearly. I think of those few years from four to eleven as a blessing, a healing. My aunts wisely kept me at home for a year from school until I adapted to local ways, and no longer spoke of our Protestant neighbours, the Clarkes, as from the next block. I explored the mountain, roving farther and farther with my dogs, to the mass rock at Altamuskin where I stayed with Aunt Anne, or the endless slope of the Pole Hill, Slievemore, with its view as far as Monaghan. There was a hazel grove where the Lynchs and I cleared a secret meeting place and the little river where we guddled trout, bathed buck naked, raced or jumped in the meadow like the boy Fianna. When later I read the Collected Wordsworth of my Uncle Thomas, dated 1903, it all swam back. To visit Dove Cottage finally was like coming home to where another bewildered boy had lost and refound himself in nature, like an Indian brave.

Then there were my summer holidays with the O'Mearas in Abbeylara, County Longford: their father had courted my Aunt Mary when he taught in Rarogan School, before Ireland was divided. There the hills flattened and the rivers widened, flowing sluggishly from lake to lake. And instead of trout we caught pike and perch from the Reillys' rowing boat. And there were village games: the tall echoing concrete of the ball alley, where the Widow Farrelly's foxy-haired son sank butt after butt, and the pitch-and-toss school in the evenings where Padna Hyland cursed and cursed. *O le nostalgie du pays plat!* I tried to pay homage to this drowned world in the second section of *The Dead Kingdom* which is also meant to be a homage to Oliver Goldsmith, country bumpkin *and* cosmopolitan. As well as an introduction to the strange ways of the South, the O'Mearas became my second family; there was a girl and boy nearly my own age whom I could love and quarrel with, as I could not with my distant, townie brothers. Flamboyant presents arrived to remind me of my American past, Red Indian outfits and cowboy chaps and Colts. And a pair of boxing gloves: I set up a gym in our barn where we pummelled each other and sparred with a swinging sack of grain. I date my love of boxing from then, the Billy Conn-Louis fight, the Reverend Henry Armstrong who held three titles, the two Sugar Rays, the bruised dignity of Tommy Farr or 'Enry Cooper, who did so well against Cassius Clay. As Gerard Lynch said at my Aunt Freda's wake: 'If those gloves could talk –'

At the age of eleven I was sent to St Patrick's, Armagh, partly to distinguish me from my brothers at Omagh CBS, partly because my aunts hoped I might follow the example of my Jesuit Uncle Thomas, or Cardinal MacRory from Shantavney, whose mother was a Montague. And religion did fascinate me; there were bibles as big as ledgers at home, my grandfather's copies of books by Cardinals Manning and Wiseman. An altar boy, I might have been drugged by the incense, the glorious ritual that heightened our country lives, but something warned me off. Those five years in Armagh were the most cramped of my childhood; just as I was learning to play with the healthy girls of Glencull I was enclosed in the black chill of celibacy. True, there were glories; the cathedral bell chiming over our heads every quarter, the ceremonies of Holy Week; but I would have exchanged all the rituals of Rome for a kiss from a girl. Someday I will exorcise it enough to forget and forgive, but at the age of sixty, images from that little hell on the hill haunt me, too harsh for long contemplation. I know many of the priests of the Armagh diocese as friends, but some as school bullies. Bitterness is a negative emotion unless you can enlarge it to a macrocosm, like Dante, whom I still read against the grain because of my unease with the Roman version of our Western faith.

I am blessed, I think, with a resilient, basically optimistic spirit. Whatever about my earliest years, only twice has my resistance really sagged: when the barrenness of Yale afforded no lift to my already depressed state, coming from Ireland, and, again, when in my early fifties I had no longer the energy to transform the narrowness of academic strife in Cork with my own private sources of release. In both instances the sterile aspects of academia came to the fore because my comic zest had wavered. It was my sense of humour which saved me in Armagh, allied to a strong sense of purpose; I felt there had to be a way out of that frustration, the swish of the cane in the dean's study, the priests patrolling the corridors at night, the endless walking around the Junior or Senior Ring. So when I was pressed on the question of vocation, the *summum bonum*, I felt I would first see if the world held any real attractions before renouncing it. Girls were constantly on my mind: I wrote long letters to a convent girl in Lurgan whom I had only met briefly on a train, but whose image loomed warmly in the chill air of St Vincent's dormitory. And when I courted Maureen Canavan after a *feis* in Ballygawley, kissing and fondling on a low bridge opposite the RUC barracks, I had material for endless letters, praising her small ears, the cloud of her fair hair. We met all that summer after college was ended, but as my stammer came back I let our relationship drift.

That last year of the war, however, brought a growing sense of release. Going to the speech therapist in Belfast once a week, which also meant a film before I caught the last train home, prepared me for a city again though I was never to know Belfast in the way I would know Dublin. The elation of speaking in debate, if only for a few months; the excitement of the first All-Ireland College championships; swooning over stars I saw in the films I escaped downtown to revel in – Betty Grable, whose legs were insured for a million dollars, Joan Leslie in *Hollywood Canteen*– a fascination connected with a sense of my lost life in America, and which probably led to my first job as film critic of *The Standard*.

So to Dublin in 1946, thirty years after 1916. My eldest brother Seamus, who had been a medical student there, following my uncle Frank Carney, was very persuasive in our Fintona family conference. While I thought of becoming a civil engineer, slide rule and all, it had become obvious that my talents were literary. And

Dublin was where the newspapers were, and the Abbey Theatre. If I thought about writing it was to be a journalist, or a best-selling novelist like A. J. Cronin or Maurice Walsh: *The Keys of the Kingdom/Above the Door* was about my level, although I had tried to read in the Russian novel. And poetry was something on exam papers, where it would remain until I met my poet contemporaries.

I travelled to Dublin by stages, the last being by train from a station near Abbeylara. Or was it a long-distance bus coming from Granard? I think it was the latter, but in any case Uncle John O'Meara left us off at the stop about two miles away. Us, because Aunt Freda came with me, and delivered me to Mrs Crinion's door at Chelmsford Road, Ranelagh. Perhaps the vision of Aunt Freda, a solid woman of her own age, endeared me to the corseted bulk of Mrs Crinion, but now I had my share of a little room upstairs, with a view of the yard and a cold-water washbasin to wash in in the mornings. I shared with a medical student called MacCaughey from the Barr Mountain outside Fintona, who was nearly as naïve as myself, though in his Second Year. He had come over to see us in Fintona to enquire if he could share with me, Mrs Crinion's being already known to us through my elder brother Seamus. It meant I had a companion from not too far away in the North, from what had now become my second home.

For although Freda travelled up with me to Dublin, and managed a few days' holidays, including an evening at the Theatre Royal, Babs de Monte and the Royalettes, Ted Heath and his Big Band blasting, I was moving away from the fields of Garvaghey. My mother sent a Northern Bank cheque for my board each week, plus a little pocket money, and I spent most of my holidays with her, for Fintona had a billiards room and a dancehall, some companions nearer my own age. And it was that adolescent world I was seeking now, determined to enjoy myself after the restrictions of Armagh. While I found university life daunting, and a little depressing, there was the wider world of Dublin outside, on a far larger scale than Fintona and Omagh. At long last I might find some pleasure, some adventure, and although I had found few companions at the university in my classes, there was the anonymity of the city to lose myself in, slaking my thirst for romance in the artificial light of dancehalls and cinemas.

I made few friends because, socially, I was at a complete loss:

there was no link between St Patrick's, Armagh, and where I now found myself. If I had gone to Belfast there would have been some fellow Armagh students at Queens, and others dotted through the city like John Kennedy, whose father was a bookie, but there was less than nobody in Dublin. I found my own lonely paths, accompanied by a boy from Derry, who also had a stammer, or a nervous hesitation, though much less drastic than mine. Self-absorbed, I skulked from classroom to library, watching the girls, waiting for the release of the evenings, when I would wander the melancholy, foggy streets.

My problem with my southern contemporaries was that they all knew the ins and outs of their little society, had homes to go to, if they were from Dublin, had already had their future paths drafted and discussed by parents. They were the sons and daughters of the first middle class of the Irish Free State, already affiliated by birth to one or other of the major parties, Fine Gael or Fianna Fáil. It could have been Tweedledum or Tweedledee as far as I was concerned; elections were distant things for us in the North, all the more because of the War which had dwarfed local party politics, which in any case were simple. We were Nationalists, they were Unionists, and cars called to bring all the electors to the polling booths. I was so ignorant that I did not know that the Treaty Debates had taken place in one of the double lecture rooms of Earlsfort Terrace, and no-one bothered to explain their significance to me. Among my classmates, Donal Barrington was already on his way to becoming a brilliant lawyer. Commerce students like Brian Lenihan and Charles Haughey were heading towards politics. I knew nothing of where they came from, Belvedere, Clongowes or Rockwell, so how could I know where they were going?

More mystifying to me than their certainty was the negative gloom of those who did not want to belong, who had seceded inwardly from the values of the state. Anthony Cronin was their leader, a brilliant orator from Enniscorthy, who could hold the L. and H., or Literary and Historical Society, spellbound with his speech on 'Jem' Larkin, the final touch a red rose solemnly laid before him. With his cronies he drank in the bars near college, Dwyers and Hartigans, and the Green Bar. He was joined by Pearse Hutchinson, already a published poet, and by his contemporary, a year younger, John Jordan, also from Rathmines. Most of the intellectuals came from the less grand schools, especially Synge Street in Dublin.

They bothered me because I thought I was an intellectual myself, with my good marks in English and History, and my furious reading from books bought cheaply on the quays where I searched the book barrows. And to my surprise I had got a first in nearly everything in my First Year, which I immediately attributed to my genius and not to the better schooling I had received in the North. But these Guinness-swilling, lecture-avoiding, gambling layabouts seemed to know something which I did not, something which the brighter girls, who were often the more pretty, appreciated. They controlled *The National Student*, the student magazine which had fostered so many Irish writers, back to James Joyce. They had the swaggering arrogance of a clique to which I, a star student, had no claim; that their comradeship was based on a social anger and genuine hurt was something it would take me years to understand, although I carried an even more potent variant in myself. Their bible was *The Portrait of the Artist*, their avatar and hero James Joyce, whose work would shortly have its cathartic effect on me as well.

It was near the end of my first year, I think, when I attended a meeting of the English Literature Society. Although I resented the presence of the enemy, who controlled it, I could not but be fascinated by the atmosphere. There, one of our future diplomats, Brendan Dillon, gave a paper on *The Portrait* which stirred me so strangely that I went and bought the book. For someone of my background who had suffered through a strict Catholic upbringing, it was like a case study of my own little psyche. Now at last I had been shown what was wrong with me, what was wrong with us, with our country. The process of independent thinking had now taken root, and the danger of arrogant solipsism.

I have already commented on this period in my preface to the revised *Poisoned Lands*, and indirectly in my fictional memoir *The Lost Notebook*. Growing more distrustful of academic success, I slowly acceded to the ranks of the alienated, the wild ones. So while I was not always at ease with my contemporaries, I am grateful to them for their embodiment of the importance of poetry. Tony Cronin's zeal brought me to Auden, while Hutchinson was a walking library already fluent in several languages. At an Arts

Ball in the Metropole Jordan rebuked me for my levity: 'In the atomic age, John, youth is no longer light-hearted.' The shrillness of *Envoy*, the slow sinking of the second version of *The Bell*, became part of a melancholy period in Irish letters when we experienced what Cronin called 'the infinite bitterness of being young', insular existentialists isolated in a post-War world.

Was such negative gloom necessary? I wish it had been easier, and comfort myself that frustration when young may stoke a later head of steam. And did (future Bishop) Frank Lenny not spot the change in me? 'I hear you have discovered your vocation': not priest, but poet.

I tackled Cronin about what seemed to me his harsh view of things, and he answered disarmingly that it was because he was so defenceless. Helping to bring Kavanagh back into the limelight, a process which ended in his legal crucifixion, left little time for anyone infected with the Irish thing, like Clarke, whom I also found fascinating. Had he not read me out on Radio Éireann, poems subsequently published in the old-world *Dublin Magazine*? After three years' flight I finally found, with Kinsella and Liam Miller of the Dolmen Press, a working relationship based on the thrust of common ideals. Liam especially had a rich generosity which transformed work into adventure: he seemed not to have a mean bone in his body. And if Tom now looks like an Assyrian king, then he was devastatingly funny, hard-working but hilarious, sharing my distaste for those who had prematurely baptized them-selves as poets, 'the knowingness of them'.

I think I now understand why *Forms of Exile* (1958) took so long to crystallize when young poets nowadays are 'exploding like bombs' (to use Auden's brilliant but dubious phrase). There was too much of a backlog of confusion for an early start: Brooklyn-born, Tyrone-reared, Dublin-educated, constituted a tangle, a turmoil of contradictory allegiance it would take a lifetime to unravel. And the chaos within contrasted with the false calm without: Ireland, both North and South, then seemed to me 'a fen of stagnant waters'. And there was no tradition for someone of my background to work in; except for the ahistorical genius of Kava-nagh, just across the border, there had not been a poet of Ulster Catholic background since the Gaelic poets of the eighteenth century. So when I describe myself as 'the missing link of Ulster poetry' I am not only joking, for, hard as it may be to understand today, there was no Northern dimension to Irish literature then, no question of going to Belfast for someone like myself, when even to get a little *bourse* to finish *The Rough Field* took nearly half a decade. I made a dutiful call on John Hewitt, but he was as ill at ease as if I had come from Mars, which was what West of the Bann was for even literary Belfast. My southern contemporaries were just as un-comprehending: I remember a sly comment in *The Irish Times* that reading my essay on Carleton, after the book by Benedict Kiely and a BBC blast by Kavanagh, gave the critic the uneasy feeling of being followed around by 'wee men'. Were the northerners going to become as clannish as the Corkmen? Even a friendly father-figure like O'Faolain found my northern twang a little ludicrous.

Austin Clarke rang me up, however, when he read 'The Sean Bhean Bhocht', recognizing that I had come home to base, begun to speak of the people I had grown up with in Tyrone, who had never before achieved the dignity of verse. But that was a compli-cated legacy and there was no point in my pretending either that I was going to stay down on the farm, or that farming was not doomed as a natural way of life. Aunt Freda dated my acceptance of Garvaghey from the day I raced home, late and breathless, saying I had been 'kepping' the cows, who had taken fright because somebody 'coped' a cart. I love the rhythms of speech, the northern which gives us access to Scottish literature, from Dunbar to MacDiarmid, the flattened vowels of the midlands which toll through the melancholy of *The Deserted Village*, the deflating Dublin dryness of a Kinsella or Behan, the extravagance of Mun-ster speech with its Irish base, rolling as the French spoken around me here in what used to be Languedoc. Only the West has not spoken to me.

It is surely time that someone came out against Kavanagh's nar-rowing notion of parochialism. Garvaghey gave me a glimpse of the old agricultural pattern but I am not going to lie and say that life is going on: I have watched my neighbours live through an agricul-tural revolution as drastic as the Enclosure Acts. There are local pieties, of course: the children of Glencull School did a video on me, and I am the laureate also of Abbeylara and receive many little tokens from Longford. And when I pass through New York I stay in Brooklyn, and the friends gather. Any place where you have lived, loved and suffered is your parish, as Pembroke Road was for P.K., or Herbert Street for myself. Heaney and I still have family homes in the North to which we can dander back for family occasions, but it is hard to think of Belfast as a parish, especially since no-one has put it on the map, as Joyce did for Dublin. Belfast is of interest as a microcosm of the tensions that rack the end of our century, the wall between the Shankill and Falls a miniature of the Berlin Wall, its sectarian strife a simpler chart to read than Beirut, the pastor Paisley a Protestant version of the Ayatollah. We are caught in a blind alley of history, and while one can appreciate the high comedy of urban intellectuals discussing the poetic equivalent of the old Abbey's peasant quality, it is a cop-out from the complications involved; a roots racket. Let me be more specific.

The only one of my books so far that has been a complete flop is A Chosen Light and I now find that historically interesting. My first wife had moved me back to Paris in 1961, and while I was, as always, entranced by the city, and found my stories were going well although no one wished to print them for large sums, I worried a little about the poetry. I showed her a sequence, overlapping with Poisoned Lands, when she asked how the work was going. She read the sheaf, and handed them back to me, without a word. 'What's wrong?' I asked, 'are they bad?' She hesitated: 'Do you really want to know?' I nodded. 'Of course they're good: you will always have style, but none of you will ever be able to write about the country the way Kavanagh did; he lived it! Besides, there has been enough cowdung in Irish poetry. Why don't you write about something you're living with?' 'Like what?' 'Like me!' she said, putting her hands on her bosom, so to speak.

The sequence, 'All Legendary Obstacles', opened my next book, the poems she read are in the second section. The irony is that I was editing the poetry of Patrick Kavanagh in the background, and clearing the way for a vision of the rooted poet to replace that of Yeats. Meanwhile The Rough Field was also being ploughed or excavated, a cross-fertilization between the longer Irish poems I admired, from The Deserted Village to The Great Hunger, and my fascination with modern experimental poetry, from Pound to the 'field theory' propounded by poets as diverse as Duncan, Snyder and Olson; Duncan had followed the discussions of the physicists who were the real pride of Berkeley. But my subject matter kept me on course: I sleep-walked through *The Rough Field* like a medium transcribing a familial and, by extension, tribal message, keeping faith with the burden of that vision for a decade. Where did it come from, why should I be the chronicler of what happened the lost intentions of the O'Neills? In my foster home at Garvaghey, as well as the family Wordsworth there was a large green volume on the earls of Tyrone and Tyrconnell and although, like Umberto Eco and the reconstructed medieval version of Aristotle's Comedy in his library, I can't remember reading it, it must have crossed my little beaver path.

There was also a copy of *Moore's Melodies*, signed by my grandfather and godfather. Who were these John (Mon)tagues? Every time I stir a genealogical stone a wild ambiguity appears. A cousin writes from the Mint in Washington, disappointed to discover that we were all Tagues, and I remember Aunt Brigid speaking with a rare fury, because I had brought back word from Altcloghfin 'to tell Biddy Tague I was asking for her' – '*never call me that again,*' she cried. I have played upon our change of name and am delighted that in the original Irish *taidgh* means 'son of the philosopher, poet or fool': I claim all three. But like the poet/genealogist of an old Gaelic family, another cousin stalks me after public readings in the North, triumphantly producing an old volume. 'I have the family history worked out,' he says: 'the Duke of Manchester had two sons who fought on opposite sides at the Boyne. Sir James of Cloghfin Castle was pardoned because of his brother William, and he took an Irish name, Tague.' Barney Horish, my guide to the lore of Garvaghey and now a gentle eighty-six year-old, partly goes along with this and, like Yeats sighing to be Duke of Ormond, I enjoy the idea, although Cousin Tommy's ultimate proof lacks historical weight. 'Look at the Montagues,' he says, 'the men never did a tap of work; they let the women do it for them, and lay back reading and talking and drinking, like lords.' True enough, in the parish of Errigal Kieran the Tagues are famous for the 'larnin'; known in Altamuskin as 'the raving Tagues', they have produced a long line of distinguished clergymen and finally, a class of a poet.

But what of Michel de Montaigne, whose tower is just across the way from where I write and with whom I share a birthday, and probably a character? My pull towards France manifested itself as early as 1948 when I cycled with a copy of Rimbaud in my knapsack from the battlefields of northern France to the Côte d'Azur. In that dance of choice and chance that constitutes a life it was the first decision which I took completely on my own, without knowing why. Brooklyn and Tyrone were chosen for me, Armagh and Dublin as well, although there I had begun to play my part. But in that first and many subsequent journeys I have rarely been disappointed, especially in the way each region has its own quality, tangy as a cheese, or the aroma of a great wine. Their controlled hedonism, their care for the earth that nourishes them, heartens me, although Paris and even French country life is changing. And their rich poetry has run underground, away from its audience, a far cry from the days when Éluard and Aragon were public figures.

Uncompleted tasks fascinate an author as much or more than his achievement. Will I be able to weave all my French translations together? What patterns will my love poems finally form? Both my wives were French, and my two daughters are bilingual, tri- if you include their Munster Irish. So I feel a natural affinity with the French attitude towards love which goes back to our poetic ancestors, the troubadours, and combines the ideal with the practical. Has my sense of experiment exhausted itself (*Mount Eagle* is full of sonnets)? In my files is a wilder, more sprawling version of *The Rough Field*. There is an ode to the Moon, and when the astronauts land there they find Johnny Danaghy sitting telling stories. My father reappears as a La Tène warrior, and David Jones mourns over these islands, and so on, with everything assumed into a final vision from Slievemore.

This is an age of self consciousness, raised to the level of art in Pal Bellow's (to use Berryman's affectionate term) novels such as *Herzog* and *Sammler's Planet*. There the confusion between author and main character, between fiction and autobiography, is part of the charm, for why should a writer abandon his hard-won views in a world where all seek direction? And few of us have refused the ritual exposure of the interview which, like the public reading, is part of publishing. Indeed, in a comic but also frightening way, appearance on television has become the necessary accolade, endorsing the public image of Behan as a drunk, Kavanagh as a sage, when the reverse was also possible. Even a literary Garbo like

Samuel Beckett confesses shyly to having a TV, but 'only for the games, of course, and only when Ireland was playing'. And if such rigour is impossible I, for one, would not begrudge my old companion a re-run of one of the comedies he loves and which he cannot easily slip in to see in a public *salle*.

There is a natural hesitancy about disclosing the hiding places of one's power, but after sixty one is conscious of certain patterns, the figure in the cave, to echo late James. Why do stones mean so much to me? It was after visiting the grottoes of the Dordogne that I began my Mexican fantasy, 'Death of a Chieftain': I was there recently and the sensual thrill of entering the earth still vibrates. On the walls of Cougnac, as little known as Seskilgreen, there were drawings of mammoths and elks which strangely resemble Barrie Cooke's cover etching for *Mount Eagle*. I sat in a flooded bar as our ship toiled through The Devil's Hole off Cornwall and translated Guillevic's long poem in short stanzas on Carnac where he was born. The green waters heaved outside, but that is a rhythm that speaks to me as well: I wrote 'Like Dolmens' watching Kenmare Bay, 'The Trout' after a morning looking into the Dordogne, 'The Well Dreams' where? Bury me under a standing-stone beside a well or spring, with a fish, trout or salmon *icythus* cut in the stone. Meanwhile a bird circles overhead, an eagle with a lark on its back? I accept the Celtic/Hindu idea of natural rhythms. I accept the North American Indian notion that God speaks through nature, the oldest values in the world as Snyder says in *Earth Household*; which we violate wholesale.

Thus music means much to me; the structure of *The Rough Field* reflects years of debate with O Riada, and my experience as a founding director of Claddagh. Old Irish music threads through the poem but there are also parlour songs, the silvery sound of the papal count which soothed our post-Treaty limbo land, drifting through *The Dead Kingdom*. But the larger units there are a homage to the symphonic structures of late nineteenth-century music, Brahms and Mahler, Bruckner's Eighth where the mountains seem to dance. I like the mathematical mind of the composer, believe they are born with a sense of the essential harmonies which is gradually drowned by the cacaphony of our world. There is perhaps a sticking-point there. I admire the researches of Boulez or Gerald Barry but the most accessible modern music is jazz in its many forms: the old bump and grind routine of Calumet City, the throb of the big instrument of Mingus in the Black Hawk in San Francisco, the cool alto sax of Paul Desmond, the jagged edge of Black Panther jazz, the classical training of Wynton Marsalis. I am delighted that Cork is now venue for one of the great jazz festivals where I can listen to sounds familiar from New York's Blue Note or Ronnie Scott's. Put a drink by my side, turn the lights down and that music up –

Some writers can pass in this world, the mighty blues rhythms of Canadian poet Barry Callaghan, William Kennedy in his films and novels, the purist canon of Larkin; nearer home, Longley and Simmons, the mind-blowing of Durcan and Muldoon. Music has many modes: in my northern home I watched my cousin John, an almost Russian baritone, breaking the family piano with a hatchet. The strangled jangle of chords might have impressed Arche Shepp, or John Cage. Perhaps we are too fixed in our ideas of form and sound when Moore shows that everything has a shape, Messiaen that everything has a sound.

Artists can be great company; and I am not just thinking of my wife's glowing mandalas. I got to know Morris Graves and Barrie Cooke in the Ireland of the early sixties; a nature-worshipping Zen monk from Fox Valley, Oregon, and a Jamaican-English hunter and fisherman. I couldn't afford Morris, but the first work I bought was a wonderful watercolour of two trout by Cooke, and then I didn't even know the sign I was born under! Their works have surrounded me since; there is a room in Grattan Hill dedicated to Hayter's vision of the universe as a net of energies, a vision coinciding with mine. Because of the physicality of their discipline, outings with them tend to be abundant and varied. A day with Cooke on the Nore haunts me with such richness. After sliding down the mill-race at forty miles an hour he was calling for me to help net a salmon when I saw a swan sailing down a branch of that great river, while a mother waterhen ushered her brood across into the swan's path. The salmon leaped, Cooke cursed, the valiant mother hen set off, a tiny feathery missile, to ward off the mighty bird. The rhythms were as glorious in their simplicity and complexity as a great sporting match, a driving jazz session, the Mozart concerto I am listening to on *France Musique*. When the veil lifts, of pain or misunderstanding, I catch glimpses of unity, a rich harmony that manages to accommodate disturbance, discord.

All this I seem to have been early aware of. I once wrote a playful variation on the usual child riddle:

> Who has a father, but is fatherless?
> Who has a mother, but is motherless?
> Who has brothers, but no family?

Myself, of course; losing a family and a country in one sweep must not have been easy, although for long I suppressed my earlier memories. The first proposition is probably at the root of my veneration for older writers of genius. I lost my letter of introduction to Ezra Pound in St Elizabeth's and did not feel confident enough to call on Wallace Stevens at Hartford, but the year at Yale was very confused and lonely. I later sought out MacDiarmid, Robert Graves, David Jones, and already knew Austin Clarke – four masters concerned with the matter of these islands. Graves was also writing in a tradition of love poetry going back to the *amour courtois* which began here in the valley of the Dordogne, a tradition in which I also inscribe myself, with modern hesitations. But I was always fond of my literary fathers, in verse and prose, and they have usually returned the compliment. In helping to get Kavanagh and Hewitt back into print I was also trying to recreate a context in which Irish poetry could flourish naturally once again

The second proposition is at the heart of *The Dead Kingdom*, and probably most of my love poetry. The last has influenced my sense of literary comradeship: I like the French idea of a fertile literary community and would not wish anyone to go through what I endured as a young writer. The unselfish generosity of our great father figure, Yeats, seems to me an ideal that has been temporarily lost, but would Irish writing have world-wide respect but for him, serving as focus for both activity and reaction? From *The Dolmen Miscellany of Irish Writing* (1961) through my 1974 Faber anthology to *Bitter Harvest* (1989), the Scribners anthology, I have tried to present the best of my contemporaries. It is in this context that I find the element of self-seeking in the northern thing depressingly close to *Ulsterkampf*, when our giant forbears, Yeats and Joyce, have given us the freedom of the world.

And outside Ireland I belong to several interlocking groups of

15

writers, quite naturally, the Irish branch, so to speak. I worked with the highly disciplined Snyder in Berkeley and at the weekends would ride pillion on his motorbike across the Bay Bridge into North Beach for a rich time of relaxation and reading. In Gian Carlo's, the San Francisco MacDaids, you might meet Jack Spicer, one of the first to cross linguistics and poetry, while Robert Duncan came sailing by in his Yeatsian cloak, his cast eye in a fine frenzy rolling. Was it luck or destiny that I walked in on a scene where poetry was briefly centre stage, with electric public readings, often with music, jazz or Country Joe and the Fish. Robert had just published his great trilogy, *The Opening of the Field, Roots and Branches* and *The Bending of the Bow*, and his broodings on the neglected H.D. were ramifying into eternity. How curious it was to have gone as far as San Francisco to find someone who believed in magic like Yeats, and who persisted in the great romantic vision of Blake and Shelley!

Compared to the Mountain-Red and marijuana-fuelled readings in the Bay Area, Paris has always taken poetry with mandarin concern. I find it strange that the flowering of French poetry in the twentieth century, with masters like Jouve, Char, Ponge, Michaux, Perse, has not been appreciated: a real anthology of modern French poetry would be staggering in its range. Again, I have been lucky in my contemporaries, beginning with Esteban who lived just across the way from me in the rue Daguerre. I have translated many of them but they have repaid the compliment handsomely with a selected poems in French for my sixtieth birthday, translated by six poets. There is also a splendid selection from Bordeaux produced by a poet/publisher who calls himself William Blake & Co. If there are very few English among my friends it is, alas, because of the Little Englandism of the Amis generation. I have shared interests with Tomlinson, sparred with Davie, and feel I understand Hughes, but not since Auden has there been a talent which deploys the resources of the great English tradition which I once learnt, and now teach and read with passion.

An astonishing and heartening development is the way the American dimension is being restored to my life in my later years. If, as some psychiatrists argue, it is the first three years that are crucial, then a lot must have already happened to me before I was sent, following an old Tyrone tradition, into fosterage. I came upon a cache of letters once, dealing with those Depression years, written from Brooklyn by my Uncle John: it was a rough time. An old tabloid clipping describes how the family were rescued from being gassed by my eldest brother Seamus, coming home from school: the baby is described as still chortling in its cot. I have no doubt that the separation from my mother, whatever the reasons for the decision, is at the centre of my emotional life, affecting my relationships with women, shadowing my powers of speech: my stammer broke out for the first time after she returned to Ireland. But though to understand, however dimly, is to begin to forgive, a writer should not forget, and my American past keeps surfacing. A journalist in the *Herald Tribune* turns pale on meeting me in a Paris bookshop; his father worked with mine on the New York subway, would cover for him when he went on the tear, rescue him, scoop him up, bring the Brooklyn equivalent of the wheel-barrow. 'My mother was terrified of Jim's late night phone calls,' said Charley Monaghan.

Brooklyn is dotted with people who share aspects of my early experience, including a poet Charles Martin, and I have always read people like Whitman and Crane with grateful recognition. And with American poets, like those I met in Iowa in the halcyon days of the Workshop, from Berryman to Dickey and Snodgrass, or much later in the releasing freedom of San Francisco in the sixties, with Snyder and Duncan and MacClure, I have always felt a strong sense of kinship, the shared adventure of modern literature, to which Ireland has contributed so much as well. And yet I have been reluctant to stay there until now, taking the greenbacks without plumbing the responsibility involved. In 1956 I was stunned to see the Joyce manuscripts and portraits in Buffalo; now mine will be going to join them, as well as those of Graves, Dylan Thomas, and my dead friend Duncan: what more can I ask? With my first doctorate from SUNY followed by a reception from both houses of the New York State legislature, destiny seems to have decided to give me back my lost childhood in America just as my Tyrone background is being destroyed by bulldozer and bomb. Ballygawley is now as black a name as the South Bronx or Brooklyn.

It is like a fairy-tale, the little child who was sent away being received back with open arms. But while awed at the reappearance of this golden cradle to rock my dotage, I am grateful to have explored Ireland so intimately. Standing-stones and streams are not part of Brooklyn, nor are *cailleachs*. To judge by my contemporaries I would probably have been a writer, certainly a journalist, had I stayed in America. But who cut the long wound of poetry into my youth? Was it my mother who chose for her own good reasons to cast me off? She could have recuperated me when she returned, and I would have become as much a part of the fabric of northern life as my brothers in Fermanagh and Tyrone. But that would have been against my father's wish and I might never have really known the streaming hair of Aunt Brigid, praying nightly for us all? Or was it the strange figure whom everybody feared as a witch, but with whom I forged a real friendship? Speaking of my aunts she said, with a nearly Scottish burr: 'They're trying to teach the wee boy to be a gentleman, like his grandfather, but where will that get him?' Women are everywhere in my work, healing and harassing presences, the other half of an equation one spends a lifetime trying to solve. I have been trying to put my love poems together and am daunted by the complexity of responses involved, from old woman to girl child.

Fragments of confession is a Goethean formula, and I approach my future with the energy of gratitude: what were once obstacles are becoming miracles, and after years of ploughing rough ground I might be allowed a period of harvesting. For a rearing can be too drastic, despite Kavanagh's theory about all art being 'life squeezed through a repression'. There was a time, seeking through the strange volumes scattered around Garvaghey, that I identified with the child martyrs, knives plunged in their proffered breasts. Henri Michaux describes how his imaginary tribe, Les Hacs, rear their artists 'in an atmosphere of terror and mystery. . . the Hacs have arranged to rear every year a few child martyrs, whom they subject to harsh treatment and evident injustices'. That dolorous discord, that forlorn note, still calls but something sustained me through those harsh, uncomprehending years. My amphibian position between North and South, my natural complicity in three cultures, American, Irish and French, with darts aside to Mexico, India, Italy or Canada, should seem natural enough in the late-twentieth century as man strives to reconcile local allegiances with

18

the absolute necessity of developing a world consciousness to save us from the abyss. Earthed in Ireland, at ease in the world, weave the strands you're given.

It has been a golden autumn in Mauriac, the hamlet near St Emilion where we now spend most of our holidays when we are not in West Cork. The *vendange*, or harvest of the grape, is in progress, and great machines lumber between the rows of vines. It is a far cry from when I nearly passed out with the heat as I and my Derry friend snipped the champagne fruit. We worked all day and danced at the cafe in the evenings: now there is only one organized Fête, but a neighbour will pass in the evening with a basket of grapes and at the weekend we gather to taste the first fermentation. I feel at home here as I did in Garvaghey during the War years when I helped to work the farm, potatoes, bog, hay and corn. A neighbour passing in his tractor, a Massey-Ferguson, salutes me at my desk under the lime tree. His lifted hand could be the same salute as the new farmers in West Cork give me while I work in the garden of Letter Cottage: modern farming is as mechanized as warfare. But the mixture of respect and complicity in his greeting represents what I love in France, where to be an artist is only an extension of the normal: '*Bonjour, maître, ça marche, le boulot?*'

I

1

TYRONE: THE ROUGH FIELD

The parish in which I was brought up lies in Tyrone, which a Belfast poet (John Hewitt) once called 'the heart land of Ulster'. A seventeenth-century survey, on the other hand, describes it as 'cold mountainous land', which may explain why it escaped resettling at the time of the Plantation. Across the road from our house were the crumbling remains of stables, a halt on the old Dublin-Derry coach road. And with its largely Catholic population (MacRory, MacGirr, Farrell, Tague), Errigal Kieran could still be taken for a parish in southern Ireland, artificially marooned. Most of the place-names were pure Gaelic: Garvaghey (The Rough Field), Glencull (The Glen of the Hazels), Clogher (The Golden Stone). On a clear day, working at turf on the top mountain, one could see straight down to north Monaghan.

But there were defiant differences. The post-van which came down the road was royal-red, with a gold crown on each side. And the postman himself was an ex-Serviceman who remembered Ypres and the Somme, rather than 1916 or the eighteenth day of November. In school we learnt the chief industries of Manchester, but very little about Cuchulainn or Connemara. And none of the farmers had enough Gaelic to translate the names of the townlands. A dark-faced fanatical priest tried to teach us some after school hours. I thought him a fearsome bore until I greeted the last Gaelic speaker in the area after mass one Sunday, and saw the light flood across her face.

The ordinary life of the people, however, took little stock of racial or religious differences; they were submerged in a preindustrial farming pattern, where the chief criterion was 'neigh-bourliness'. True, there were social differences which betrayed the historical cleavage. The depressed class of farm labourers were largely Catholic, just as the majority of the stronger farmers were Protestant. There were also the sexual fantasies which emerge when, as in the American South, two cultures rub uneasily to-gether. Pedigree bulls were mainly owned by Protestants: indeed, there was a curious legend that Catholic bulls were rarely as potent. And when I went to fetch the local gelder for our young bulls, it seemed oddly appropriate that he should take down his cloth-covered weapon from beside a stack of black family bibles.

But in the seasonal tasks that pushed the wheel of the year the important thing was skill, based on traditional practice. Turf-cutting, which began in late spring, revealed all the instinctive layers of a craft. First there was the stripping of the bank, the rough sods being saved for the back of the fire. Then the three-man team moved in, one to cut (using the traditional slane or flanged spade), one to fill (grasping the wet turves in rows) and one to wheel (emptying the barrow sideways, so that the turf fell uncrushed, but open to the sun). At mealtime, they sat around the basket in a circle, their hobnailed boots shining with wet, and talked of turfing teams of the past. 'John Donnelly and his two sons were the best team ever seen round here. They could go through a bank like butter.'

Cutting was only the first stage in the 'saving' of only one kind of turf. There was the spreading, tossing the barrow loads aside to dry. After, depending on their degree of dryness, came 'footing' and 'castling', placing the turf in structures through which the wind could whistle. Finally came the clamps or stacks from which they were hauled home in late summer to the barn. Even then skill was called for, the filling of cart or barn so that maximum space could be combined with least damage being a delicate question. And this careful building had to be repeated again in the dusty enclosure of the turf shed, although there were always hiding places near the roof, where the pigeons congregated on the beams. I loved to crouch in those high, dry corners, away from everything.

But turf-cutting was not as delicate a task as building a stack. To begin, a circle of stones and whins was laid, 'to let the air in under her'. Upon this the stack rose, the builder riding with it, to catch

24

and place the sheaves forked to him, until he slithered down to round the conical roof of thatch. One of our hands, slovenly enough in other ways, was held to be a master builder. In winter, when the thresher came, his kraal of stacks unpeeled in smooth slivers, like an orange.

Such tasks determined the character of the people, hard-working, frugal, completely escaping the traditional view of the Celt. Kitchens were usually well lit, with a dresser of delf along one wall, a curtained settle bed in another, a shotgun or fiddle resting on a third. But the centre was the great blackened tent of the hearth, where the crook swung, supporting a hierarchy of pots and pans. From this fire to the dairy, with its meal bins and churns, the farmer's wife bustled, until the men came tramping in for their evening meal.

The hearth was also the focus of the strongest custom in Ulster farming communities, the habit of dropping in, for a visit or *ceilidh*, after milking time. One rarely knocked, your approach being heralded by the dog's bark, the shadow crossing the window. Sometimes a worn pack of cards was produced, for a game of 'twenty-five'. Sometimes a song was called for, but the district was not rich in balladry, except for a version of the north-country 'Barbary Allen' and one or two patriotic songs, like 'The Mountains of Pomeroy'.

It was at such times that one came closest to the secret life of the countryside. Starting from practical details, the chat drew a thick web of speculation over local affairs: who was 'failing fast', who was threatening 'the law' on some neighbour, who was going to give birth (inside or outside the blanket, several of the children in the local school being illegitimate). Fact soon drowned in fancy: how so-and-so had broken his leg after ploughing down a fairy fort, how a B-Special's hair had turned white because he arrested a priest on his way to a dying man, how Father Mackey had put a poltergeist in a bottle.

For behind the flat surface of daily life beat memories of a more resonant past, now half-regretted, half-feared. When I was five I was brought to my first wake and remember the neat row of clay pipes beside the snuff and porter. But by the time I was going to secondary school my aunt had given up plaiting the rushy St Brigid's Crosses which used to hang over the lintel in kitchen and byre. Even barn dances had become a thing of the past, although I made the last one in the Fintona area famous when, climbing to get a swig of poteen from the local fiddler, I fell straight through the loft into a nest of squealing pigs.

For a long time Carleton's Tyrone survived in the remote areas, under the shadow of the mountains, but since the War the pace of change has become relentless. The replacing of the hearth fire by a stove dealt a blow not merely to turf-cutting and breadmaking (most farmers' wives now buy shop bread) but also to the practice of ceilidhing. The battery wireless was an endearing faulty messenger from outside, but with the arrival of electric light and television the Rough Field has become a part of the twentieth century. The old coach-road is now a magnificent highway, running straight as a die through the built-up valley. The public-house, surrounded by cars, looks like a roadhouse; the shop sells ice-cream to children from the pre-fabricated village where the road workers and lorry drivers (formerly farm labourers) live.

But one must avoid seeing all this through a haze of nostalgia. The last time I was back I was talking to a strong farmer in his byre. Behind us the milking-machine hummed, the pans and cylinders swaying under the cows' udders. He was lamenting the decline of neighbourliness, how farming had become mechanized, how the young had no time for anything but cars and dancehalls. Then a smile crossed his face, and he described how the oldest crone in the district had come down to see his television set.

She had a stick in either hand, and her bent over like a hoop. She came into the kitchen – we had to pull back the dogs off her – and she said she be to see the picture box. She sat in front of it for an hour and then rose to go, saying that a wee man you could turn on like that would be a great comfort on a cold winter's night.

[1963]

2

THE WAR YEARS IN ULSTER

I loved the War. It was a spectacular background to my small existence from the age of ten to sixteen. When it broke out I was still in Garvaghey School and my ambition was to be a pilot in the RAF. A past pupil was operating one of the big flying boats from the Erne base, and he looped over the school one day in an act of defiance and homage: he had not been a star student. His gesture is hidden in *The Rough Field:*

> a white Catalina
> From the Erne base (an old pupil)
> Rose out of a hole in the hedge,
> Sudden as a flying swan, to circle
> Over the school in salutation
> And fold into cloud again.

Another day, a damaged flying boat was towed down the Derry Road – it looked like an enormous prehistoric creature, a pterodactyl with folded wings. I was still at the Percy Westerman stage of reading, and collecting cigarette cards of battleships as well as fighting planes: I must have known every ship in the British navy as well as the make of every plane in the RAF. The day a Spitfire zoomed low over the sodden field behind our house was like a storybook come true; I yearned to be the goggled, death-defying pilot!

Those were the days of the Phoney War, as unreal as the troops I deployed on our parlour floor. I loved toy soldiers and had whole regiments of them, supplemented by spent cartridges kept for me by our Protestant neighbours; special occasions brought a new addition, a gun-carrier or a fighter plane. By the time I moved to

Glencull School the *Blitzkrieg* was on, and no one sang of hanging out their washing on the Siegfried Line. Like a commanding officer, I had a map, and moved pins to mark the progress of the German armies as they pushed through northern France and on to Paris. My letters to my cousins in Longford were full of war plans, and signed in true army style, Captain or Lieutenant or General (later, Field Marshal) Montague. I was neither pro-British nor Republican, just a boy living on the edge of a giant historical drama.

Not quite as innocent as that, perhaps. I was also at Glencull when de Valera declared against conscription for all of Ireland, and was aware of the relief this caused, especially among our Protestant neighbours. A schoolboy is not a very sophisticated witness, but it was noticeable that while many poor Catholics I knew, both in Tyrone, and my twinned southern county, Longford, joined the army (one came home in a sealed coffin, like the father in 'Clear the Way'), very few of the local Protestants did. In the evening they donned their black B-Special uniforms, drilled before the Orange Lodge, and pestered us on the way home from school concerts and parish plays. I am in a car with half the cast of *Professor Tim* when we are waved down by red torches, and questioned as to our identity. The harassment continues until the driver roars out in exasperation. 'George Allen, stop acting the clift! Are you being paid to not recognize your neighbours? Away and fight Hitler, where you're needed.'

The soldiers from 'the other side' that I knew of were mainly from the towns; the farmers could rightly argue that they did more at home. Ulster was a market garden for the British war effort, and every available field was under cultivation, including some that have since reverted to heather or forest. There were subsidies for everything, and I can still close my eyes and see Garvaghey, every field ploughed and sown, the children allowed to stay at home to help with the harvest, trim patterns of haycocks and golden stooks, summers spent working on the upper bog. Again there is a glimpse of this in *The Rough Field*, the last time that Garvaghey was still functioning as a real farming community, when

the stacks
Still rode the stone circled haggard

28

And the tall shed was walled high
And dry with turf, for the war years.

But the War effort also accelerated progress in farming: the mass
production of eggs (I sat with my aunt scrubbing them for sale) led
inexorably to the new model hens in their tiny concentration
camps, a chilling spectacle I tried to describe in 'Henhouse'. As the
War ended, the first Fordson tractors bumped through the lanes
and farmyards; the farmhorse, as well as the old style hen, was being
hustled into oblivion.

Our distance from the Continent made Ulster a natural train-
ing-ground; when the small boy in 'The Oklahoma Kid' goes to
town, he finds it packed with British soldiers. Sidney Keyes was
garrisoned in Omagh, and found Ulster an unhappy place, 'brooding, waiting', though his antennae were probably more subtle than
those of the class-conscious author of *The Valley of Bones*, Anthony
Powell, who detested the neo-Gothic castle in which he was
stationed (probably in County Down), beyond 'the grubby pubs of
a small, down-at-heel town a mile or two away'. 'At Castlemallock
I knew despair,' he writes, but his description of confused manoeuvres along that coast could have been of the kind of thing I
happily took part in. Rarogan Hill was taken over by a detachment
of British soldiers, and while they waited to be dislodged I ferried
billy cans of tea to them for twopence. It was still early in the War,
for canisters of gas were lobbed across the hedges, as well as the flat
smoke of blank cartridges. The laconic infantrymen found me
amusing and useful, with my specialized knowledge of the local
territory: I told them how the others would attack because I knew
how Dympna MacGirr sneaked up from her parents' house to meet
a foxy-haired friend of mine there, in an old cottage.

The threat of invasion never seemed real. We loved the grotesque snouts of the gasmasks we were issued with at school, but as
science-fiction playthings, not responses to a real threat. When I
first saw Belfast there was a barrage balloon floating over it, like a
swollen silver fish. But Belfast descended on us, in the form of a
dozen evacuees, children with a precocious vocabulary, and activity, that astounded our slower country minds. Big Billy might
mount the girls on the way up Glencull Brae, shouting 'whee!' as
he coped his willing victim in the ditch, and threw his leg over her,

but one of the Belfast boys took out his tool in class and pointed its pink top at the girls, who took a good look, while they protested. And the stories: 'There was a lassie from the Markets that took to wearing tin knickers whenever she went out with a soldier. Then she met one of the Royal Engineers.'

Sex was like a musk in the air, with Vera Lynn's voice, and Betty Grable's legs. Since I had to bring our cows to Coote's bull I was not backward on the technical aspects of the subject, but visits to Omagh, as in 'The Oklahoma Kid', accustomed me to the sight of soldiers groping girls in every cinema and alley-way. Catholic girls who went with British soldiers were liable to moral comment, sometimes ostracism, but the contraceptives clogged the drains in the morning, or floated down the Strule; where glass-bottomed boats had fished for pearls, there were now flotillas of finger-sized, semi-translucent balloons. The soldiers brought their own women, of course: Georgie Allen said the WAACs, pronounced Whacks, were great rides, if you could prise the British soldiers off them. Ruby Anderson joined up, and was rumoured to have been ridden by a member of the King's African Rifles, and wouldn't look at a white man, Protestant or Catholic, after.

There's a poem in all that; but hardly a delicate one, and Ben Kiely has written most of the stories. One aspect of the War which was not accessible to most of my northern contemporaries but slightly familiar to me was the way the South reacted. My holidays were usually spent with my O'Meara cousins in Longford, and I can testify that, in its own way, the Twenty-Six Counties was on a War footing. Uncle John's car was up on blocks, so now I travelled by bus to Tynan, and then by a turf-fed train to Cavan town where I caught another bus, if I was on time. Signposts were gone, school names blocked out, and in the local church hall, the LDF were drilling. My tall cousin Brendan, who played for St Mel's and the Leinster Colleges, kept his Lee Enfield beside his bed. At long last his little brother John and I had access to a gun: we watched from the benches as the men drilled and then imitated them in the garden. Large-scale manoeuvres were organized and we hung around, although Abbeylara was too small and sleepy to be a major target:

> So we learnt to defend
> this neutral realm,

each holiday summer,
against all comers. . .

What would have happened if Germany had invaded the South is only speculation: they would certainly have been confused for a while, like the Irish-speaking German spy who sauntered into Danny Mac's in Dingle and nonchalantly demanded, with a perfect *blas,* "a pint of whiskey". The Irish army was swollen with volunteers for the Emergency, and the Local Defence Force seemed to me more numerous than the B-Specials. It may be bias on my part, but I had the impression that they were ready to at least harry and hinder whoever came, using their knowledge of the bogs and mountains.

Meanwhile Allied officers took the train to Dublin to rest from rationing. The hotels welcomed them and, indeed, many were only returning home for holidays: two of Uncle John's past pupils were in the Commandos and dazzled Abbeylara with their account of training procedures, rolling sideways over walls so as to present no target, crawling on their elbows as through bales of barbed wire, illustrating how to gouge eye- and other balls. Again, they were not the most brilliant pupils, scholastically, but they now had special aptitudes, which did not protect them from dying in Normandy.

Even Field-Marshal Montague could see, however, that the South could not have held Hitler in open battle; it would have been a delaying action until a larger army came. As the Invasion troops mustered in Ulster, I moved from Garvaghey to Glencull School, three miles away. Open-sided American jeeps flashed by (one dropped into Shantavney bog, the driver slumped drunk and snoring as I cycled by in the morning), or a fleet of double-wheeled troop lorries. Then one day I came out of school and the Broad Road was crawling with tanks and clanking gun-carriers. It took three hours for them to pass, and it was a wonderful sight for a small boy. I tried to ride along the verge but ended up by taking the Hill Head Road, past Errigal Keerogue. But they were still clanking past our house, like a rally of steam-rollers, when I came out at Falban.

America's entry into the War decided my political allegiances: after all, I had been born there, a matter for confusion and pride. Hill's *History of the United States* became part of our curriculum in Armagh College but most of the boys welcomed another chance of seeing our traditional enemy flattened. Belfast had been bombed several times, which sent us scurrying to the air-raid shelters, but raiders rarely wandered inland. Still, there were

> nights in Armagh school
> When, cramped in mud shelters,
> We heard planes prowling overhead,
> Saw, across Belfast, the night-sky
> Swollen with fire, like blood.

And, of course, we knew all about rationing, especially of chocolate: a match against Monaghan or Cavan led to an orgy, like the Allied soldiers on leave, our pockets stuffed with Mars Bars and Milky Way as we chugged towards Goraghwood where the Customs Officers waited. But our progress towards the Ulster Championship meant more to us than the War; Iggy Jones flashing towards goal on a toe-to-hand run, Jim Devlin rising for a ball at full back. One frosty morning I heard that Roosevelt had died and it seemed to me the world had changed, but when we had a school debate on the War my attempt to describe its significance was lost in laughter when a lad from Keady referred to the King and Queen as 'Stuttering George and Bandy-Legged Lizzie'.

There was so much happening by this time that my chronology becomes a little confused. I was beginning to visit my mother now that I could cycle the seven miles from Garvaghey to Fintona, and a large contingent of Yanks had been settled in Nissen huts on the edge of Browne-Lecky's estate. They transformed Fintona life or, more exactly, revived and extended an old tradition. There is a peculiar saying, which you can interpret as you like, perhaps even as jealousy: 'I was never married but I was twice in Fintona!' To my naïve eye, the GIs did not seem to lack company in the town, but they were, by local standards, big spenders, and the women from the back lanes had never seen such glamour. But there was a charitable side to it as well; many of the more respectable girls took pity on these unlicked youngsters on their way to Omaha beach, and invited them home for tea and cake, only to find themselves writing for years afterwards to heart-broken parents, some of whom made the pilgrimage to the Ulster village which had briefly harboured their slaughtered sons.

Those were mainly young officers: the other ranks, since the supply of light of loves was numerically limited, drank as long as the

Military Police would allow them (the RUC kept carefully away). My granny's public house was popular because so many of us had been in the States, but I don't think they paid much attention to her politics. Both her sons had been interned during the Troubles and she was still a fanatic republican, listening intently to Lord Haw-Haw every evening. 'D'ye hear him; the English are getting it this time,' she enthused to some poor GI slumped over his drink: 'Hell slap it up them!' Polite, uncomprehending, they agreed with her unholy glee as she retailed Joyce's supercilious exaggerations; Coventry and London disintegrated in her Fenian dreams.

Old Browne-Lecky was as sceptical about his compulsory American visitors, the officers who had taken over his stately home. He told me in his quavering voice that they had disturbed his great-aunt by their bad manners. Although dead many years, she made a nightly tour of the Georgian mansion and greatly resented being challenged by a sentry. One night as she sailed past on her tour of inspection the baffled poor man fired right through her. According to Raymond, an actor of the old school as well as an aristocrat, she turned on her well-bred heel, and came back towards the sentry. 'Young man,' she said, waving a fleshless finger, 'whoever you are, and wherever you are from, you have no *savoir faire*. One simply does not fire on anyone, especially a lady, and especially dead, in their own home.'

Convoys on the Broad Road, Sherman tanks crushing our hedges, Yankee soldiers slumped in Fintona public-houses or hunting for women -- suddenly it was all gone, like a company moved to another theatre. We gathered around the radiogram in our gymnasium to hear news of the landings: 'This is the News, and John Snagge reading it. Allied troops landed this morning on the coast of Normandy.' Now I followed the race in the reverse direction, so that on my honeymoon years later I was able to identify Patton's route through Normandy, the sinister slitted shapes of pill-boxes, the floating harbour at Arromanches. A strange diversion for such an occasion but also an acknowledgment of the way that War had marked our world, geographically.

Although most of my fellow students had inherited a republican sympathy for Germany, we were still thrilled by such a massive adventure, the end-result of all the mysterious troop movements we had seen through the Ulster countryside. Cherbourg, Caen,

Cotenin, the Ardennes, Arnheim – it seemed the greatest cowboy chase of all time. Then Germany was breached and strange news began to reach even our childish ears. We were used to war films, like the piper leading the troops ashore in *Desert Victory*, but what was Mersa Matruh or the Siege of Tobruk to us unless you knew some poor neighbour who had died there? We did not belong to *This Happy Breed*, but when we were brought down to see the first newsreels of the prison camps I felt a chill more profound than propaganda. Our world had indeed changed; and what had seemed like a spectacle concealed a slaughterhouse. I tried to deal with it as humbly as possible in a poem, fifteen years later:

> That long dead Sunday in Armagh
> I learned one meaning of total war
> And went home to my Christian school
> To kick a football through the air.

I say humbly because violence is one of the central themes of our century: and only recently have we been really exposed to it, and then only in our northern crevice. I first heard about the atom bomb in a Protestant neighbour's house, where the wireless sat under the racked shotguns. The men were in for dinner, and after a minute the conversation returned to more mundane necessities. But I was deeply excited and troubled by a mixture of awe and fear. Because while I could accept war as some kind of a bloody game, remote from our local concerns, this was a direct challenge to the source of life; the seal had been broken. I remember rushing to Omagh to buy a special issue of *Picture Post*, and trying to work out the implications of Uranium 235. And in my files are poem after poem which try to deal with the problem posed by that satanic mushroom.

But though I made morbid pilgrimages to Oak Ridge and Los Alamos, as to Mulberry Harbour and the diorama of the landings nearby, I have yet to finish a poem about the atom bomb. The trouble in writing about nuclear dangers is that they present too good a subject, in the old-fashioned sense. Most of the poems I have read so far about the atom bomb have been, unconsciously, poems of praise, drawn to its dark power. If nuclear horror is only to be an excuse for rhetoric, however magnificent, then we should leave it

34

to more public media, like cinema, press and television. Thomas Kinsella, for example, dignifies 'Old Harry' with a moral complexity alien to his character: 'he was', said General Groves of Truman, 'like a small boy on a toboggan,' an all-American boy. So to compare the hapless inhabitants of Hiroshima and Nagasaki to 'the notorious cities of the plain' is a frightening inference. Apart from Alain Resnais, I cannot think of any artist who has found anything approaching a redemptive language to deal with what is, in a historical and moral sense, man's supreme challenge to himself; we have reached the end of the road, and must turn back. Already the terrible balance of power that has held the world back from a major war suggests that the sacrifice of the victims of Hiroshima was not entirely in vain.

I began by saying that I loved the War, but that small boy has had to live with its implications ever since. It is probably why, although I am a republican, I do not believe in physical force except as a form of resistance. It is as if I have spent half a lifetime trying to digest what man has done to man in this century, the way violence has been accelerated by technical progress, from the spectacle of an enormous toy balloon over Belfast to the deadly mushroom. Even my school stories went wrong: the dream of Jules Verne came true, but the moon was a political football, and the silvery super planes of P. C. Westerman were menaces that I would never wish to pilot. I may not be a convinced pacifist, but I am convinced that poetry must speak for man. Although

> I lived in Armagh
> In a time of war   the most dreamy
> Time of my life

I know now that it was not a dream but a nightmare, from which we must, indeed, try to awake.

[1979-80]

3

THE UNPARTITIONED INTELLECT

Yeats died in 1939, Joyce in 1941, a double blow to modern and Irish literature. In Tyrone I heard of neither event but we did gather around the green baize of our old Philco radio to hear Eamon de Valera's reply to Winston Churchill after the War: the vindication of that neutrality which made the South of Ireland seem so strange to a little Ulster boy like myself. Despite their Coronation jugs, my aunts were moved by memories of their youth, Sinn Féin and Cumann na mBan. Simple, stirring patriotism, a bony repudiation of Churchill's stammering rhetoric.

Wakes and weddings, I noticed, would be interrupted by intense discussion of the doings of this dark man; the Economic War, the giving back of the ports. Finally I saw him standing some rainy evening on College Green, droning on majestically about the Irish language, and the price of bread. It was the election of 1956, and I described it in a piece for the Ulster magazine *Threshold*, only to have my best phrase, comparing that lonely black-coated and hatted figure to a 'sacerdotal heron', censored.

So around de Valera a nexus of associations began to form, a symbol of dark intransigence, of fiery austerity. Investigating the South of Ireland also meant exploring his mind, of which it was partly the creation. No wonder Sean O'Faolain did two studies of this much-beloved despot, who aroused both hatred and total respect. The writers of the 1930s in Ireland were obsessed by him while acknowledging his power, like that portrait in Liam O'Flaherty's *Shame the Devil*.

The post-War South I discovered was a limbo land which made even the North seem lively. The tosspit and the concrete dancehall were the main distractions through the countryside. It was a land that was over 90 per cent Catholic, with a hundred thousand domestic servants, with late marriages, if ever, and half the population overseas,* and it was natural that the writers should withdraw. O'Faolain's story, 'A Broken World', is a post-Joycean vision of the bleakness of that little state, and I remember many a spat between him and Frank O'Connor and the advocates of our priest-ridden, censored country. All hail to their bravery, but it did them much harm; if you spend too much energy on a negative cause you will absorb some of it: Tsarist Stalin helped to make Solzhenitsyn into an old-fashioned Russian prophet, the scourge of the Revolution, a magnificent bore. 'You become', I partly agree with AE, 'what you contemplate.'

So the South seemed to me to be a procession of sad and broken poets and complaining novelists. Why should I not go and see the patriarch of all this misery, the great apostle of gloom himself? After all, we had a common destiny, being both New York born and then pitchforked by history back into rural Ireland. Winter, gathering darkness over Aras an Uachtaráin, the old Vice-Regal lodge. I have come for tea and tea it is; not a scent or glint of a whiskey bottle in sight. I try a little Ulster Irish; he is clearly under the impression that I am speaking a foreign language. I turn to Irish literature and, to my astonishment, he seems to know only Pearse. *Buile Suibhne* he has never heard of, or my ears lost his low tones: or *Aisling MacConglinne*. He accepts graciously that they are the two masterpieces of medieval Irish literature but seems to have expected me to bring copies. They are out of print for years, since the foundation of the State.

Desperately, I speak of the home areas I know best: Tyrone and Fermanagh, lost green fields. He does not know that the Foyle is also the Strule, where Omagh stands. He has heard nothing of Knockmany Hill and little of Clogher. I tried a joke about us both being born in New York. I said he had changed my life by his victory in the 1932 election because I came home in 1933. He seemed to take these as serious statements, not bantering homage. He had no feeling for his birth-place, he said. What would he have become there? Cardinal or Chief of Police?

*I take these grim details from Terence Brown's splendid study, *Ireland: A Social and Cultural History, 1922-1985*.

Twilight falling, his wife whispering in and out of the room, where was I, beyond intruding on a great ghost? There was a strange atmosphere in the room, strange but familiar. Was I in the presence of a parish priest? No, the aura was more powerful: and he was married. Was this, as his enemies declared, the great ogre, an Ayatollah of Ireland? No, he seemed distant, but kindly. An odour of chalk, of simple severity, of unassailable certainties – was I with the Dean of Studies?

Which brings us back to James Joyce. His is a Dublin-centred Ireland, dominated by the high drama of Parnell and his fall. De Valera's Clare is only distantly represented in the Gaelic ideals of Stephen's friend Davin, later parodied in the Citizen. But, although his world is pre-Independence, there is no doubt in his, or his characters', minds that Dublin is the capital of Ireland, of all-Ireland, because the concept of Great Britain *and* Ireland allowed for that, a position more definite than that of Edinburgh and Scotland now. Parnell, in any case, did not recognize such barriers between Irishmen, the Protestant patriot being an example of the open sensibility I wish to praise.

Because Parnell looks back to Thomas Davis and beyond that to the United Irishmen, old Si Dedalus and his Catholic cronies can recognize him as their uncrowned king, a Protestant *ard-rí* of a largely Catholic people. Was there not a song: 'We'll crown de Valera king of Ireland'? What Ireland? The even more stagnant and narrowing one from which Beckett fled, the ingrown toenail known as Saorstát na hÉireann? The minds of Joyce's characters are not as partitioned.

So it is fascinating to place Joyce beside de Valera, another lean and obsessive man – I almost said Manichee – who believed that he was chosen 'to forge the uncreated conscience of his race': political this time, of course. There is much evidence in *Finnegans Wake* that Joyce was intrigued by him, and rightly, because since Parnell no politician had been so sure that he understood the psyche of the Irish people, because it was his own. But the larger vision of Avondale was gone, and we are right to think of Ireland after Parnell as suffering a split in sensibility which the simplified dream of the boy from Bruree ignores.

The ironies are many and painful. The massive ritual of Roman Catholicism, the most universal aspect of Ireland, forms a large part of Joyce's vision. But his is not a peasant faith for a peasant people; his Jesuit training has placed him socially above the boots of the Christian Brothers whom he sees marching along the Bull Wall. Although he is our Dante, forging in imagined and angry exile the uncreated conscience of his race, he spurns the part of it from which de Valera derives his strength: 'I fear him. I fear his redrimmed horny eyes.'

So Joyce's view of his race is also exclusive. What race, indeed? Protestantism, either northern or southern, is not part of his vision, but neither is the dispossessed world of Corkery's Irish-speaking peasant. The first great voice of the Irish-Catholic consciousness in English, Joyce's achievement is based upon a repudiation of most of the ideals by which his countrymen lived. There is the fundamental difference between these two bony, implacable men: Joyce's proud definition in A *Portrait* of the nets he must fly by in the *persona* of Stephen is almost a definition of the Ireland de Valera was sustained by, sought to bring into political existence.

Together they can be seen as our long-delayed Dante, and his attendant Savonarola. De Valera did not initiate censorship, but he did not haul the books from the burning. He did not flee nets, he welcomed their embrace, cultivating their intensities of narrowness. Contemplating the contradictory visions of these two great Irishmen, what ideals can we offer for our country? Some critics, influenced by Corkery, would have us believe that Irish literature escaped the Renaissance. But James Joyce did not, and if Joyce is not Irish, where are we? 'All too Irish,' he said himself, meaning southern Irish Catholic, the only kind he really knew, but his Catholicism was more that of Rabelais than of Brother Rice. The negative Catholicism we practise is far from that of Italy and France, as far perhaps as Ian Paisley is from Luther's or Calvin's theology. Contemplating two forms of bigotry, the benighted Ireland over which de Valera ruled, whose list of banned books exceeded that of Rome and rivalled Russia's, and the Orange vision of Ulster as the last stand of the True Blues, who in his right mind would choose either? Both de Valera and Paisley are examples of the partitioned intellect, the result of that split in sensibility the country suffered after the fall of Parnell. Let us propose a greater vision, a creative synthesis to warm them together again in some life-enhancing embrace.

At the end of my *Selected Poems* (1982) is a sign, a device, the same as is on the cover of the *The Rough Field* in its third edition. In both cases it was chosen as a symbol central to my work, as an emblem to sport on a shield, not for battle but for courteous exchange, if you please, despite my republican background. It is the seal of the United Irishmen, a harp, of course. This harp is swathed in a motto: *It is new strung and shall be heard.* My purpose is that we should realize its various tones. I would link it remotely with the harp of Aeolus, the murmuring breath of Romanticism, but more immediately to the events in my own country. Richness and narrowness, the world and our province: we must have both. Or rather we must have them all, remembering what Seamus Deane has brilliantly diagnosed as 'the central fact of Irish tradition – that it is always an attempt to describe what we have yet to build'.

So I would like to introduce a new element into the discussion of Anglo-Irish literature, an inclusiveness towards which we might all aspire, a passionate welcoming, a fertile balance. The unpartitioned intellect is a sensibility which is prepared to entertain, to be sympathetic to, all the traditions of which our country can be said to be composed. I am thinking in terms of archaeology, history and religion. But why not football as well? Let us declare an end to all narrowness, in our thoughts at least. The unpartitioned sensibility should be able to accept, or listen to, the many voices, agreeable and disturbing, which haunt our land. 'The isle is full of noises', but they should be made to blend, as a symphony contains its dissonances, structures of healing.

An Ulsterman, ironically, can approach this ideal, an emancipated Ulster Catholic or a Protestant Jacobin. An Ulster Catholic has suffered from the narrowness of that northern statelet, and can recognize its mirror image in the South, however much more he feels at home. Liberal though the attitude towards Protestants was in the Free State, the peculiar equation of religion, race, and language was dangerously close to *Kulturkampf* – doctrinaire, loveless, life-denying.

So, adapting the motto of the Royal Irish Fusiliers, let us 'Clear the Way' to celebrate Armistice Day as well as Ivy Day. Should we not praise peace? Ireland runs all the way from the flints at Larne to the Boyne mounds, the harsh covenanting of Ian Paisley and the soothering vagueness of the southern politician. Ireland's children

40

lie buried on the Somme as well as in Kilmainham. Francis Ledwidge, mourning the execution of the leaders of the 1916 Rising while wearing the British army uniform in which he was to die, is a fitting symbol of the contradictory imperatives of our country. A man may make the wrong choice and still belong, if generosity can prevail.

[1985]

4

NOTES AND INTRODUCTIONS

i A PRIMAL GAELTACHT

All around, shards of a lost tradition:
From the Rough Field I went to school
In the Glen of the Hazels.

In the summer of 1970 I was lying on the side of a hill, looking at one of the loveliest landscapes in Ireland. I was just back from a short reading tour in America, where I had earned more in a month than a term's teaching at home would bring. But at no point in my journey, even crossing a sunlit campus after my morning's stint was done or relaxing in some heated pool, was I as happy as that May day on the slopes of Slieve Gullion.

Behind me lay the scattered stones of one of the two hill-top cairns. Its pattern was obscured by heather but that only made it seem a more natural part of the landscape. If the cairn was nearly four thousand years old, the small hills from which it was quarried were older, left by the glacier which melted to form the drumlins in south Ulster. Everything seemed to share that prehistoric timelessness: the stream that ran down the edge of the mountain path, the sheep that scattered as one climbed to the dark glitter of the Hag's Lake.

The Hag's Lake! Immediately I knew why this landscape satisfied me so much: it was only a more dramatic version of the landscape of my Clogher valley childhood. Near Glencull School was Seskilgreen, which I later found out to be one of the few decorated passage graves in Ulster: a plaster cast of one of its stones greeted me when I entered the National Museum in Dublin for the first time. And, beckoning across the valley, was the mysterious saddle shape of Knockmany Hill. I walked there one Sunday to discover what the locals called the Grave of the Dead Queen.

> But in high summer, as the hills burned with corn
> I strode through golden light
> To the ogham script of the burial stone. . .

There is a mistake in that poem, though an understandable one. Recently I heard a distinguished artist explain that the difference between early Irish civilization and the great civilizations of the Middle East was a matter of language; we have no idea of what our earliest ancestors spoke, or if they had managed to develop a system of writing. Ogham came much later, so that when I described the curious circles on the Knockmany stones as 'ogham script' I was committing archaeological heresy. But in another sense I was right, because one of the most fascinating things about early Irish is the way it enshrines earlier traditions. Take the name Knockmany.

One could explain it as 'Cnoc Maine', the hill of Manaig or Menapii, a tribe of the Belgae who travelled as far as Lough Erne; after all, they gave their name to the adjoining county of Fermanagh. But the local translation of the name is Ania's Cove, and Ania or Áine or Ana is the Danaan mother goddess, whose name is also found in the river Boyne, the Boan or Good Mother.

> And thou, great Anna. . .

I am beginning to sound like Robert Graves's *White Goddess*, but there is an extraordinary identity between the linguistic and archaeological evidence concerning Knockmany. The curious cup marks and circles have been described as the eyes and breasts of a mother goddess whose cult spread from Syria. I doubt if the late O. G. S. Crawford knew early Irish, but his eye goddess theory bears out the derivations I have suggested, since the same shapes are found at Newgrange on the Boyne.

So the least Irish place-name can net a world with its associations. At the foot of Knockmany is the little town of Clogher: according to one interpretation this means *cloch oir* or golden stone, a curious name for a bishopric. Not long ago, however, I came on a reference to a golden stone or idol called the Crom Cruach, or Crooked One, which was worshipped by the Goidels.

And sure enough there was supposed to be another, farther north, in the area of Clogher. . .

> From the Glen of the Hazels
> To the Golden Stone may be
> The longest journey
> I have ever gone.

What I am trying to say is that the Irish landscape is a kind of primal Gaeltacht, and that anyone brought up in it has already absorbed a great deal of the language. And to return to my Knockmany poem; when I wrote those lines about the hills burning with 'golden light', did I realize that I was crossing Bealtaine, the ridge of the god of fire? The racial aspect of a poet's inheritance should be unconscious as breathing. Where I was brought up, Irish is no longer a spoken language, but it is still very much alive in the place-names and the local idiom. Like Máirtin Ó Direáin writing of Aran, or Sean O'Riordáin from Cork, I must tap tradition where I find it, in my part of the landscape.

That taproot tells me that the last poets in my area, those from whom I naturally inherit, were the Gaelic poets of the Fews. Not far from where I was lying on the slopes of Slieve Gullion is Creggan churchyard: is it an accident that the only song I remember from school is Art MacCooey's 'Úirchill an Chreagáin'? . . .

> bím trathnóna ag Teamhair is
> ar maidin i lár Thír Eoghain. . .
> (At evening I'm in Tara and
> At morning in mid-Tyrone. . .)

In that aisling we find, perhaps, the debased, final version of the earth-goddess theme: it was then, due to political unhappiness, when the feminine, fertile land was identified with a national cause, that Irish poetry began to grow sentimental.

That poem, and that landscape, also provide an interesting example of unconscious literary partition. When southern Ireland achieved its local revolution, it began a Celtic *Kulturkampf* based mainly on the Munster dialect. There is only the most passing reference to the south Ulster school in Corkery's *Hidden Ireland*; Art MacCooey scrapes in on a footnote. And yet Peadar O'Doirnín,

44

Séamus Dall, Art and Cathal Buidhe were as gifted as many of the Sliabh Luachra poets, with the towering exception of the magnificently monotonous O'Rathaille. And their influence, in English at least, persists in a much more beneficent way; there is not that tendency to buck-lepping which mars the professional southern Irishman. Kavanagh's 'Art MacCooey' is a simple, though oblique, homage, and when I was editing his *Collected Poems* I came upon another early poem in which he regretted not having been born in Forkhill, O'Doirnín's home-place. I am not suggesting that Kavanagh studied these poets, but he was aware of their presence as the last poets to write in his part of the world.

Similarly, a more recent poet from the North like Seamus Heaney can describe *An Bunnán Buidhe* as his touchstone for the tradition (I am reporting a conversation but not, I think, betraying a trust). The important thing for Irish poets in English is not that we should hurry to the Gaeltacht, but that we should contact our common tradition through whatever of it is still alive in our own area.

[1970]

ii I ALSO HAD MUSIC

> The country people asked if I also had music,
> All the family had had. . .

Yes, music is part of my memories, part of my essential nourishment. One of the two aunts who brought me up played the harmonium in Garvaghey Chapel; we grouped around her in the choir-loft while the calor lamp hissed over the bowed heads of the worshippers below. During the War we had only candles, which guttered on the lid of the wheezing harmonium. Sometimes a pedal or note or pipe stuck and we sang bravely through the dissonance – was that an obscure preparation for my love of Stravinsky years later?

In Armagh, it was the same stately Gregorian chant, with the cathedral bell striking its solemn note every quarter. Our music master was a noble eccentric, an Englishman called William Holden whom we irreverently called 'Dickie Doh'. My inability to read even the simplest scales brought down his old-fashioned wrath on my head: 'What you need is a jolly good sixer!' (pronounced 'six-ah' – we were an improving school).

What strikes me now is the way I lost my sense of traditional music at college – or not truly traditional, but all we had at home. As we churned, my aunt and I sang 'The Blackbird', 'The Castle of Dromore' and 'The Spinning Wheel'. And no matter what house I went to in the countryside, Protestant or Catholic, I always used to sing, like my father before me. In the rafters of our kitchen an old fiddle rotted; my aunt wanted me to learn the violin at school but I could make nothing of it, briefly lost between two traditions.

Art music entered my life slowly. Eimar O'Broin was in the same class at University College, Dublin, and I was awed by such early purpose as he studied scores in class. But when my civilized friends led me to the Phoenix Hall, I was baffled. I liked the noise but it seemed remote from my experience; if I put on the Third Programme at home even the dog howled. 'What's that old stuff you're listening to. . . ?'

Still I persevered. In Vienna and Paris during a *wanderjahre*, disguised as a pilgrim, I went religiously to both opera and ballet. But my most real memory is of a horse coming on the stage in the Volksoper, and when my German girlfriend brought me to hear the Hamburg State Opera in Dublin's Gaiety I was as much impressed by the delicately exposed boozelems of the leading lady (which she seemed proud of unlike the Irish ladies of my acquaintance) as by the light energy of Mozart's music. Much later I would love his elegance, but my adolescent senses still responded more to the sight of the swans in *Lohengrin*, or to the Slavic chorus of *Boris Godunov*.

And yet my first published poem (a real horror, so I won't reveal where it was) was about playing the piano, and music is an influence on my work, whether in short pieces like 'The Country Fiddler' and 'The Siege of Mullingar', or in larger structures such as 'Patriotic Suite'. And to my surprise I find myself director of a music company, helping to write sleeve notes for a piping record, working over translations of Irish songs with Seamus Ennis, helping to name a musical group, The Chieftains, translating from the German for Bernadette Greevy.

Two things helped to open my ears. Part of my suspicion of classical music was of the kimd of people who seemed to thrive on it, well-fed, well-dressed snots who seemed to have no interest in any other art. (I exaggerate, but you must allow for what I now see to be a countryman's prejudice against an urban art). But after I had helped him with the syntax of an article on music, a friend presented me with an old Phillips 'Black Box', and I began to buy records. After a period of indiscriminate listening preferences began to weave their pattern – the symphonies and song-cycles of Mahler, the drive of Stravinsky (his 'Oedipus Rex' gave me back my Church Latin with a vengeance), the quartets of Beethoven.

The same friend, Garech Browne, reintroduced me to traditional music. It was like coming back to a home I had never known to see Paddy Moloney crouched over the pipes, or grave Willy Clancy. And to hear Seán Potts or Festy Conlon weave their way through 'Donal Óg', or another of the great slow airs. If I could usually only listen to art music alone, or with an intimate, I rejoiced in the communal aspect of Irish music as part of a heritage. And yet I know of no sound more lonely or more intense than that of Máire Áine singing 'Úna Bhán': all deeply racial art, like flamenco and fado singing, stirs the root of the spirit like a great poem. Irish poetry retreated to the cabins as the language faltered.

The music I prefer, it would appear, is that of infinite variation, like a Mahler or Bruckner symphony, or of quarter tones, like the great Irish songs. I find no difficulty in moving from the severest traditional to modern music, just as I can listen to Miles Davis or Charlie Mingus after the great Blues men. There is a tune of Denis Murphy's which he calls 'The Queen of the O'Donnells', though I am nearly sure it is a lament (*Caoine*, not Queen) for the Ulster family. Listening to its hesitating, wavering rhythms, which stop only to start again, is to experience the circular aesthetic of an art older than Western music. In the first version of *The Rough Field*, I place blocks of material against each other, in dissonance as well as harmony. But through the larger contrasts weave recurring images: a bird in flight, a zig-zag line (which could be a geographical fault or a physicist's notation of energy), a flickering light, a wave. If the content suggests that I sometimes see myself as successor to the last bard of the O'Neills, the structure is meant to be musical, in Mallarmé's sense:

we are at this point precisely to seek, when confronted by the breaking of the great literary rhythms and their scattering into articulated shudders

47

approaching instrumentation, an art of perfecting the transposition from the symphony to the book. . .

And then there are the songs and tunes that link the poem together, something that emerged poignantly in its stage performances. It was the last art of the Irish people and it disappears from *The Dead Kingdom*, which is full of the sentiment of the stage-Irish songs of McCormack, the nightingale who soothed our limbo land. But it is symphonic as well, the larger structures absorbing their melancholy. Two different shapes for two very different blocks of material.

[1971]

iii A NOTE ON RHYTHM

I believe very strongly that a poem appears with its own rhythm. When I was learning to write I practised all kinds of metre (including syllabics) and if a pattern emerges I try to fulfill it. But I think of a poem as a living thing, which one must aid, not forceps-haul into birth. This sense of the organic nature of a poem goes with a conviction that rhythm and line length should be based on living speech: I am sure that there was a relationship between Elizabethan language and the iambic line which no longer holds except as an example of how to harness an energy. The cant phrase about 'finding one's voice' has relevance when it means that the poet's voice is heard in the poem, not as an educated mumble, but with all the pressure of his personality and province behind him: consider Mac Diarmid's harsh skirl, Pound's western yawp.

I would like to use the page more, both for visual and musical effect, as French and American poets have been doing for nearly a hundred years, but apart from 'Hymn to the New Omagh Road' and 'Life Class' which follows the curves of the female body, I have rarely succeeded as well as I would wish. There is an inhibiting traditionalism in contemporary poetry in English on this side of the Atlantic which saps inventiveness. It is only a habit of the mind which makes us expect a poem to march as docile as a herd of sheep between the fence of white margins. And what about all that waste paper, not reserved for silences but left fallow at the poem's edge? No farmer would allow such poor ploughing. When the poet is

aware of space, then the poem achieves a Giacometti tension, surrounded by silence, but otherwise spacing is blankly automatic. I
like lean as well as visually diverse poems, especially for emotional
subjects, 'to ayery thinnesse beate'. Sometimes I take a wicked
pleasure in ending lines with insignificant, barely stressed words
like 'the', 'and','or', in order to defeat expectation, but also to ease
the flow into the following line. I feel words visually and musically
as well as aurally when they are part of a poetic line – 'and', to take
a simple example, is a three-letter statement, occupying a definite
space and time, so that if it is only a simple connective I need, I
prefer the ampersand. Ideally, there is no limit to the resources now
available to us, but who, except David Jones, tries for the great music, where the human voice weaves structures on a page, as physical
as sculpture, as resourceful in counterpoint as a Mahler symphony?

[1972-73]

iv TIDES

A book of poems is, for me, a temporary exhaustion of an obsession.
So *Tides* ends where it began, with the sound of water, rising/
falling. In 1966 W. S. Hayter asked me to provide poems to go with
a series of his engravings on the sea. I protested: the only water I
knew was inland (already a discovery). But soon I cast off, and
found myself in deep water, dealing with subjects I might previously have protected myself against through irony, implication (I
don't mean that I scorn these weapons but I reach for them only
when the monster can't be caught by more direct means. Crossing
the Irish Sea, I was re-reading the third chapter of *Moby Dick* when
in walked my cabin mate. He was as highly coloured as the
harpooner Queequeg).

So the real subject of the 'Sea Changes' sequence, and the rest
of the book, is the interior, the human sea, with its rhythms of life
and death. In the first section they are inextricable: an emergency
operation, lovers quarrelling bitterly, the attempted rape of an old
woman. Another meaningful coincidence: I was translating from
the old Irish and for the first time found myself able to face up to
that concentrated masterpiece, 'The Hag of Beare,' in which the
old woman compares her life to the ebbing sea.

In the second section we meet the muse as death, death naked.

I would prefer not to discuss these poems casually, except to say that I am glad I was able to write them, for the experience behind them had been festering a long time. They may seem morbid but I think they are true and, having mirrored the Medusa, the artist may return. Some of the best modern poetry inhabits this area, but there is also the great opposite, life-giving rhythm.

So the third section is ruled by a different kind of nakedness: the muse as energy, love, the full moon. Here, and elsewhere, I was delighted to find the shape of the poem growing more open: much Irish poetry, at least, is conventionalized by the iambic line and lacks the energy of the spoken, as opposed to the 'written', word.

The moon, mistress of the tides, appears in another phase, in the second last section of the book, which deals with death as process, a wearing down, a waning. As in 'Omagh Hospital': if we have drifted far enough out, we are ready to submerge again.

[1970]

v ON TRANSLATING IRISH, WITHOUT SPEAKING IT

My attitude towards Irish is ambiguous and haunted. I first learnt it not during but *after* school, when an enthusiastic priest came to teach us poor northern children our lost heritage. I loathed it, and him, thought only of the three long miles I had to cycle home. Besides, an ironic reversal took place during that hour, for many of the children who were good at Irish were not ordinarily regarded as bright, while the clever often foundered. Perhaps we felt that we had worked enough and resented that wall chart with its pigs and hens and cows; all the rural world we would soon be leaving presented as a primal culture.

Enough excuses – when I went to Armagh College I found that my little Irish was a great help. Our master was Sean O'Boyle, and even a small philistine like myself, crammed with English school stories, could recognize a dedicated man. In his nasal voice he intoned the Ulster aislings, and I felt so obscurely moved that I quenched a rebellion against his zeal, which exceeded examination requirements. But while honouring, I felt no desire to imitate: once again, I passed up a chance to go to the Donegal Gaeltacht. There seemed no connection between his enthusiasm and the world in which I thought I was going to live. And when I came to

Dublin my Irish withered: the oral examiner at UCD found my northern dialect a comically barbaric survival.

How do I find myself translating from the Irish, twenty years later? It is intimately connected with my discovery of poetry: after a certain point I felt I had to examine what had been done in this country before the spread of English. One of the exercises that fanatical priest had given us was to collect place-names; so I learnt that I was brought up in the Rough Field, and was going to school in the Glen of the Hazels. Like a stream driven underground, Irish still ran under the speech and names of my childhood. Especially my own, as was proven to me in a very touching way. After I had appeared on RTE I had a letter asking me if my name was not an anglicization of Tadgh or Tague; it came from Nuala Costello, daughter of the collector of the *Songs of Mayo*. She had seen through my family's protective colouring.

So far I have not translated any of the songs or poems I learnt at school, being drawn more to the brevity of the early Irish, or its crude mythologizing humour. Where the idea was more important, with the versification only a vehicle for it, as in 'The First Invasion' and 'The First Lawcase', I have been content to clarify the story-line. We should not be deprived of such an energetic vision of our national origins because the verbal texture is relatively undistinguished. One wonders how many of those who speak of our national heritage are aware of the sensual Mohammedan vision that lurks behind it.

One poem has a gloomy significance for me. I asked Sean O'Riada to bring me the Irish poem he liked best, and we worked on it together for several days until he was satisfied. If there is little philosophy as such in our mainly lyric literature, 'Under Sorrow's Sign' might be called a theological poem. Its stately bleakness is one aspect of the medieval tradition which we have not lost, though its co-existence with the orgiastic pleasures of *The Book of Invasions*, and the delight in nature which flowers in a monastic quatrain or a Fenian lay like 'The Deserted Mountain', indicates the variety of response possible then. And if there was no drama either, there is the delight in dialogue and human psychology which we glimpse in 'Emer Reclaims Cu Chulainn'.

Finally, a complete translation is impossible; even if one could match all the internal and half rhymes of the Irish original, there

51

is still the metre: something must always be partly sacrificed to achieve a readable version in English. I will continue to translate from the Irish for the rest of my life with, I hope, increasing accuracy and awareness, and it will continue to influence my own work, for, whether we write in Irish or English, all Irish poets share the same tradition.

[1972]

vi A SLOW DANCE

I begin this note on Vancouver Island, in a bar full of Nootka Indians, one of whom lies supine under the other side of the table. I feel at home, as if I were in a West of Ireland pub, surrounded by high-cheeked aboriginals smiling at the clouded mountains outside. An Irishman of Gaelic background is, in a sense, a White Indian, sharing that affinity with nature which is celebrated in the opening title sequence of A Slow Dance. The poet-king Sweeny, who was translated into a bird, might be a figure – Raven, Crow – from Haida legend. And the green mitre of St Patrick, snakes writhing on his Tallcrook, reappears as the Damballa of Haitian voodoo, whom I contemplated for the cover of this book, before we found the nightmarish images of Jack Coughlin.

These glosses are after the fact, of course, which is that I was brought up among the hill forts of the Clogher Valley; the passage grave of Seskilgreen was behind our school, with the cairn of Knockmany inviting or glowering across the valley. They both figure in discussions of the Eye Goddess, from Crawford to Herity, but I met her as a childhood presence (dare I say playmate?). A less ritualized landscape gleams in the second part of the book, the wet lushness which excited me so much when I returned to Ireland, after a decade in exile. The detailed sharp beauty of early Irish poetry is what I was trying for in these nature lyrics, but as an Ulsterman I cannot forget that history has sown another crop, of dragon's teeth, the kind of racial and sectarian hatred which is synonymous with my native province.

Anyone who has read my long poem, The Rough Field, will know my personal and historical view of the Ulster morass. Now it has darkened to nightmare, with only the grim laughter of the survivor as consolation. One can relate the violence to the La Tène warrior cult ('Hero's Portion'), the War Goddess ('Wheels Slowly Turning'), or even further back to the glacier which held Ulster in its icy grip and left a sketchy geographical border ('Coldness'). But it still must be endured, and accepted, even when language breaks down and a harsh dance of healing is our only answer, as in 'The Cave of Night', the main poem of the third section.

In the second last section, we are back with family and friends, a less extreme landscape of life and death. The mad colonel of 'The Cave of Night' appears in more human guise as my first wife's father, and my own father and godfather, who figured in earlier books, return to haunt me. The maternal presence is also felt, in its daily form, and will, I hope, warm later books. This counterpoint of mythical or extreme experience with our more usual burdens is part of the structure of the book, with two lengthy elegies, 'A Courtyard in Winter' and 'A Graveyard in Queens', one formal and impersonal, the other familiar and experimental, dominating the quieter sections. This dance of death and life gathers to a climax in the music of O'Riada's Farewell', an elegy for a dead composer friend who was fascinated by magic. An exemplar of the artist broken on the wheel of nationalism, so that the bright vision of the aisling becomes a death wish, his fate leads me to see the artist as lamenting the world itself, just as in the beginning I had praised it.

[1975]

vii POISONED LANDS

Revising these poems [2nd edition, 1977] has been a strange experience, the reverse, almost, of Henry James's late story, 'The Jolly Corner'. It became not so much the case of an older writer wishing to correct his younger self as of trying to release that earlier self from chains of time and place.

A marooned northerner, I began to write as a student in post-War – sorry, Emergency – Dublin. A third of the poems in the book date from the early fifties when I was discovering with awe that I might possibly be able to write something like the kind of modern poetry I admired. But the literary atmosphere was against it, and, while I found lonely allies in people like Valentin Iremonger, what prevailed in the poetic world of Dublin was acrimony and insult:

53

a poem was to be kicked, not examined; the begrudgers ruled. I admired Patrick Kavanagh but his baffled fury was that of a man flailing between two faded worlds, the country he had left, and the literary Dublin he never found.

Such an ingrown, discouraging climate meant that my leaving for America became partly a flight. I recovered slowly there and met writers of my own age, whether Snodgrass and Bly in the Midwest, or Snyder and Ginsberg in California, for whom poetry was a craft and a vision. On the wing, and wounded, I wrote little, but by 1956 I felt strong enough to return to Ireland; was, indeed, helped to by the generous friend [Roger McHugh] to whom this book is dedicated, who found me that most useful of things, a decent job.

So the second group of poems begin in the late fifties when I had revived the dialogue with my earlier self. The atmosphere was more cordial, thanks also to the Dolmen Press, which produced *Forms of Exile* in late 1958. My taste was becoming surer, and I remember receiving a letter from Robert Graves, one of my heroes, altering a word in 'The First Invasion of Ireland' (I leave you to guess which) with a charming apology: 'Few poems are worth a comment nowadays.' But when I came to gather *Poisoned Lands* (1961), I still suppressed poems in a way that now seems part of the malaise of the period, an unconscious censorship, a fear of emotion, of deliberate Irishism, of ruralism. How could we anticipate that the harshness of factory farming would revive the bucolic dream?

After sixteen years a few changes are inevitable. If the rhetoric of 'Rome, Anno Santo' refused to be shaped into shorter stanzas, 'The Water Carrier' regained a lost stanza. An archaeological anachronism had to be removed from 'The Sean Bhean Bhocht' and the Éluard awaits a future anthology of recent French poetry. Altogether, this new edition of *Poisoned Lands* is much closer to what it should have been, and, if I drop a few poems I can no longer stomach, I include several that I then smothered. I notice the reticence where love is concerned but plead that I have tried to make up for it since. As for the oppressive note that glooms through the whole collection, may it not have been prophetic?

A final period vignette. An editor-poet I studiously avoided was T. S. Eliot but when the volume was being considered for American publication, it crossed his desk. Old Possum risked a friendly

pat: 'I have, indeed, found Mr Montague's poems worthy of study.'
I hope they still are; and that they give pleasure as well.

[1977]

viii THE ROUGH FIELD

This poem begins in the early sixties, when I went to Belfast to receive a small poetry prize, the first, I think, to exist in that part of the world. (Ironically, the Irish papers hailed it as 'Dublin Poet wins Belfast Prize', so little were they accustomed to a poet of my background.) To deepen the paradox, the award was presented in the Assembly Rooms of the Presbyterian Church in Belfast, a drab Victorian building in the heart of the city. And as 'Like Dolmens round my Childhood' was being read, I heard the rumble of drums, preparing for 'the Twelfth', the annual Orange festival.

Bumping down towards Tyrone a few days later by bus, I had a kind of vision, in the medieval sense, of my home area, the unhappiness of its historical destiny. And of all such remote areas where the presence of the past was compounded with a bleak economic future, whether in Ulster, Brittany, or the Highlands of Scotland. I managed to draft the opening and the close, but soon realized that I did not have the technique for so varied a task. At intervals during the decade I returned to it, when the signs seemed right. An extreme Protestant organization put me on its mailing list, for instance, and the only antidote I could find against such hatred was to absorb it into 'The Bread God'. And ten years later I was given another small award, again from the North, to complete the manuscript.

Although, as the Ulster crisis broke, I felt as if I had been stirring a witch's cauldron, I never thought of the poem as tethered to any particular set of events. One explores an inheritance to free oneself and others, and if I sometimes saw the poem as taking over where the last bard of the O'Neills left off, the New Road I describe runs through Normandy as well as Tyrone. And experience of agitations in Paris and Berkeley taught me that the violence of disputing factions is more than a local phenomenon. But one must start from home – so the poem begins where I began myself, with a Catholic family in the townland of Garvaghey (*garbh achaidh*, a rough field) in the county of Tyrone, in the province of Ulster.

The illustrations which appear on the title page and which precede each section of the poem are details from the suite of woodcuts in *The Image of Irelande* with *A Discoverie of Woodkarne* by John Derricke, printed in London in 1581. Derricke seems to have been an English artist who came to Ireland as a retainer of Sir Henry Sidney. Sidney served as Vice-Treasurer in Ireland from 1556 to 1559 and as Lord Deputy from 1565 to 1571 and again from 1575 to 1578. He mounted two major campaigns against the O'Neills in Ulster. Some of these woodcuts are thought to be based on sketches made by Derricke during Sidney's campaigns, and may well be the only eye-witness accounts of the Ulster wars.

The crest is that of the United Irishmen, founded by Theobald Wolfe Tone in Belfast in 1791, and is reproduced from the original wood engraving of the device.

[1979]

ix THE DEAD KINGDOM

The 'thread' or plot of *The Dead Kingdom* is the long drive North, from Cork where I now live, to Fermanagh-South Tyrone where I was brought up. There is an old Irish poetical form, *dinnseanchas* or place wisdom. It was part of traditional bardic training, a sense of the historical layers and legends which give character to an area, a local piety deeper than the topographical. Some people would argue that Ireland has had too much history; I partly agree, but perhaps it has not been properly understood?

The last long poem I tried was *The Rough Field*, begun in 1960, and growing over a decade. When it was published, beautifully, by the Dolmen Press in 1972, I hoped that I would not find myself in the same position again for a long time, confronting the Matter of Ulster through a variety of forms.

But a year later my mother began to die, and I found myself heading North again and again to visit her. She had laughingly reproached me for ignoring the distaff side of our family and after she died the material began to precipitate. It chose a deceptively simple medium, a seven-syllable line which I had already placed at the centre of the previous long poem, a meditative metre which can carry both narrative and comment.

I believe that a long poem should be readable but with changes of pace, contrasting textures. So *The Dead Kingdom* is in five movements, and I was especially pleased with the second, or slow movement. My wartime holidays were spent in the Irish midlands, the Goldsmith country, and I have always wanted to pay homage to that melancholy plain, the now stripped Bog of Allen, the chalk-white towers of *Bord na Móna,* the turf board, or industry.

As the poem approaches the Border, the atmosphere darkens. The area I was describing, that lost finger of Leitrim/Cavan which intrudes into the North, is now known for killings, and the Tidey kidnapping. It has been suggested that there is some link between all this and Nordic violence but the historical basis is different, though I include the one relevant section of the *Njal Saga*.

Before the poem drowned in gloom, my father's ghost began breaking in. He was, after all, my mother's husband, and partly re-sponsible for my creation. He brought his sense of humour and his rough tenor voice to leaven the grimness. The last section, 'A Flowering Absence', is a bitter-sweet homage to the maternal; it is hard to work so close to the bone.

As the book emerged I became aware of a need or desire for a further dimension. After fifty, a man should not be afraid to generalize from his own particulars, to adapt Pound. I like medita-tive, timeless poems like 'The Well Dreams', and hope I will write more. In the meantime I am grateful to the Poetry Book Society, about which I am beginning to feel like Gordon Richards and the Derby; this is my third Recommendation! But *The Rough Field* was an also-ran, so my speed over the distance is improving.

[1984]

II

5

OLIVER GOLDSMITH:
THE SENTIMENTAL PROPHECY

Perhaps this is the true point of happiness, on one side of which lies savage wretchedness, and on the other, excruciating refinement. A life like this, of society, frugality, and labour, is the object of every philosophic wish, the theme of every enraptured imagination.

'A Comparative View of Races and Nations'
Royal Magazine, July 1760

> On a summer midnight, you can hear the music
> Of the weak pipe and the little drum
> And see them dancing around the bonfire. . .
> Rustically solemn or in rustic laughter
> Lifting heavy feet in clumsy shoes,
> Earth feet, loam feet, lifted in country mirth
> Mirth of those long since under earth
> Nourishing the corn. Keeping time,
> Keeping the rhythm in the dancing
> As in their living in the living seasons. . .
> T. S. Eliot: *East Coker*

Their bards, in particular, are still held in great veneration among them: those traditional heralds are invited to every funeral, in order to fill up the intervals of the howl with their songs and harps. In those they rehearse the actions of the ancestors of the deceased, bewail the bondage of this country under the English government, and generally conclude with advising the young men and maidens to make the best of their time, for they will soon, for all their present bloom, be stretched under the table, like the dead body before them.

'Carolan, the Irish Bard'

The Deserted Village, like *The Vicar of Wakefield* and *She Stoops to Conquer*, is one of Goldsmith's acknowledged masterpieces, probably the most distinguished long poem by an Irishman. And yet, one is surprised, despite its popularity and apparent simplicity, by the general confusion of views concerning it: enough, indeed, to suggest something curious about the poem. The description of the village, in particular, has proved a stumbling block. According to Macaulay,

It is made up of incongruous parts. The village in its happy days is a true English village. The village in its decay is an Irish village. The felicity and the misery which Goldsmith has brought close together belong to different countries, and to two different stages in the progress of society. . . by joining the two he has produced something which never was and never will be seen in any part of the world.

For the Irish literary nationalist, of course, the question is simple: the village is Lissoy, as sketched by Newell (Goldsmith's *Poetical Works*, 1811) and signposted by the Irish Tourist Board. The Rev. Annesley Strean, who succeeded Goldsmith's brother in the curacy of Kilkenny West, has related the incident upon which the poem is supposedly based:

The poem of *The Deserted Village* took its origin from the circumstance of General Robert Napper. . . having purchased an extensive tract of the country surrounding Lissoy or *Auburn* ; in consequence of which many families, here called cottiers, were removed, to make room for the intended improvements of what was now to become the wide domain of a rich man. . .[1]

This is valuable information, tracing the development of the theme from the poet's boyhood, but it does not prove that Lissoy is Auburn, and that *The Deserted Village* is a specifically Irish poem. More subtly, Yeats saw Goldsmith as part of the Anglo-Irish tradition: 'Goldsmith and the Dean, Berkeley and Burke have travelled' on his winding stair. But his picture of *The Deserted Village* in 'The Seven Sages' is curiously selective: he seems to regard it as a vision of the ills of Ireland before the rise of nationalism.

> Oliver Goldsmith sang what he had seen,
> Roads full of beggars, cattle in the fields,

> But never saw the trefoil stained with blood,
> The avenging leaf those fields raised up against it.

Robert Graves, who also regards himself as an Anglo-Irish poet, gives the most forceful expression of this point of view in *The Crowning Privilege*, relating the poem to the Gaelic Aislings or Vision poems of the eighteenth century:

> . . . *The Deserted Village*, despite its aim of formality, is a true poem, because, like Swift, Goldsmith was in earnest. He was offering, disguised as an essay on the break-up of English village society, a lament for the ills of Ireland, modelled on contemporary Irish minstrel songs – walk, description, meditation, moral vision, invocation of the Goddess; even the distressful crone is there, and the damsel who tears out her hair in handfuls. Auburn really lies in County Roscommon; the poem is full of personal recollections, and glows with sorrowful anger.[2]

Against this, of course, there is the fact that the poem is specifically about 'England's griefs'; that the whole argument is a development of the vision of England in decay in lines 393-412 of *The Traveller*: that the Dedication speaks (like a correspondent in the *Public Advertiser* of September 29, 1780)[3] of what Goldsmith had seen in the English countryside, 'for the four or five years past'. On this, and the evidence of Goldsmith's remarkable early essay 'The Revolution in Low Life', R. S. Crane, one of the most intelligent of Goldsmith's academic critics, concludes:

> . . . that the immediate social background of that poem must be sought in England, not in Ireland, and that, historically, the lament over the ruins of Auburn must be regarded as simply the most memorable of a long series of pamphlets called forth in the sixties and seventies of the 18th century by the English agricultural revolution.[4]

But even at that level, there is a certain confusion, for, as some critics have pointed out, Goldsmith seems less concerned with the agricultural revolution than with the growth of a commercial aristocracy, the 'Nabob' class described also in Samuel Foote's plays and Langhorne's 'The Country Justice'. In *The Traveller*, such men, enriched with the gains of empire, threaten the liberties of England: their purchase of estates is part of their movement towards position and power. In England, says Dorothy George, 'it

63

was a general ambition to own land, the chief source of social consideration and political influence'.[5] It is 'the man of wealth and pride' in *The Deserted Village* who 'takes up a space that many poor supplied'. This process is somewhat different from the desire for agricultural improvement which gave rise to the Enclosure Acts, of which there were over a thousand in the period 1760-80 alone, as opposed to a hundred in the first half of the century. But at least some of the 'Nabobs' were improving farmers; the result, in any case, tended to be the dispossession of the small holder, and the beginnings of the flight from the land: the better conditions of the earlier part of the century when the rural population had increased, became by contrast an Arcadia, a Golden Age. Here again, the nationalist element cannot be discounted, for it may well have been Goldsmith's early experiences in what Mr Desmond Stewart calls 'the rural slum' of Ireland which created his bias against landlordism; the agrarian problem has been one of the major subjects of Irish literature in English from Goldsmith's near neighbour and contemporary, Lawrence Whyte, a Westmeath schoolmaster,[6] to Maria Edgeworth's *Castle Rackrent* and Allingham's *Lawrence Bloomfield*; perhaps even to Mr Patrick Kavanagh's *The Great Hunger*, which is, like Crabbe's *The Village*, a repudiation of the traditional rustic idyll, a sort of anti-Goldsmith.

We have said enough, I think, to suggest that the simplicity of *The Deserted Village* is rather deceptive. A song of exile from Lissoy, a protest against the Enclosure Acts and/or the new commercial oligarchy, a vision of the ills of Ireland: the poem does indeed answer partly to each of these descriptions. But it is also something more, something which includes and transcends all these things: seen in the context of Oliver Goldsmith's career it has the force of a final statement, the culminating vision of that decay in his own time, which haunted him from his earliest essay, *An Enquiry into the Present State of Polite Learning* (1759), onwards. Whether Auburn is an Irish or an English village is, from this point of view, irrelevant: it is a composite picture, deliberately striving beyond details to a general view. Whether the weight of meaning Goldsmith places upon the poem does not, in fact, have an effect other than he intended is something we can discover only from a closer examination. In dealing with it we are in the unusual position of possessing something very near a first prose draft in 'The Revolution in Low Life', published in *Lloyd's Magazine* eight years earlier, on January 14-16, 1762.

The Deserted Village stands in a very close relationship to *The Traveller*: it might be described as a sequel, although the later poem is much the better known. There are indications in the picture of Italy where 'nought remain'd of all that riches gave/But towns unmann'd and lords without a slave', but the obvious source is the passage 397-412, including

> Have we not seen, at pleasure's lordly call,
> The smiling long-frequented village fall?[7]

The Deserted Village is, in fact, an expansion of these lines, and for a specific purpose: to dramatize the ravages of opulence in Britain by its effect upon the most vulnerable part of society, rural life. In *The Traveller*, the moral is cumulative, leading to a rhetorical appeal: whatever autobiographical involvement there is is mainly in the analysis of 'the traveller'. In *The Deserted Village*, the autobiographical and the didactic meet: the result is an emotional appeal calculated to wring the withers of the reader. What form it takes we shall soon begin to see.

> Sweet Auburn! loveliest village of the plain,
> Where health and plenty cheer'd the labouring swain,
> Where smiling spring its earliest visit paid,
> And parting summer's lingering blooms delay'd:
> Dear lovely bowers of innocence and ease. . .

What one notices in this passage, I think, is its delicate conventionality. Although Goldsmith was a countryman, there are surprisingly few fresh 'images of external nature' (to use Wordsworth's phrase)[8] in the poem; much less, for instance, than in *An History of the Earth and Animated Nature*, where the descriptions often combine great beauty and exactness. One does not expect close natural observation in eighteenth-century poetry – though there is a good deal in Thomson's *Seasons* – but here, one feels, the pastoral clichés of eighteenth-century poetry are being used to a very definite artistic purpose, the evocation of a 'Golden Age' of rural life. Auburn is not a particular, but a universal village, the loveliest of the plain, a pastoral Eden evoking the essence of every Virgilian eclogue and Horatian retreat: it even has special climatic privileges. Notice the enumeration of 'every charm', with its appropriate adjective:

> The shelter'd cot, the cultivated farm,
> The never-failing brook, the busy mill...
>
> 10

leading to the ritual of pleasures, 'in sweet succession':

> And still as each repeated pleasure tir'd
> Succeeding sports the mirthful band inspir'd...
>
> 24

What is being described here is Goldsmith's ideal society, a local culture based upon ritual and frugal content, as seen in *The Vicar of Wakefield* (particularly the opening of Chapter IV) and in the opening of 'The Revolution in Low Life'.

I spent part of the last summer in a little village, distant about fifty miles from town, consisting of near an hundred houses. It lay entirely out of the road of commerce, and was inhabited by a race of men who followed the primeval profession of agriculture for several generations. Though strangers to opulence, they were unacquainted with distress; few of them were known either to acquire a fortune or to die in indigence. By a long intercourse and frequent intermarriages, they were all become in a manner one family; and, when the work of the day was done, spent the night agreeably in visits at each other's houses. Upon those occasions the poor traveller and stranger were always welcome; and they kept up the stated days of festivity with the strictest observance.

If one remembers that the impulse behind generalization in eighteenth-century literature was often a vision of the universe as divine order – the work of 'the Great Disposer' of *Animated Nature* – then here we have an example of poetic diction being specifically used to recall a section of that order. The relevant comparison is not with Thomson or Wordsworth, but with the passage of *East Coker* quoted at the beginning of this essay.

After this accumulation of images of rural content – the opening is, with the ending paragraph, the longest in the poem – the final half-line has a deliberate curt brutality: 'But all these charms are fled.' Having involved us in his 'smiling plain' (a Virgilian phrase as Tillotson points out in his essay on 'Eighteenth Century Poetic

Diction'), Goldsmith now – abruptly and dramatically – shows its complete ruin, and it is typical of his talent that this should be one of the most powerful and closely observed passages in the poem.

> No more thy glassy brook reflects the day,
> But chok'd with sedges, works its weedy way.
> Along thy glades, a solitary guest,
> The hollow-sounding bittern guards its nest...   44

From the sentimental to the pathetic: after these two paragraphs, we are ready for a solemn statement of the thesis of the poem.

> Ill fares the land, to hast'ning ills a prey,   51
> Where wealth accumulates, and men decay...

What strikes in this section of the poem (lines 51-74) is its directness and simplicity: an immediate and very explicit under-lining of the moral behind the destruction of Auburn. What is less obvious is the slurring of the time sequence, so that the rural para-dise of Auburn exists both in the immediate past – 'But times are alter'd' – and in the fairy-tale never-never – 'a time there was'. Goldsmith's technique in *The Deserted Village* is to carry his thesis by the emotional effect of his skilful alternation between images of original innocence and malignant destruction: the relatively few didactic passages are made as simple and clear as possible. It is not that his argument is unimportant – it is rather so important to him, so much a part of his total vision, that he is prepared to use all the poetic means in his power to invade the reader on its behalf. That is why we cannot, like Alice, read *The Deserted Village* just for its pictures, because its pictures are part of a calculated attack upon our sympathies.

The imaginary walk through a deserted Auburn (73-135) gives the game away: it is pure 'Mother Machree', the lament of the returned exile who finds nettles growing across the doorstep.[9] One of the more impressive aspects of *The Traveller* is the way the narrator admits the permanence of his exile. Although his wish is often 'to find/Some spot to real happiness consign'd', he recognizes his fate: 'not destin'd such delights to share'. But the exiled narrator of *The Deserted Village* does return, and his personal lament for the transience of things mortal adds to the emotional bias of the poem.

The destruction of the village is not only the destruction of the narrator's childhood, but also of his dream of an ideal retreat and escape:

> O blest retirement, friend to life's decline,
> Retreats from care, that never must be mine,
> How happy he who crowns in shades like these,
> A youth of labour with an age of ease;   100
> Who quits a world where strong temptations try
> And, since 'tis hard to combat, learns to fly!

An interesting example of this poetic 'whitewashing' is the way lines of 'Description of an Author's Bed Chamber', from Letter XXIX of *The Citizen of the World*, change on their assimilation into *The Deserted Village*. The original, with its humorously sordid details, has great vivacity, like Swift's 'A Description of the Morning' or Eliot's 'Preludes'; it shows that Goldsmith was capable of energetic, realistic observation.

> Where the Red Lion flaring o'er the way,
> Invites each passing stranger that can pay
> Where Calvert's butt and parson's black champagne
> Regale the drabs and bloods of Drury-lane. . .

But when the room reappears in *The Deserted Village*, 'The humid wall with paltry pictures spread' becomes 'The pictures placed for ornament and use'; 'the twelve rules the royal martyr drew' change to 'the twelve good rules'; 'The rusty grate unconscious of a fire' becomes 'the hearth. . ./ With aspen boughs and flowers and fennel gay' and – most revealing – 'the five cracked tea-cups' reappear as 'broken tea-cups, wisely kept for show'. The reasons for the change are obvious but there seems to me a thwarting of the original motive behind the lines which is highly suspect.

The portraits which follow (lines 137-250) are the most praised part of *The Deserted Village*: 'a skill and concision seldom equalled since Chaucer', as Eliot says in his essay on 'Johnson as Critic and Poet'. The comparison, we can see, has a deeper relevance, for it is a medieval, i.e. Chaucerian, social order Goldsmith is evoking. But with a difference, because Chaucer's portraits contain a good deal of subtle irony and criticism, which Goldsmith, as special pleader, cannot allow: the only relief from unadulterated virtue is humour,

> And e'en the story ran that he could gauge.
> And news much older than their ale went round.

which hardly compares with the delicate implications in Chaucer's portrait of the Prioress:

> There was also a Nonne, a Prioresse,
> That of hir smylyng was ful symple and coy;
> Hire gretteste ooth was by Seinte Loy;
> And she was cleped Madame Eglentyne.
> Ful weel she soong the service dyvyne,
> Entuned in hir nose ful semely. . .

Chaucer's people are human, too human often, he seems to suggest, for their callings. Goldsmith's portraits tend to the ideal, and are saved only by their humour and homely detail. Again, this is not to be attributed entirely to the conventionality of eighteenth century poetry. Compare the way, for instance, irony plays around the central character in *The Vicar of Wakefield;* or the more bitter portrait of a parson father in The Man in Black's tale in *The Citizen of the World:* nothing of this appears in *The Deserted Village.* The 'sweet oblivion' of the village inn seems far from Goldsmith's very unIrish attack on alehouses in 'Upon Political Frugality': 'alehouses are ever an occasion of debauchery and excess, and either in a religious or political light, it would be our highest interest to have the greatest part of them suppressed'.[10] That Goldsmith was capable of more balanced portraiture in poetry we know from 'Retaliation': I am not objecting to the procedure, only defining its calculated appeal.

A very curious thing happens in the next, and openly didactic, section of the poem (lines 250-300). One notices the implications Goldsmith makes in passing from 'the woodman's ballad' to 'the midnight masquerade'; from the natural order of 'spontaneous joys' to the unnatural 'freaks of wanton wealth'. There is a great rhetorical power in his picture of trade,

> Proud swells the tide with loads of freighted ore,
> And shouting Folly hails them from her shore. . .   270

where the personifications (as Donald Davie points out in Augustan poetry generally) are energized by the verbs, and joined in a minor dramatic situation or 'plot', like the ocean and rampart in the description of Holland in *The Traveller*. This sweeping vision of energy, however, is broken by the abruptness of the half-line – 'Yet count our gains' – and then reversed in painting the other side of the picture, the usurpations of the commercial magnate.

> The robe that wraps his limbs in silken sloth   279
> Has robb'd the neighbouring fields of half their
>   growth. . .

Here the robe becomes a reptile, its strangling presence dramatized in the hissing end of one line, and the dragging length of the next. The rich man's estate 'spurns the cottage from the green'; again the transference of personification works through an active verb. But it is the last couplet in the paragraph to which I especially wish to draw attention, the epic simile which arises from it (lines 287-308), and its implication in the whole context of the poem.

Here the landscape is compared – one can hardly escape the meaning – to an ageing woman in the hands of a seducer;

> . . . adorned for pleasure, all   285
> In barren splendour [she] feebly waits the fall.

One would hesitate to insist on the sexual implication of 'fall' and 'barren' if they were not so consistently carried through in the following paragraph.

> But when those charms are past, for charms are frail,
> When time advances, and when *lovers* fail,
> She then shines forth, *solicitous* to bless,
> In all the glaring *impotence* of dress.
> Thus fares the land, by luxury *betray'd*. [my italics]   295

At least some of the 'triumphant felicity' Donald Davie attributes to the phrase 'the glaring impotence of dress' – a more striking version of 'barren splendour' – comes from its sexual connotations, its summary of the pathetic drama in which the rake (luxury) betrays the 'fair female' (land), who can now only hope to appeal through artificial skills.[11] The only trouble is the basic confusion in the comparison, which leaves the land both waiting for 'the fall' and 'betray'd': if I make heavy weather of the point, it is because I feel that Goldsmith's excessive involvement with his theme manifests itself in such sleights of word.

Donald Davie has analyzed the effects in the rest of this paragraph; 'the startling force given to "smiling land" when it is seen to smile with heartless indifference on the ruined peasant': the way the cant of the landscape gardener – his 'striking vistas' and 'surprised views' – is used with ironical intent (I am not quite so sure of the way the peasant 'scourg'd by famine from the smiling land' sinks – presumably in the sea – 'without one arm to save'). What has not been commented on, I think, is the contrast between this picture of the landscaped countryside and the picture of desolation presented in the second paragraph of the poem, where 'the long grass o'ertops the mould'ring wall'. One could argue that this is not Auburn, but the land around it; yet in both, the same drama is taking place, and the peasant is in flight 'from the spoiler's hand'. Goldsmith is presumably presenting the two kinds of rural usurpation, the one of the improving farmer where 'half a tillage stints thy smiling plain' and the other where the land is redesigned as a private garden. It might seem another example of Goldsmith's determination to carry his argument, but it is also justified in view of the fuller picture it gives of the problem. The village, the countryside, and even 'the common's fenceless limits' (line 303) are all divided by 'the sons of wealth'.[12] Auburn is as symbolically representative a village in its downfall as in its original order.

The next section (lines 309-384) deals with the Flight from the Land, and it is the climax of Goldsmith's emotional treatment of his theme. All the clichés are there, the ruined maid (the palpable realization, so to speak, of the parallel between the 'ruined' land and the fallen woman), the family, from 'the good old sire' to 'his lovely daughter, lovelier in her tears,' exiled to the 'horrid shore'. And yet, one is not really shocked by it, partly because of its position in the whole movement of the poem; it represents a last emotional appeal before the prophetic vision of the closing paragraphs. Besides, there are passages of considerable power; the picture of urban desolation, for instance, has a Johnsonian vigour and loathing in its contrasts: not quite what one expects in Goldsmith.

> Here, while the courtier glitters in brocade,
> There the pale artist plies the sickly trade;
> Here, while the proud their long-drawn pomps display,
> There the black gibbet glooms beside the way.
> The dome where Pleasure holds her midnight reign
> Here, richly deck'd, admits the gorgeous train;   320
> Tumultuous grandeur crowds the blazing square,
> The rattling chariots clash, the torches glare.

This, together with the glimpses of the outcast prostitute, might be said to anticipate aspects of Blake, or even Baudelaire, in 'Le Crépuscule du Soir':

> A travers les lueurs que tourmente le vent
> La Prostitution s'allume dans les rues. . .
> On entend cà et là les cuisines siffler,
> Les théâtres glapir, les orchestres ronfler. . .

The 'gorgeous train', of course, contrasts with another, very different, the train of poor people driven from Auburn; in one phrase ('thy fair tribes', l. 337), Goldsmith seems to link their fate with that of the Jews. They go

> . . . To distant climes, a dreary scene
> Where half the convex world intrudes between. . .

The unusual but geographically correct adjective (their destination is America) and the active verb ('intrudes', like an unfriendly stranger) dramatize the distance separating them from all they have known. The picture of North America that follows is unreal, but dramatically so, one feels: a land enlarged by the exile's anticipation and fear of the unknown. Even the sentimentality of the group portrait can be justified: it is a family which is being driven away; the traditional and sacred unit of society is being violated.[13]

> The good old sire, the first prepar'd to go
> To new-found worlds, and wept for others' woe. . .
> His lovely daughter, lovelier in her tears,   375
> The fond companion of his helpless years,
> Silent went next, neglectful of her charms,
> And left a lover's for a father's arms. . .

The punning irony of 'new-found worlds' – glamorous to explorers and traders but not to them – is saving and bitter while the lovers, separated by luxury's baleful influence, remind us of Pound's Canto XLV:

> Usura slayeth the child in the womb
> It stayeth the young man's courting
> It hath brought palsy to bed, lyeth
> Between the young bride and her bridegroom.
> CONTRA NATURAM

The ending, of course, is powerful; the rhetorical outbreak in the short second-last paragraph, the long sadness of the close. Now the real motive force of the poem appears: it is not merely that villages, like Auburn, are being dispossessed, but that this dispossession is part of a whole pattern of economic greed which will in time, destroy society. 'Those who constitute the basis of the great fabric of society should be particularly regarded: for in policy, as in architecture, ruin is most fatal when it begins from the bottom': Goldsmith's comment in the essay 'On English Clergy' might well be applied to the argument of *The Deserted Village*. It is this vision of decay consequent upon imperial expansion and excessive trade, which haunted Goldsmith throughout his career: like the Roman Empire, like the commercial oligarchies of Venice and Holland, Britain will sink into obscurity, destroyed by her 'rage of gain'. Just as Goldsmith has described in Auburn a medieval order, so his rebuke is based upon the medieval analogy between the human body and society;[14] he even invokes, like Pound, the religious sanction against usury, as CONTRA NATURAM.

> O Luxury! thou curs'd by Heaven's decree,   385
> How ill exchanged are things like these for thee!
> How do thy potions, with insidious joy
> Diffuse their pleasures only to destroy!
> Kingdoms, by thee, to sickly greatness grown,
> Boast of a florid vigour not their own;   390
> At every draught more large and large they grow,
> A bloated mass of rank unwieldy woe;
> Till sapp'd their strength, and every part unsound,
> Down, down they sink, and spread a ruin round.

This paragraph occurs at exactly the same point in the poem as the magnificent outbreak in *The Traveller*, 'But when contending chiefs blockade the throne. . . .' It is an indication of Goldsmith's almost mathematical planning of his effects. The ending sequence of the earlier poem – a vision of destruction and waste, a scene of mournful exile, with a global invocation, leading to a final moral – is triumphantly repeated in *The Deserted Village*: Goldsmith is a master of the melancholy diapason.

> E'en now the devastation is begun,   395
> And half the business of destruction done;
> E'en now, methinks, as pond'ring here I stand,
> I see the rural virtues leave the land. . .

The 'rural virtues', for Goldsmith, as for the Agrarians in Ireland or America, are actually the root virtues of the good society. And since literary and political health are interconnected, poetry joins them in exile: the prophecy at the end of the *Enquiry* is fulfilled, and the Muse is heard weeping 'her own decline'.

> And thou, sweet Poetry, thou loveliest maid,
> Still first to fly where sensual joys invade!
> Unfit, in these degenerate times of shame,
> To catch the heart or strike for honest fame;   410
> Dear charming nymph, neglected and decried,
> My shame in crowds, my solitary pride;
> Thou nurse of every virtue, fare thee well!

Imperceptibly, therefore, the destruction of Auburn has come to signify the destruction of many things: the narrator's childhood and his dreams of escape and peaceful retirement (with which the reader presumably identifies), 'rural virtues', 'all the connexions of kindred' in the family unit, 'spontaneous joys' as opposed to unnatural artifice, virginal innocence, and, finally, poetry itself, even perhaps religion.

> And piety, with wishes plac'd above . . .   405

Auburn, in fact, is identified with the good of society and of England, and *The Deserted Village* is one of the first statements of a great modern theme, the erosion of traditional values and natural rhythms in a commercial society: the fall of Auburn is the fall of a whole social order. It looks forward to Wordsworth; even, to Lawrence and Pound, and to Faulkner's protest against the destruction of the Big Woods. Our attitude towards the poem, therefore, partly depends on our attitude towards modern history: one cannot help feeling, for instance, that Eliot's admiration for *The Deserted Village* may be partly due to the fact that it represents an anticipation of certain aspects of his own work: a sort of rural *Waste Land*. That Goldsmith deduced so much from what he had seen of the Agricultural Revolution may appear, according to one's viewpoint, misguided or miraculously prophetic. Whether the symbol of Auburn can support the tremendous burden of meaning the poem places on it is another matter: if sentimentality is a display of emotion in excess of the given facts, then *The Deserted Village* might justly be called a sentimental prophecy. And that may be the most Irish thing about it: as 'sad historian of the pensive plain', Goldsmith has a good deal in common with the emotional exaggeration of the Irish bards, described in his essay on Carolan, the harper. For although the idea of an Irish literature in English was outside his experience, *The Deserted Village* rehearses one of the most Irish themes of all, a forecast of the downfall of Britain through imperial greed. He produced the first anti-imperialistic poem in the period of England's greatest imperial expansion. We have, perhaps, a special claim on the poem: but so, I think, has the whole tradition of modern literature.

NOTES

1. Rev. Edward Mangin, MA, *Essay on Light Reading*, 1808; quoted also in Newell's edition of the Poetical Works (London 1811).

2. Lecture 2. 'The Age of Obsequiousness' (Cassel & Co. 1955). Lissoy, of course, is not in Roscommon, and there is no damsel in the poem 'who tears out her hair in handfuls'. These vigorous errors in detail do not detract from the element of truth in Graves's feeling about the poem, any more than the supposed 'cattle in the fields' does from Yeats's.

3. 'In one of his country excursions he resided near the house of a great West Indian, in the neighbourhood of which several cottages were destroyed, in order to enlarge, or rather to polish, the prospect.'

4. *New Essays*, Introduction, p. xi and 'The Revolution in Low Life', *ibid*. 116-124. In a review of *The Oxford Book of Irish Verse* in *Poetry*, July 1959, Desmond Stewart also points out that 'it is an Anglican village that Goldsmith is writing

about, where the pastor is shepherd to all', which would hardly be the case in Catholic Ireland. 'Only perhaps in the poet's description of that "horrid shore" to which the poor are driven in exile is there something of a recognisably Irish exaggeration.'

5. *England in Transition* (London 1931). Dr George is opposed to the idea – put about by Goldsmith and others – of a Golden Age of British agriculture; while the changes may have struck the yeoman or freeholder harder than any other class, the result was a rise in the overall standard of living. Most modern social historians are so eager to accept this view that one suspects a certain guilt and/or anti-poetic bias.

6. Whether Goldsmith knew Whyte's *Original Poems on Various Subjects, Serious and Diverting* (published in Dublin in 1740 and again in 1742, and presumably easily available to a Trinity student) is problematical, but despite the difference in literary quality, there are sufficient resemblances to indicate that the experience behind *The Deserted Village* was initially Irish:

> Their native soil were forced to quit,
> So Irish landlords thought it fit
> Who without evening or rout,
> For their improvements turned them out. . .
> How many villages they razed
> How many parishes laid waste. . .
> Whole colonies, to shun the fate
> Of being oppress'd at such a rate,
> By tyrants who still raise this rent,
> Sail'd to the Western Continent.

7. In *A Prospect of Society*, the early version of *The Traveller*, the lines appear as:

> Have we not seen, at pleasure's lordly call
> An hundred villages in ruin fall?

which – with 'The Revolution in Low Life' – shows Goldsmith's quite extraordinarily early awareness of the significance of the Agricultural Revolution.

8. Essay supplementary to the Preface to the *Lyrical Ballads*, 2nd ed. 1815. 'Now it is remarkable that, excepting the Nocturnal Reverie of Lady Winchelsea, and a passage or two in the Windsor Forest of Pope, the poetry of the period intervening between the publication of Paradise Lost and The Seasons does not contain a single new image of external nature. . .' This is sheer pamphleteering, of course, because an image like 'sweet as the primrose peeps beneath the thorn' is as botanically exact as anything in Wordsworth.

9. One is not surprised to read in Newell's edition of the Poetical Works, of the local belief 'that "the Poet" as he is usually called there, after his pedestrian tour upon the Continent of Europe, returned to and resided in the village some time. . . It is moreover believed that the havock which had been made in his absence among those favourite scenes of his youth, affected his mind so deeply, that he actually composed a great part of *The Deserted Village* at Lissoy'. There seems little doubt that Goldsmith never returned to Ireland, but he often expressed his acute sense of change. cf. *New Essays*, p. 13: 'To grow old in the same fields where we once were young; to be capable of every moment beholding objects that recall our early pleasures. . . . 'Happy could so charming an illusion continue,' as he says in the second issue of *The Bee*.

10. *The Bee*, November 3, 1759.

11. The parallel is repeated in Crabbe's *The Village*, lines 79-84. See Donald Davie, *Purity of Diction in English Verse*, (London 1952) and (ed.) *The Late Augustans*, (London 1958) for some of the most valuable recent discussion of Goldsmith.

12. 'In almost every part of the Kingdom, the laborious husbandman has been reduced, and the lands are now occupied either by some general undertaker, or turned into enclosures destined for the purposes of amusement or luxury', 'A Revolution in Low Life', *New Essays*, p. 120.

13. cf. The corresponding passage in 'The Revolution in Low Life': 'The modest matron followed her husband in tears, and often looked back at the little mansion where she had passed her life in innocence, and to which she was never more to return; while the beautiful daughter parted for ever from her lover, who had now become too poor to maintain her as his wife. *All the connections of kindred were now irreparably broken* . . . (my italics).

14. This analogy is also used in the parable of 'The Kingdom of Lao' in Letter XXIV of *The Citizen of the World*: 'Their commerce with their neighbours was totally destroyed, and that with their colonies was every day naturally and necessarily declining. In short, the state resembled one of those bodies bloated with disease, whose bulk is only a symptom of its wretchedness. . . .' See also Tawney's *Religion and the Rise of Capitalism*, Chapter 1, especially, 'The Medieval Background'.

[1962]

6

WILLIAM CARLETON: THE FIERY GIFT

William Carleton, the peasant novelist from Clogher and the valleys of South Tyrone, is the only Irish prose writer of the nineteenth century who could in any real sense be called great. To open the *Traits and Stories of the Irish Peasantry* is to discover a world as vigorous and wonderful as that of Dickens, the first real picture in English of that dark gesturing world of the 'Hidden Ireland' which, until Carleton's coming, had only found halting expression in the novels of Maria Edgeworth and the Banim brothers. If we approach Maxwell or Lover or Lever, with their distinguishing upper-class accents, and their belief in gaiety rather than truth, or even native sentimentalists like Kickham or Griffin, we are more liable to be bored or disappointed or irritated than anything else. We admire their gusto, their rapidity and invention, but cannot condone their misunderstanding of the people. 'There is more difference', wrote the man from Clogher of his contemporaries, 'between Banim and Lever than there is between pantomime and the legitimate drama – between John Kemble and a buffoon.'

There is that period in every country's history when a writer or group of writers achieve a national expression which gives their country the dignity of consciousness. Carleton stands alone in his period because he was the first Irish writer to discover the ordinary people of Ireland; the first who, having lived as a boy in the cabins and pretended work in the fields, later turned to them for his subjects. Compared to the patriotic rediscoveries of the *Nation* group, his achievement was on a much larger scale; he stood out like a giant among them. Almost single-handed he effected a literary discovery of the Irish people.

In that important sense, then, Carleton's work is the only authentic expression we have of rural Ireland, before the appearance in our own century of writers like O'Flaherty and Patrick Kavanagh. The very unfinished, rough nature of his achievement, the rubble and the broken shapes lying around, products of a particularly powerful and confused memory and creative imagination, are the artistic counterpart of the Ireland of the early nineteenth century, when a degraded peasantry were struggling towards the first gleams of relief and security under the vehement leadership of O'Connell. These two men, seen in perspective against later abortive movements, and false attitudes, stand clearly above their contemporaries; the one striving, on a political plane, to raise a whole people into the beginnings of a democracy, the other raising them, not by helping the lovely lost Jacobite lady of Ireland across the muck, like the Gaelic poets of the eighteenth century, but by writing of them as they were, confronting the brute reality and giving it a form. Carleton's instinctive truthfulness in the portrayal of the Irish people parallels the realistic attitude of O'Connell in politics; both stand clearly against either sentimental falsification, in the name of a lost national tradition, or arrogant condescension on the part of those in the saddle.

W. B. Yeats, looking back across the century and invoking ancestors to guide him in his work towards a national literary revival, showed a remarkable clarity in defining Carleton's merit. Cutting right across all distinctions between kinds and creeds of Irishmen, Yeats saw him as the greatest novelist Ireland had yet produced. 'The true peasant was at last speaking, stammeringly, illogically, bitterly, but none the less with the dark and mournful accents of the people.' Carleton's magnificent natural talents, perhaps, never felt the clarity and restraint of discipline that would have made him a great writer on any grounds; isolated from the literary training of London and the Continent, and formed by writers of notable excess like Le Sage, the wonder is that he was able to see clearly for so long, that his prose shows such a natural undirected power, a descriptive agility that at times rivals Balzac and Scott. 'Wildgoose Lodge', for example, is more terrifying than all the histrionics of Maturin and the Dublin Gothic school; its brevity and macabre power remain unequalled in Irish literature until Seumas O'Kelly's 'The Weaver's Grave'.

He uttered one wild and terrific cry, as he fell back, and no more. After this nothing was heard but the crackling of the fire, and the rushing of the blast: all that had possessed life within were consumed, amounting either to eleven or fifteen persons.

When this was accomplished, those who took an active part in the murder, stood for some time about the conflagration; and as it threw its red light upon their fierce faces and rough persons, soiled as they now were with smoke and black streaks of ashes, the scene seemed to be changed to hell, the murderers to spirits of the damned, rejoicing over the arrival and the torture of some guilty soul. . .

It was only when the last victim went down, that the conflagration shot up into the air with most unbounded fury. The house was large, deeply thatched, and well furnished; and the broad red pyramid rose with fearful magnificence towards the sky. . . the dark clouds above, together with the intermediate air, appeared to reflect back, or rather to have caught the red hue of the fire. The hills and country about us appeared with an alarming distinctness. . . the floods that spread over the surrounding plains. . . appeared to be one broad mass of liquid copper, for the motion of the breaking waters caught from the blaze of the high waving column, as reflected in them, a glaring light, which eddied and rose, and fluctuated, as if the flood itself had been a lake of molten fire.

This hellish conflagration could be contrasted with the blessing light at the beginning of 'The Midnight Mass' as an example of his fiery gift. Unlike Yeats or George Moore, Carleton had not to engage in a continual struggle with false angels of vision. Yeats fought towards reality like an always rejected lover, taking thought daily and adding to his stature; Carleton, before the final landslide of his abilities after middle age and a Civil List pension, wrote of people and places familiar to him as the alphabet. The frieze-coated peasant of genius, from the Clogher Valley, makes all subsequent folk-tale trafficking, all lost-world recording of old tales inside half-doors, from Lady Gregory and Yeats onwards, seem little more than watery gruel.

Carleton's unfinished *Autobiography*, with its exact moral style and its intelligent analysis of motive, seems to me one of the most remarkable books in Irish literature: it shows a high degree of self-consciousness, all the more unusual since Carleton was one of the native Irish educated at random in various hedge-schools. It is written in that controlled 'uphill' mood, which is so delightful in any form of literature; the craftsman in his prime deliberately matching emotion and incident with slightly underplayed statement, a sense of powers held well in check; the extravagance that mars so many of the novels, the natural wild exuberance that erupts into *Valentine McClutchy* like a volcano, is muted and subdued, the nostalgia for the cramped green fields and hazel glens a mature, not sentimental, feeling. It shows that while Carleton, being naturally lazy as sin, could postpone writing a novel until a contract or necessity compelled him, and then rattle it off with an upflow of energy that made parts read like genius undiluted, the rest like the intemperate ravings of a bigot, he could also take himself and his gifts in hand, and write with common sense and artistic intelligence. It is a pity that he did not live to complete the manuscript, though the second part dealing with his literary adventures in Dublin might not have been so restrained. But what we have is clearly the work of a born writer, of someone to whom experience was incomplete till he had written of it, and, finally, the only writers of interest are those born for the chase, with a sentence instead of a golden spoon in their mouths.

It tells how Billy Carleton, a small farmer's son from the Clogher Valley, one of a family of fourteen, a lazy local hero who never did a tap of work if he could avoid it, and never missed a dance or hooley or any other kind of mischief the whole country round, was eventually forced to take to the high road to seek his fortune. After very many years of idleness obtained on the pretence of being intended for Holy Orders, and after holding and losing many small odd jobs, he eventually met the Reverend Caesar Otway and became a novelist. The confusion of Goldsmith's career in the previous century comes to mind, with its mixture of piety and nostalgia; although one cannot see Carleton playing even the Orange flute. His picture of life in Ulster is the only genuine record of the period: we see him robbing an Orange orchard, following Anne Duffy home after chapel, performing remarkable feats of strength, like throwing the weight higher over the beam than the big muscled local miller, Frank Farrell. Irish peasant life was at its most lively, before the dark plunge downwards of the famine years, and Carleton, a born mimic and sensitive, gathered his material instinctively, as a bee secretes honey.

A large part of Carleton's genius was that, although the urge was in him to go far afield, to win fame in cities by the power of the written word, he always remained a countryman at heart, irascible and emphatic, marked for life by that kind of broad ruthless simplicity which sees things in their lowest common terms and refuses to be deceived by the trappings; a reaction which to the townsman seems only one stage removed from mysticism. The peasant has observed the natural growth and progress of things and comes in time to think of man as something also with roots in the soil, growing through a natural span on top of green earth. Questioning in the metaphysical sense is alien to him; however much he wonders and admires, it is always with a brute sense of acceptance, for it is but natural that man should behave so, as weeds do, or as corn springs from minute green tips to heavy grain. As Shane Fadh says of the antics of the courting couples: 'It's all in the nathure of the baste.'

Much has been made, too much perhaps, of the way Carleton came under the influence of Caesar Otway, and the fact that he left the religion of his childhood. The poor people among whom he had been reared were under many burdens, not least of which were the monstrous Penal Laws, meant to extinguish the entire intellectual life of the Catholic Irish, but there were times when Carleton saw the well-fed clergy, not as consolers and friends of the people, but as living off a pauper peasantry in much the same way as Darby Skinadre, the miserable gombeen man.

Before Carleton met Otway, he had already discovered that it was easier to get a job in a Sunday School or through Protestant influence than by playing up to the Catholic clergy, though he would, in his desperation, have played the game of priest as well as parson, had it been a paying one. A poor man, particularly one of Carleton's abilities, with a gathering grudge against a world that did not grant his talents recognition, is liable to be as trusty as a weathercock. Carleton took the golden chance offered him by Caesar Otway of publishing his work, with suitable bigoted additions, and probably if someone had asked him for a Gothic novel like those of Maturin he would have written that too. The urge to write was too strong in him to resist the temptation; Otway released him from artistic frustration.

It was lamentable, certainly, because it raised a barrier of misunderstanding between Carleton and his people, and gave his later writing that doctrinaire twist which destroyed his talent. When people taunted and taxed him with his excesses, as in *Paddy Go-Easy*, he shook his head, pawed the ground and defied anyone to place a finger on any of his work and say that it was false. When he said: 'As for myself I have been so completely sickened by the bigots on either side, that I have come to the determination as every honest Irishman ought, of knowing no party but my country, and of devoting such talents as God has given me to the promotion of her general interests, and the happiness of her whole people', he was either attempting to rationalize betrayal, or making a gesture as rhetorically magnificent as that of O'Connell.

Carleton's instinctive sympathies always remained on the side of the Catholic poor, but in casting over what he took to be the native superstitions of Catholicism he felt no difficulties, no modern drama of conscience: he was not like Mauriac, one of those who 'realize. . . that they will never be able to escape. . . they are inundated with light'. Carleton was prepared to begin his career by writing something like anti-Catholic propaganda as another writer in present-day Ireland might be prepared, for a time, to write Catholic propaganda. Now the reverse pays best: we have advanced little enough, only reversed our positions in the pointless jig that is Irish sectarian history.

For a youngster living on the edge of the Clogher Valley, the stories of William Carleton were not fiction but fact; gradually one learnt the genealogy of the various houses, gathered a hint of the intricate law-cases and local feuds, saw Orange drummers practising before a tin-roofed lodge. There were people still alive who could remember Anne Duffy, the original of all his idealized gentle heroines, the blind fiddler Micky MacRory, and in a famous fight at a barn-dance only thirty years before, two whole townlands had battered away at each other until dawn was breaking and there were no more untouched skulls. Clamping turf in an upland bog, one could see, across the cramped heathery hills, the double-wooded swell or saddle of Knockmany, the mountain which had haunted all of Carleton's work, particularly his longing imitative verse, an image of thoughtless happy youth in green fields.

As good a way as any of judging the merit of a novelist like Carleton or Scott or Dickens is to enumerate the characters that remain in the mind; Denis O'Shaughnessy, playing the priesteen on his scrawny nag, symbol of a country's absurd respect for learning in the period of their greatest oppression, Mat Frayne and all the other grotesque philomaths holding school in the butt of a green hedge, and mouthing words so long that they could nearly walk round them, Ned McKeown clacking homewards with his ungreased cart, Feardorcha, so miserly that he would hardly allow the flesh to stay on his bones; the list is as long as today and tomorrow. Carleton, like Dickens, saw people with an intensity that approached caricature, a kind of fierce, creative joy which cannot be explained merely as memory. This natural picaresque, a sheer joy or excitement in excess, can be found in writers as apart as Carlyle, coming from Craigenputtock with his head full of prophecy, and Joyce breaking out through the elbows of language in the funferal of *Finnegans Wake*. It springs from that transcendent moment when the world seems to mime and dance, and the soul kicks up its heels in joy of its own creation.

With Carleton's writing in the *Traits and Stories*, *The Emigrants of Ahadarra*, *Feardorcha the Miser*, and *The Black Prophet* with its terrible panorama of a country in disease, began the indigenous tradition in Irish prose writing, though not until Joyce did Carleton meet his match for natural gifts. There is more than one point of comparison between the two men; both exiles, one remembering ever after the people of an Ulster valley, the other leaving a city and building it up again in his mind, both aloof and disliked by the majority of their countrymen because of their knack of seeing filth and disorder, and not being frightened by it. There is their extraordinary instinct for authentic dialogue and character; in Joyce the dirty bobbing stream of Dublin pub life, in Carleton the droll Ulster dialect, which has never been used with such effect since.

Carleton defined his own work with a characteristic mixture of humility and pride.

There never was any man of letters who had an opportunity of knowing and describing the manners of the Irish people as thoroughly as I had. I was one of themselves, and mingled in all those sports and pastimes in which their characters are most clearly developed. That, however, is not much of itself, because many have had the same advantages, but not only a cultivated intellect but strong imagination and extraordinary powers of what I may term unconscious observation, existed in my case. I take no pride from these, because they were the gift of God.

He showed more concern for his family than his fame, but probably the most amusing tribute paid him was that of John McCormick, the Omagh Bard, who while in prison for debt was trying to raise the wind to publish his manuscript of poems, *Dreams of Genius*. He wrote:

> Carleton, son of old Tyrone,
> Could genius raise thee to a throne,
> Supreme you'd reign, my glorious boy,
> From old Strabane to Aughnacloy.

[1952]

7

GEORGE MOORE: THE TYRANNY OF MEMORY

If we naturally judge the importance of a writer for a later generation by the number of critical studies or articles on his work that
appear, or the number of casual copies to be found on public library
shelves, then George Moore is well forgotten, as his contemporaries, Yeats, Thomas Hardy and James are not, and his only certain
fame out of a mass of novels, memoirs, critical essays and unsuccessful plays is from the relaxed and wicked chronicle of the minor
lunacies of the Revival in *Hail and Farewell*. Even this carefully
wrought three-decker – probably the most mature book we possess
– is read mainly for its nostalgic flavour as a period piece, the sentimental history of a now fabulous time when Dublin had wit,
enthusiasm, and a natural rivalry that produced good work. By
contrast with the later drastic dearth, it has become the literary
portrait gallery of a lost world: the talkative, malicious, literary
Dublin which Joyce rejected and which now seems as much a
matter of history as the battle of Benburb, though its memory can
still be used to belittle any attempt to build on new ground. But
behind the chastened, meditative style, that catches all the nostalgia of Dublin in the spring and summer, and the alert eye that pin-
points character in a phrase, lie long years of heartbreak, a single-
minded devotion to writing, which was almost as saintly, if not as
impressive in achievement, as that of Flaubert or Joyce. The slack
anecdotal movement – the sentences of Moore's mature style
which Yeats compared to toothpaste squeezed out of a tube –
conceals a carefully plotted and planned narrative: 'enriched at
every moment by new and unexpected matters', as Moore himself

put it. Gogarty's picture of that same Dublin in *As I Was Going Down Sackville Street* has been praised, because, like *The Imitation of Christ*, you can open it anywhere, but the description is still more true of Moore's book: you can open any of the volumes at almost any page and pull out a plum of descriptive malice. And from that point of view, at least, and because he is our only 'civilized writer', Moore is a good example for the prospective prose-writer in Ireland today: he presents the case for discriminating industry with a vengeance, though one immediately questions his greatness, since form and skill are not sufficient: Carleton and Joyce are compelled by an urgency of imaginative vision which he never experienced.

But for Moore's other work – does the obsessive craftmanship, the impossibly sensitive weaving and reweaving, the devotion to stylistic delicacy that produced *Heloise and Abelard*, or *The Brook Kerith*, which Moore loved to hear referred to as the only two prose-epics in English, count for nothing in the end? Beyond the inevitable few admirers – and people like myself who wish to write on him – have his most studied masterpieces (and he did set out consciously, like Milton, to add a masterpiece to English literature) failed because their perfection was too rare-aired and empty, a wistful feminine style that aspired to be pure prose, and only existed in a kind of vacuum, all the strength of real experience drawn off? It is easy to state the case against the prose epics in their lovely expensive binding: Moore was an entertaining, plausible crafts-man, with a strong sense of the ridiculous that tilted neatly over into self-parody – writing on his own misadventures, as in *Memoirs of My Dead Life* and *Hail and Farewell*, he is always entertaining, for he has a gift of making the real unreal – but he lacked any deep, as apart from finely contrived, feeling, and in the end, from the lack of heart or red blood, his work crumbles away like dust in the hand. The tension, the pain, the conflict, that mark the great as opposed to the greatly skilled writer is missing; writers as apart as Balzac, Melville and Shakespeare are great perhaps because they are identical with their material, if only for a time, theirs being the pain that sustains the writing; the long struggle of Moore to achieve greatness only accentuates this central deficiency, reducing him to one of the great unread second-rate writers who miss genius through no fault of their own, stretching their original talent to its natural limits but cut off from the beginning by some flaw of personality, as, in Moore, the early adopting of an aesthetic approach to experience. Sensitivity, developed good taste, a way with words, these are not enough: sensitivity can be indiscriminate, overdone, as in Elizabeth Bowen, where the antennae are so refined that words and scenes are in a constant restless quiver that never quite achieves either truth or beauty: too much time is spent in the picking up of invisible pins.

When Eliot wrote of Shaw and Wells and Bertrand Russell in 1926 that they were part of the 'present which is already dead', he could have been speaking of the isolation of Moore in 'lack-lustre' Ebury Street, ignored by the leading writers of the period, and plaintively wondering to the assembled bookmen, why Yeats does not call on me now, or if *Ulysses* is really as good a book as *The Brook Kerith*. Far too early in life his literary personality interposed between himself and his experience, as you will see if you read through the many nostalgic refinements of his past, from the *Confessions of a Young Man* onwards. He became the lonely, slightly wicked bachelor dedicated to literature, deciding that a wife would interfere with his writing, using people and places unscrupulously only in so far as they could furnish material, always in search of a subject, and damned from the start in his effort to achieve greatness by his aesthetic approach to life, the inhuman eye of the practising writer to whom every one of his friends is a possible sitter for a portrait. And yet the many naturalistic novels were part of the apprenticeship of James Joyce, who gave one or two of them condescending praise, and in their day they broke the hold of Victorian prudery on the circulating libraries by their general success.

The truth is, perhaps, that Moore is a very special kind of writer: a mixture of novelist, essayist, and story-teller, with a thin lyrical touch, a kind of verbal impressionism, which has little relevance today, but which will return to favour when the period it springs from, too recent for revival, comes around into fashion again. Leaving aside the novels and tales and epics for the time being, the best introduction to his peculiar cultivated grace of sentiment – a favourite word – and style, is through the many books of conversational criticism and embroidered reminiscence. He had been lucky in his many shifts of interest and liked to believe that some form of Providence had guided the art-hungry steps of George

Moore, an ignorant landlord from Mayo, who could neither spell nor paint, first to the Nouvelles Athenes, where he was on the fringe of a great new movement in painting, poetry and fiction, and a friend of Degas, Manet, Mallarmé, Zola; and then to England, where his acquired enthusiasm made him the pioneer of the naturalistic novel. When his talent for novel writing was wearing thin (the impossible literary courtships of *Evelyn Innes*, and the attempt at fashionable social scenes, all have a tired, cliché-ridden air) then he came on impulse back to Ireland, and found himself in the middle of a new and delightfully mad movement, with a few cracked poets meditating a Gaelic Athens, all the necessary stimuli for a complete renewal of his talent. Moore was not a reticent man, nor was he given to praising his contemporaries, so that a good number of anecdotes, truthful or heightened, have been drawn as red herrings across his actual work: in Dublin especially where a good story is much more likely to succeed than a good book, the tale of Moore and the Protestant bishop, or Moore and the lady from Texas, is more likely to be quoted than the disciplined prose of *Ulick and Soracha*.

For this side-tracking of a man's work by the enlarged legend of his imaginary feats as a Gaelic Casanova, Moore himself was to blame, though very little of his supposed 'Pre-Raphaelite nastiness' ever got into his work, beyond a few randy stories in *A Story-Teller's Holiday*, and the squirming sensual affectation in the *Confessions*, which is much closer to Ethel Mannin than to Joyce's *Portrait of the Artist*, the other 'education novel' of a Parisian Irishman. Moore's skill in telling a story to his own satiric disadvantage – and this skill may have become precisely so dominating because he began as an illiterate, pleasure-loving squireen, to whom the simple sentence was more difficult than the water-jump – in the end became so great that he could muse incessantly on paper, with no more than a gentle melancholy boredom, and a curious lovable note of self-parody, particularly when he wrote of his mock-battles with house-agents and neighbours, the workmen who tried to destroy his rooms while he shooed them away, perched on the windowsill in his pyjamas, the vagaries of the cat next door, whether a friend would call or not, or must he sit in the chair before the fire alone. In this sense he became the greatest of the armchair authors, making dream mountains from molehills: in *Avowals* he writes, 'on an autumn evening by the fire, thinking is pleasanter, more soothing than writing: but talking, aestheticising, with one's feet to the blaze, is delightful'. This has always seemed to me a peculiar achievement of Moore's; a small one, but requiring a skill that no one else possessed; he could give to the commonplace, the small intimate things, a specific reflective glow of their own: he was the minor poet and chronicler, not of the obvious grandeur of gesture and thought as with Yeats, but of little fretful incidents, contriving to convince us that they have their own small-scale poignancy.

To some this may read like a misuse of the poetic effect, like the lyrical bubbling in Virginia Woolf's *The Waves*, a kind of random febrile feminine prose, divorced from life, but Moore – if it is of any importance – had mastered the 'stream of consciousness' method long before any of the delicate ladies from Chelsea. The sun setting over Baggot Street bridge, he cries somewhere, is more beautiful than the sunset anywhere else in the world, and despite the usual playful exaggeration, it was a cry from his heart, for Moore knew that it is not parochial pride but the deep understanding of the writer that can give splendour to every petty suburb. Part of his writing treats Ireland in the off-hand supercilious way of his predecessors in Irish landlord literature, Lover and Lever, but finally his own country gave this affected Francophile and Parisian playboy four of his best books: the famous trilogy, the contrived simplicity of *The Lake*, the short stories in *The Untilled Field*, from which, like Gogol's *Overcoat*, came Corkery and other short-story writers, and the retelling of the old Gaelic tales in *A Story-Teller's Holiday*, as no one has ever told them before or since. And even his later carefully composed landscapes of antiquity, Palestine or Boetia, with their reiterated idyllic warbling of streams and birds, go back beyond his Mediterranean excursions and his camel rides in Lebanon, to the lake at Carra and remembered views of the Mayo of his boyhood. Despite his fretful love of praise, and his egotistic pranks, Moore is at his best as a contemplative writer: the sombre, stylized melodic melancholy that he saw in Turgenev and Corot: 'I then had only an inkling of the beauty I have learnt, and that I am still learning to comprehend – a tale by Turgenev and a landscape by Corot. . . these have been and still are the holy places where I rested and rest: together they revealed to me all I needed to know.'

The autobiographical instinct – at its greatest in writers like Stendhal, Rousseau, Montaigne, all prime and attractive egotists – was one part of the talent Moore drove so hard, though one cannot always guess, as in some of the novels, that the whip is only out of sight. 'The mature writer', said Moore, 'takes the material closest to his hand', and one of his many arguments for indulging his love of reciting his own past, as long as anyone would listen to him, was that, if a man could not be interesting on the subject of himself, then there was little point in his assuming the responsibility of the novelist and guiding the lives of created characters. The prolonged boast of the *Confessions* – how like the sensuous manifesto of the young Gide in *Les Nourritures Terrestres*, a writer of trained skill and taste, the 'man of letters' rather than great creator, very like Moore in many ways – that hectic, frivolous, juvenile work begins a lifelong monologue, with George Moore as the scrawny, acid-tongued Hamlet from Mayo, who lived as if between the covers of his own greatest book. Preaching complete artistic detachment – Whistler frightened him by saying, you care for nothing but your writing – he came to regard his own life as his best material: alone in his room in the morning reweaving the texture of past incidents, creating a world in which George Moore was loved and liked and capable of being immensely witty, a world where actions were smoother than in life, his attractions greater, and even when the tables were turned on him it was an acceptable joke, a reverse which was really part of the special pattern that Providence had prepared for his strange career. From would-be steeple-chaser to Old Master in Ebury Street: the whole story held for him the fabulous picaresque quality of one of his favourite tales of antiquity, Apuleius, or Petronius, or quite simply Ulick and Soracha. Not that there was self-pity beyond the ordinary, despite his favourite elegiac tone – no, it was rather an indwelling on the mystery of himself, not introspection but bemused self-inspection, till in stories like 'The Lovers of Orelay', fact and fancy merge, he becomes a fantasist of self. Which is not unusual among Irishmen: but Moore is almost alone in carrying his own literary character beyond conversation in pub or salon on to a special, self-erected stage, where he plays before his own admiration.

There is an early portrait of Moore used to preface an edition of *Memoirs of My Dead Life*: the long nose, the already shrewd eyes, the lank hair plastered to one side, the frail shapeless body: the child that was to grow up into a rather ugly man, with shoulders that sloped like a bottle, the true Moore face, 'like a fiery sheep', and 'the blonde hair that Manet loved to paint'. This was the unusual little boy, who never learned to spell, and whose chief ambition was to ride at Aintree, until a colt named reverently after the holy mountain of 'Croaghpatrick' earned his fees by winning at Goodwood, and Master George had his first taste of clerical discipline at the 'hateful Roman Catholic College' at Oscott, where his slightly daft, and wholly naïve anti-clericalism first gained fuel. After several years of determined idleness that undermined the zeal of every teacher who tried to take him in hand, he was withdrawn, after one very typical incident of defiance, which he loved to relate in after life. George had commenced an intrigue with a serving-maid, screwing his neck around to observe her in the chapel, and then presenting the timid little girl with a bouquet ; he later refused to go to confession to tell his grievous sin of immorality, plaintively saying that there was no point in confessing when you had nothing to tell. That little incident, half-fantasy, half-rebellion, has the stamp of all of Moore's life: including the partiality for serving-maids, though his affairs were never as wicked and sensual as he would have them to be: in reality he had the daring of timidity, a strong sense of his own distinguished ugliness, and a delicacy in writing of love that is almost that of the sensitive celibate. But never again could George Moore complain that he had nothing to tell.

The *Confessions* have not worn well: they are very much a document of the period, full of the impressionable callow egotism of the spring tide, but even then Moore was able to tell a bad story to his own disadvantage. There is the contrast between the superficial brilliance of his friend Marshall, and his own plodding discovery of his gift for writing prose after failing as a painter and decadent poet: the little volume, with skull and crossbones on the cover and still more dead bones and carnal delights within, becomes a joke, the first milestone safely passed. The perverse young hero – he was reviewed in England as 'The Bestial Bard', a unique honour in English criticism – is playing the nineties' game of shocking the Victorian bourgeoise out of their shirts; nothing is too daring for him to pretend. Others are judged merely on their

relation to the figure in the centre of his drama: when his admiration lags, Zola becomes, not a powerful writer whose approach to
the novel had yielded Moore two or three of his own, but a sorry
prolific hack, at the mention of whom he kicks his heels in the air
and laughs. The whole book is a summary of Amor Moorcini, the
adolescent demon that Moore was to try all his life to exorcise, and
because of whose activities and bad taste he was obliged to suppress
much of his book from the Collected Edition. Already the eye for
sly deliberate comedy is evident: Moore heading off to the Derby
with a party of tarts and mashers, his copy of Kant in his pocket,
with the page turned down because he hopes to get an occasional
glance on the racecourse: the bizarre jumble of the Studio in the rue
de Tour de Dames, with a Buddhist altar in one corner, censers and
candlesticks and palms, and a python tied to the bed, sleeping off
its monthly meal of guinea pigs.

In the *Confessions* there are touches of the individual melancholic style which Moore was later to perfect, the prose of a
frustrated minor poet of landscape. At times the words hustle, fly
off into broken-winged raptures, praise some new poet or painter
or subtle mistress in a flurry of dots and dashes, dropping at last into
inflated prose poems, with a modicum of affected blasphemy.
Moore always maintained that it was Pater's *Marius the Epicurean*
which had finally opened his eyes to the possibility of writing
'serious', 'aesthetic' prose narrative in English. He praised the mild,
overwritten pages of his chosen master at the expense of the whole
traditional group of English novelists, all of whom in his opinion
– except for Jane Austen, Anne Brontë, and maybe one or two
others – lacked the art of telling a story, or even the ordinary graces
of style. Moore was, thank God, incapable of seeing both sides of
the matter at once. He had the natural bias of even the minor
creator, and was not as cool and detached in his judgments on his
fellows as the bookmen like Gosse, Morgan, Freeman and Hum-
bert Wolfe, who gathered around him, thinking him fair game for
gentle homage. In fact Moore was never quite sure whether he was
a plain novelist, a story-teller of the picaresque or a contemplative
essayist, and *Memoirs of My Dead Life*, one of his best books, is a
gentle compound of all three methods. 'You are aware of the
sadness in things, and it is your pleasure to indulge it', said a friend
of Moore, and these haphazard essays are weighed with some

attractive, even affected, melancholy, not strong or very real, but expressed with mild precision. This is the sentimental education of George Moore: the style, not of the brash young Parisian Irishman, but of the lonely bachelor author whose happiness lay in revising the enthusiasms of his youth. Granted a certain *fin de siècle* preciousness of phrase, and an aesthetic attitude that treats the world, including women, as some kind of vast museum or gallery (here a pleasant hill or tree or setting by the Unknown hand) the book remains nevertheless a remarkable, even unique achievement, the merely precious preserved by some special alchemy.

What is really unusual is the French analytic approach: Moore, like James Joyce after him, served an apprenticeship to the continental novelists, and turned his foreign skill on subjects nearer home: tutoring himself to stand wryly aloof and amused, 'paring his fingernails'. The careful relating of the 'Lovers of Orelay', with its final vision of a scrawny Moore and his beloved, whom he has travelled a thousand miles to seduce, like Jason in search of the Golden Fleece, coming to a little medieval town in southern France, with a regal hotel bedroom and a bed as big as a battlefield, and then finding that George's valet had not packed his many coloured silk pyjamas, hunting the sleepy little town from end to end but finding nothing but flannel nightshirts, which emphasized the unlovely line of Moore's physique; this must be one of the best-told stories in the world, one that ranks with Constant or Flaubert, though the humour is all against himself. Nothing could be further from the lean amorist who repudiated his pleasures, and went to the traditional garret in London, tying himself to the treadmill of his talent and producing over ten novels which had great temporary success, but are now largely forgotten, partly through his own wish.

Moore's return to Ireland was something he had never foreseen when he gladly left for Paris in the morning: 'I have two dominant notes,' he cried, 'an original hatred for my own country, and a brutal loathing of the religion I was brought up in.' At home in Mayo, separated from his little volumes of the Parnassian Poets, he would have been as much an exile as Adam and Eve driven from paradise. In *Parnell and His Island* (1887) there is a memorable scene where tenants come in an uproar to the gate, and the host turns with his guests into a secluded room, reading aloud a sonnet of Mallarmé. That was why, perhaps, he was so fond of 'dear Edward

Martyn', saying to himself, 'that there but for the grace of the Nouvelles Athenes goes George Moore, a contemplative and impotent landlord, with faint literary ambitions'. But the mysterious Angel that called Moore in Chelsea, telling him to go to Ireland, his manuscripts in his case, was, maybe, no angel in the ordinary sense of the word, but the most shrewd literary conscience that Ireland ever produced, the conscience of a skilful man of letters who knows when each separate seam has yielded all its gold. Detecting a failure in his talent, a tiredness, a recurrence of the clichés of naturalism, he realized that there came a day when one could no longer go on producing competent novels – he came to Ireland in fact in search of new words to conquer.

Whimsy, pardonable enough in the period, was part of Moore's stock in trade, and has to that extent worn thin, but the magnificent performance of *Hail and Farewell*, magnificent certainly, but also a performance, is very nearly as entertaining as Boswell or Sterne, though Moore, argumentative and shrill, insists on dragging in long anti-clerical passages which have not even the merit of wit. The scenes take on an eternal quality; Moore dawdling down to see John Eglinton in the National Library, and walking home arguing with him in the heavy summer evening, the scent of lilac and laburnum and hawthorn in the air, Moore cycling to Monasterboice on a blistering hot day with AE and taking off his long woollen drawers behind a hedge, offering them in exchange for a cup of milk; Yeats in the tossing boat during the storm, trying to pray, but only remembering chunks of *Paradise Lost*: these scenes are as great comedy as has ever been written, the kind of malicious yet loving detachment in *Don Quixote*, with Moore as Cervantes to his own Don Quixote, a lean and foolish writer, coming to Ireland on a grammatical crusade, and lost among the many windmills of a priest-ridden, fanatic little island. There is much in the Moore of the collaboration with Yeats, and the devastation of certain elderly critics who opposed the Revival, of Toad of Toad Hall, the outrageous landlord of Kenneth Grahame's animal story, with his inquisitive finger in every new-fangled pie, always reckless, and always being rescued by his long-suffering friends, especially poor dreamy Edward, the friendly Badger, who preferred the quiet wood. 'We have gone through life together,' said Moore, 'myself charging windmills, Edward holding up his hands in astonishment.' They became types and eternal figures, ineffectual and foolish immortals: 'there is something eternal about Edward, an entity come down through the ages, and myself another entity.' With his faculty for making the small incident monstrously witty, the final triumph of the novelist's craft, Moore had his fantasy, and his puppets, right at his hand: the lanky Yeats in his black cloak, cawing gently; the bearded and charitable AE, a fount of wisdom, lost to us in being cloudily phrased, and all the minor bees that buzzed in the bottle; these and their antics diverted the tedium of Moore's life in Ely Place, dissipated his gentle ennui. For Moore was honest enough to admit that he was driven to continue writing, not by a great urgency as in Joyce, but just by boredom; he had lost enthusiasm for reading, and the only thing he could do was to go on writing, for he knew no other trade: 'Man was born to labour, as the oldest texts say; he must continue to drive his furrow to the end of the field, otherwise he would lie down and die of sheer boredom or go mad.' Prolific and sensitive to the last, he propped himself up on his bed, hoping to complete his last version of the Odyssey of George Moore, *A Communication to My Friends*.

Moore is, therefore, like so many modern writers, obsessed by memory: after a certain age, thoughtless action ceases, and he finds himself committed to a perpetual stocktaking. The heavy latent shadow of nostalgia lies across much of the best writing of the last fifty years, whether the indefatigable burrowings of Proust, Graham Greene describing intimations of mortality in a Lost Childhood, or even Evelyn Waugh, relaxing the astringency of his satire to flounder in luxuriant memories of his salad days. Proust is the archetype of all those to whom life is a glance over the shoulder, his influence being plain in *Brideshead Revisited*, and his slack, melancholic tone very like the Moore of *Memoirs of My Dead Life*, and the many embroidered memories scattered through the works of criticism and conversation. Like Waugh, though there is a different convention of wickedness and irresponsibility in Moore, his work is burdened at times with all the purple ecstasy of a man remembering a perpetual land of undergraduate – or Bohemian – joy. The recurrence of Moore's pet trademarks of glamour and art – in the café correcting his proofs, when Degas speaks to him, and the day that Manet said, 'You are no longer le plus Parisien de tous les Anglais' – these typical clichés of place remind us of the director in Scott Fitzgerald's *The Last Tycoon*, to whom a young girl surrounded by dogs going out to pat a horse on the rump became a symbol, a scene that was repeated in all his films.

There is a suggestion in this attitude that only recollected emotion can be a fit subject for art, that remorse and nostalgia are the real Muses. It shows too that Moore is not so far from the temper of our own time as the surface of his prose suggests; he shares the general evasion, the self-indulgence which is one kind of good writing. In this attitude – and it seems to me a valid criticism of nearly all modern writing – there is a fundamental lack or absence, not of maturity in the ordinary sense, but of 'adultness'; such writers rarely take satisfactory or forceful action in their own time, apart from their work: Malraux's criticism of Proust applies: he said that he would like to line up all the characters of *A la Recherche du Temps Perdu* in front of a firing squad or a barricade. They are naturally displaced persons, absorbed in the contemplation of minutiae, always searching for an enclosed garden of romance, never entering their own time except through the sideways method of satire, and their appeal, I think, is part of this, perhaps justifiable, evasive action. This side-stepping of adult responsibility leads to the private world: the style is negative, and dreamy, infinitely pleasing in nuance, but dissatisfying in ˙he end. But nothing is as indestructible as a good book, and AE discoursing under the trees in the garden of Ely Place is almost as universal as Hamlet. For every intellectual skirmish there is a 'painted' landscape, and when George Moore, spinsterish and petulant and talented, came home from the company of the great in Paris to observe the tantalizing oddities of his native town, he wrote at least one lasting book. He revived the art of the conversation as a literary form, he gave us fine models for the short story and the retelling of the more lively legends, and not one of his eighty items, pamphlets, poems, plays, and especially his novels, is without its merit. We could do with a little of his disinterested zeal, and his industry.

[1951]

8

JAMES JOYCE: WORK YOUR PROGRESS

The most impressive thing about Joyce, as a writer, is that he did not flounder. The first efforts of a writer are often tentative, various, before they focus. There is the light tinkle of *Chamber Music*, of course, but then everyone wants to be a poet (except, in my experience, those who find themselves *bemused*) and Joyce's poetry is a series of musical experiments, far better than Faulkner's and more singable than *Echo's Bones!* But look how even someone as bright as Beckett twisted and turned before he found his lonely voice. I have not read *A Dream of Fair to Middling Women*, but *More Pricks than Kicks* is the work of a Trinity scholard. As for the early Yeats, it stands so far from his mature achievement that I sometimes wonder if the fairies didn't steal him. Some twenty and more years ago, I nicked a copy of his early *Collected Poems* from the Tyrone County Library, but I limped back with it a few months later: I could see no connection between it and anything I knew about the world or writing.

Whereas *Dubliners* was immediately accessible. I was helped to fathom that melancholy, decaying city through a Guild paperback bought in my first year at University College, Dublin. Dublin hadn't changed all that much, though I was so ignorant that I didn't understand many aspects of it, like the musical. When I met Jimmy Plunkett and joined little *soirées* with the stout bottles behind the piano, and he and his wife playing the violin, I recognized a tradition, a rich, warmer one than the vindictive chat of pub intellectuals. The ladies-in-waiting had disappeared, of course, in the wake of the British army, so the dissatisfied young had only the dancehalls, instead of the Kips, to let off a head of steam. But those meticulous stories, so well written, so well arranged, were an intelligent antidote to what lay around my naïve northerner's eye, and my *Dubliners* ended with one of the great short stories of the world.

Warmth was missing, perhaps: Joyce was reacting against the Celtic Twilight and the auld chat about a Literary Revival. Instead, he picked up the scalpel that Flaubert had passed on to Maupassant, who was not long dead when Joyce started, and in so doing he put paid to the amateurism of nineteenth-century prose in English. *The Untilled Field* was already there, but Joyce had a prejudice against even Gallicized bogmen. I have no sympathy with the attempt of some writers to belittle *Dubliners* on minor grounds; the occasional excesses of style seem to me deliberate, a counter-point to the 'scrupulous meanness' of his system, little arias of *fin de siècle* solipsism. And yet there *is* much feeling in *Dubliners*, exact, and not gushing, a compassion for the trapped, especially in 'The Dead'. Perhaps I should modify that remark about bogmen, because Joyce's eerie sympathy for the West his wife had come from was demonstrated for me once in a way that he would regard as the magic of coincidence. On an early Claddagh record a young red-haired woman sings 'The Lass of Aughrim'; she was Dolly MacMahon, whose maiden name was Furey.

I wish he had gone on to write more stories, but bow to the relentlessness of his progress. He had squeezed the form dry before the age of twenty-five, and left us with an ideal, a standard. Naturally, there was a romantic reaction, but (despite *Spring Sowing, Guests of the Nation* and *Midsummer Night Madness*) *Dubliners* remains the best single collection of stories in our literature. Lawrence and Faulkner have done more, but they were not in pursuit of perfection, the Flaubertian *mot juste* and master-work, with not a comma amiss. Fifty years later, when I assembled *Death of a Chieftain*, I tried for a similar pattern, from childhood to manhood, though I was dealing with the Ulster countryside, and a much later Dublin. No one noticed this oblique homage but I may still restore my original epigraph from *A Portrait*, where Joyce grapples with the spectre of the Irish countryman:

I fear him. I fear his redrimmed horny eyes. It is with him I must struggle all through this night till day comes, till he or I lie dead, gripping him by the sinewy throat till. . . Till what? Till he yield to me? No. I mean him no harm.

No one could overestimate the effects of A *Portrait of the Artist as a Young Man* on later Irish writers, from Austin Clarke to John McGahern. Or on the national psyche: many young Irishmen came to painful consciousness reading those corrosive pages. The Dublin of my student days was strewn with versions of Stephen Dedalus, including myself, though I wonder what the women thought of it! Again, the bravura passages, like the sermon, are deliberate, and the ecstasy on the seashore is central, like the vision Beckett records in *Krapp's Last Tape*. Joyce had found his vocation, and his analysis of an Irish Catholic education has been cathartic for us all; compare it with *Le Grand Meaulnes*, *Huckleberry Finn*, or even *Sons and Lovers*, as a novel of growing up, and you will get a chilling sense of the intensity of our national psychosis. Little failed saints, we knew eternity too early. I notice with relief that few novelists have tried to cover that ground again; when it reappears, it will be in poetry like Clarke's *Night and Morning*.

Having shown us how to write short stories as good as any French naturalist's, he produces our classic *künstlerroman*. Perhaps the long delay in the publication of *Dubliners* helped him to escape the chronicle of *Stephen Hero*. I would be fascinated to read those burnt pages, but it would be for selfish, scholarly reasons: the next move had not taken place and Stephen is still a hero to himself, in the pages we have. Whereas the breakdown into diary form at the end of *A Portrait*, like the notes at the end of *Watt*, is a mock-heroic coda, after the job is done. He had given himself ten years to produce his misterwork, to use the phrase of Myles, and 'Dublin, 1904 – Trieste, 1914' is a first defiant signal from abroad.

And then he widens his scope again. Such intensity is awesome and sets standards no writer, Irish or otherwise, has tried to match. Frank O'Connor or James Plunkett or Seamus Heaney, to name three different generations, once they have found a rich vein, contentedly mine it: a Cork, Dublin or South Derry childhood, slowly understood, becomes substance for a body of work. But Master Joyce took the English novel and wrung its neck in *Ulysses*, singlehandedly inventing the modern novel. He also chastised his own earlier self or *persona*, for Stephen Dedalus could not have written such a rich work. His aesthetic indifference is set against the uncertain humanity of Bloom, who, as we now know from the letters to Nora, is much closer to the older Joyce than that eternal student.

But back to the historical achievement. The whole modern American novel springs from *Ulysses*, especially the Jewish, and especially Bellow. (I mentioned Moses Herzog to Bellow once and he laughed his usual wry smile: 'I think we owe more than a name.') That a middle-class Dubliner should have introduced two of the major themes of modern fiction, the urban scene, and the wandering Jew, is, well, genius, of the order of Dante, Melville, Proust – naming continents our conscious mind had shirked. And no one has caught up with his technical innovations. Dos Passos uses 'The Cave of the Winds' in his *U.S.A.*, and Burroughs and Pynchon, those darlings of the young, also try to match his inventiveness. William Faulkner had a good try in *The Sound and the Fury*, but then Faulkner is an erratic provincial genius in his own write.

The *Portrait* ends with Stephen communing with himself in an undisguised diary, *Ulysses* ends with the monologue of Molly, and then we have seventeen years of *Finnegans Wake*. It is at this historical point that Beckett lurches onto the scene, helping the blind penman dictate, as well as initiating a transmogrification of parts of *Wake* into French, with his pal, Albert Peron. I leave the detection of influences to scholars, but the great, later Beckett is also a master of monologue, and his first published work in French was in that translation. He has never yielded in his admiration for *Finnegans Wake*, while oddly declaring that Joyce was for order, organization as against the chaos he felt himself prey to, impotent as Earwicker.

I don't think novelists have caught up with Joyce, nor do I think they have to react in the intense personal way that Beckett did, as disciple and friend. By now Joyce should have sunk into the Irish consciousness, to be read and recited the way Florentines remember Dante. He did exactly what he set out to do, and forged the 'uncreated conscience' of the long-submerged Irish Catholic race. How lucky we are to have such a legacy and, if it is more important to re-read a chapter of *Ulysses* than the latest masterpiece, it is because such skill sets standards which free us from illusions.

Which we have all around us, the jockeying for the Booker, or the newest poetry rosette, writers ranked like racehorses. It is an aspect of our advertising age; and also a new weariness. The lonely artist of the early twentieth century is now an historical figure, part of what we call the Modernist movement; Joyce and Yeats died before the Holocaust and the Bomb that has frightened us into peace. What is striking in most recent writing is the shrinking of the scale of achievement: from D. H. Lawrence to Ted Hughes, from David Jones to Geoffrey Hill, from Yeats and Joyce down to all of us. There are still idiosyncratic documents, Beckett's *Watt*, as well as the trilogy, *Black List Section H* as an Irish version of Céline, Flann O'Brien's *Third Policeman*, but what Stuart calls the barnyard fowls rule the roost, clucking over chaos like a delf egg.

Misunderstood from America to Australia, travelling bagmen bombarded by crisis-hungry media, we cannot take ourselves as seriously. In any case, Joyce's exile was tactical; he could never have written *Ulysses* in Dublin surrounded by his litigious originals. He invented his drama, declared his own past dead. Perhaps what we have still to learn from Joyce is his ferocious sense of humour. He complained that nobody ever said that *Ulysses* was funny: a mock-heroic epic, like *Tom Jones*. But *Finnegans Wake* is achingly worse, the cackle of our global village heard for the first time in literature. Joyce's Tower is the Tower of Babel. 'Here form is content, content is form.' Beckett's phrase becomes McLuhan's well-heeled cliché: *The medium is the message*.

Hugh Kenner once remarked that Irish fiction had never matched the magnificent dinner scene in *The Portrait*, its detail of comedy and pain. Modern poets might also learn a little about structure and language from our great blind master. When people ask me about the chorus at the end of 'The Cave of Night', I refer them to Joyce's great culminating vision of orderly chaos where 'Gricks may rise and Troysirs fall'. And 'The Bread God' owes as much to Joyce's rendition of a hot-gospeller as to William Carlos Williams, or the lunatic notion of 'open form'.

Yeats may be our seer, in the tradition of the poet-aristocrat. But Joyce is our all-seeing ear, a great democrat of literature, as Saul Bellow once explained, comparing him with Henry James. But those voices raised in sentimental song, those tears above the glass? I am afraid I must let a cat out of the bag here; a decade in Cork has convinced me that *Ulysses* is largely the work of an exiled Corkman, the son of Si Dedalus. In the Long Valley, the old records of John McCormack still soar silvery above the glasses, and as the boss once said to me in The Ivy Leaf, near Parnell Place: 'Musical gatherings are the essence of Cork.' As for Stephen and his Judas, perhaps we can leave them to Dublin, but the ghost of Dedalus *père* should pour into the portals of the ear of Daniel Corkery and his brigade the simple truth, that he helped to inspire the greatest work in our literature.

[1982]

9

SAMUEL BECKETT: SPOILED HERMIT

I floated quite naturally into Beckett's company in the early sixties, when we became Montparnasse neighbours. A. J. ('Con') Leventhal of Trinity was the catalyst, and if one was naturally wary of intruding on the great man, such caution was soon dissolved in cataracts of drink and good conversation. Besides, canonization was only in progress, and Beckett was still able to circulate freely through the night haunts of his chosen city.

We usually met around 10 p.m. in the Falstaff, an old watering-hole of the twenties still frequented by writers. Was that Sartre in the corner, or Ionesco with his Chinese wife? Probably, but after a friendly farmer's nod had been exchanged, we did not cross lines, because that was the convention of our village. Sartre lodged with Simone de Beauvoir in the rue Schoelcher around the corner, so everyone converged in the evening after the day's work to relax among friends. After the Falstaff changed hands, we moved lower down to the Rosebud, or the vast spaces of the Coupole.

And relax Beckett usually did, the lined face suddenly crinkling with laughter, the seagull eyes sparkling. His bony reserve was daunting, but his beloved Con was a gentle subversive. Leventhal and I were discussing love in a leisurely fashion, when Sam saw a chance to shove in his oar. 'No love!' he said with satisfaction, 'only fuck.' Startled silence, as Beckett moves in again. 'Eat-drink-fuck' he declared, 'that's all!', unconsciously echoing Eliot. How a shocked Con recovered to stalk his man and discomfit Beckett is a longer story; but he succeeded because he knew his friend.

Friendship clearly means a great deal to Beckett, and he is

fiercely loyal; the widows of his friends in particular can testify to his care and generosity. Although he is of the select company of those who, like Sophocles, would prefer not to have been born, he would do everything he could to ease a friend's suffering. Contemplating the cheerful grimness of his work and days, I once asked him if he had ever thought of ending it. 'Out of the question,' he said brusquely. 'But I have thought about disappearance.' His best plan, he elaborated, was a boat with a hole in the bottom, to be dredged up by the divers. Then a philosophic sigh. 'That's legally impossible too. The widow wouldn't inherit for seven years.'

He lived without the protective outer skin of custom, and sees naked pain and suffering everywhere. Chased out of a publishing party by a belligerent young Irish novelist, he first disappeared under the table, emerging at the other end to plead on his hands and knees for a kiss from a pretty young woman. In a taxi afterwards, he mutely pointed to the signs for various charities adorning the inside of the car. HELP THE BLIND, SAVE THE STARVING, MERCY FOR THE MUTILATED; they seemed to sing an answer to his call. Sharing a coffee, he confided, 'I see it everywhere. The human spirit is on its knees. Everything is on fire.' For him, only a few artists, like the weeping canvases of Bram Van Velde, or the ferocity of Louis Ferdinand Céline's novels, are equal to the Goya-like darkness of our crematorium century.

Ireland is a sore subject, to be carefully handled: he has recognized Joyce's reservations, and though a firm family man, he has no great desire to return. While he can speak with extraordinary fondness of the landscape, the land itself, and would praise essays like Synge's Wicklow Travels, he is suspicious of the inhabitants and their attitude towards art. The famous misquotation about our being driven into writing because we are caught between the English and the Church is only partly right; we've also buggered ourselves. I had an early book savaged by an older Irish poet, and Beckett was relentless; 'Don't answer, they're not *worth* it.' Whatever about his youthful literary persona, Belacqua, he does not like bad manners, literary or otherwise, and regards them as endemic to the great Hibernian bog.

Withal, he seems to me deeply Irish, with his control masking volatile swings of mood from unshakable gloom about the human condition through ferocity at any surrender to lower standards and, underlying all, the quick redeeming flash of humour, the sudden surge of generosity. We never mentioned Deirdre Bair's biography, not even my long repentant review of it in *The Guardian*, but when I teased him about the confusions concerning his birthday, he still stuck to Good Friday, 13 April 1906 – despite the birth certificate, which records 13 May. 'I have it from a good source,' he said. 'Not the Dublin City Records,' I replied. 'A far better source,' he grinned, 'someone at the heart of the problem.' Then with one flat Dublin phrase, he swept my friendly prodding away: 'The mother!' His look dared me to contradict that ultimate authority.

And for the Irish male, getting drunk together seems a necessary preface to intimacy; Sam is no exception. One 14 July I was sitting calmly on the terrace of the Select with a serious young French critic. Suddenly Sam lurched by, clutching a woman, a distinguished painter. He spied me and drew to a swaying halt at our table. He was clearly on the tear, that most un-French of occupations. And nothing would do but that I should accompany him. The cricket, as his companion kept calling my poor French friend, was also swept along, awed and astonished at our antics. Again space fails me, but as dawn was breaking we tottered out of the last dive. I propped Beckett along while Leventhal mooched ahead, swinging wide his lame leg. 'Con's a great man,' said Sam admiringly. We parted ways at the top of the Boulevard Raspail, and I managed Beckett to his door. Next day there was a note through the post. 'Thanks for your help up the blazing Boulevard.'

It wasn't only Leventhal who was a 'great man' in Beckett's eyes. I watched once as a crafty journalist seeking his confidence lightly mentioned that he had played rugby with Ollie Campbell. Beckett's eyes lit up, and all his weary embarrassment vanished. 'Do you really know Campbell?' he said excitedly. 'What's he like?' My cunning confrère confided that no more modest humble man ever pulled on rugby boot. 'He's a genius!' cried Beckett. 'But you're not supposed to have a television,' I reminded Sam. 'You're supposed to be against all that.' 'Only for the games,' was his furtive apology, 'and only when the Irish play.' But the journalist had the hook in, and soon Sam was discussing with him a rugby team of Irish writers. Spoilers like O'Flaherty were easy to place, but the half-blind Joyce was a problem, and Beckett would not relegate his old master to the bench. 'Very crafty, very nippy, try him at fly-half. He might surprise you when the light is fading.'

If I were asked to sum up my neighbourly exchanges with Beckett I would say that, while acknowledging that we live in the worst of all possible worlds, cheerfulness keeps breaking in. Every time I come away exhilarated by his tough-mindedness, his humility, his uncomplaining acceptance of his fate. When I moved back to Ireland, a decision about which he was mildly apprehensive, our meetings naturally became rarer. In any case, his retreat for such occasions to the ultra-modern hotel opposite his flat is a sign not only of his advancing age, but of general change. The Falstaff has changed hands, the Rosebud is thronged, the Closerie de Lilas too public. Impossibly harassed, he no longer answers the phone but negotiates more formal, though still friendly, meetings. Our catalyst Con is gone, but the old fire still smoulders in Beckett's weary but warm gaze.

We were once discussing the view from his window, 'Don't you get bored looking down on La Santé Prison?' I asked mischievously. With shy vanity he flashed back: 'But I can see the Pantheon as well, John.' We rarely mentioned Irish writing, although he confessed to sneaking away from the pubs to all the Abbey first nights of O'Casey and Yeats. When I lamented the fact that Irish literature seemed to have gone backwards and that there was no longer any link between French and English literature as in the great days of the Modern Movement, I was so eloquently gloomy that I finally let my head hang, declaring, 'There's no point in going on.' There was a sigh and a stir above me until I looked up into his solicitous gaze; 'But John, you must go on.'

People sometimes wonder if Beckett's retiring modesty is genuine, considering his professional exactitude. In our most recent conversation, after we had moved away from that monstrous hotel to a little workers' café where he even sank a brandy, he became his old relaxed self. 'What are you writing now, Sam?' 'Senilities,' he said with pleasant sharpness, 'But I'll manage something yet. Did you have that terrible choice at school between Science and the Greeks? I wish I had read Sophocles and all the rest. I might have done something.' A phrase from our differing backgrounds intrigued him suddenly. 'John, what do you mean by a spoiled priest?' I explained, and there was a wry pause. 'Well, I suppose that I'm a spoiled hermit,' he said reflectively. 'My father was always worried about me and wanted me to do a Guinness clerkship. I'd be retired by now.' 'And unknown,' I said. 'Ah yes,' he said with a genuine sigh, *'never heard of.'*

[1986]

10

IN THE IRISH GRAIN

I

Gaelic is my national language but it is not my mother tongue.
W. B. Yeats

Every poet must dream of an ideal anthology of the poetry of his country, all the major objects declared and arranged. And no literature stands more in need of such a spring-cleaning than Irish: we have a tendency to applaud work for its local or national interest which has hampered any consistent attempt to apply poetic standards. There are good historical reasons for our uncertainty. After living abroad for over a decade, I came to the conclusion that, unlike prose writers, it is almost impossible for a poet to change languages. And yet this is what happened to Irish poetry in the nineteenth century, after the native tradition seemed to peter out in the doggerel of Raftery. So what we find in the work of Mangan, Walsh, Ferguson, Callanan, is a racial sensibility striving to be reborn; is it strange that it comes through with a mournful sound, like a medium's wail? The true condition of Irish poetry in the nineteenth century is not silence, as Thomas Kinsella has argued, but mutilation. Loss is Mangan's only real theme, and in Ferguson's most original ballad, 'The Welshmen of Tirawley', the choice proposed to the Lynotts clan, between castration and blindness, might be a symbol of the plight of a subject people; many of the later poets in Irish, from Carolan to Raftery, were physically blind, like the great blues-singers of the American South.

Since then it has been a natural practice for our poets to translate from the Irish. Even Yeats, who knew little, gave his early blessing to Hyde's *Love Songs of Connacht* and Kuno Meyer's version of *The Vision of MacConglinne*, and forty years later improved, then borrowed from, the early translations of O'Connor. After the foundation of the Republic, the majority of Irish poets (including those brought up in Ulster Catholic schools like myself and Seamus Heaney) became to some extent bilingual. But the anomaly remains: Irish literature in English is in the uneasy position that the larger part of its past lies in another language. That this could be a strength, I hope to show later, but in order to appreciate the dilemma properly, one must take up the story at the beginning, over a thousand years ago.

The first thing that strikes one in early Irish literature is the importance attached to poetry. In an oral culture, the *scop* or *file* is a blend of historian and priest, a repository of information and magic. So we find Amergin, the official poet of the Milesians, apostrophizing Eire on behalf of his patrons; official Irish poetry may be said to have begun on that day. But devotion to Ireland is only part of a religious vision of the universe, an aspect of nature worship. Even if one hesitates before Robert Graves's imaginative reconstruction of 'The Song of Amergin', we have that prospect of a prelapsarian, almost Mohammedan paradise which is one of the recurrent themes of Irish poetry, from *The Wooing of Etáin* through *The Vision of MacConglinne* to the Middle English *Land of Cockaigne*.

> Steadily may Bran row!
> It is not far to the Land of Women. . .
> (Version: Kuno Meyer)

And here we should remark another aspect of early Irish poetry: it is the only literature in Europe, and perhaps in the world, where one finds a succession of women poets. Psychologically, a female poet has always seemed an anomaly, because of the necessarily intense relationship between the poet and the Muse. Why then did poetry always seem a natural mode of expression for gifted Irish women? I think this was because there was no discrimination against them: the first woman poet of whom we hear, Liadan of Corcaguiney, was a fully-qualified member of the poets' guild,

which could mean as much as twelve years of study. It was as an
equal that the poet Curithir wooed her, and though she drove him
off, for religious reasons, her lament rings in our ears to this day.

There is a long line of such poems, culminating in the majestic
'Keen for Art O'Leary', composed by Dark Eileen, his wife, as late
as the end of the eighteenth century. But the greatest of all the early
Irish poems supposedly written by women is not a lament for one
love but for many. It might be more accurate to say that it is a
lament for mankind in general, a piercing outcry against age which
anticipates Villon by several centuries. Behind 'The Hag of Beare'
lies the struggle between paganism and Christianity, between
bodily pleasure and the doctrine of salvation through repentance.
It is the ebb and flow of her misery, with sudden crests of remembered pride, which gives this dramatic lyric its structure; it ends as
it begins, following the circular aesthetic of Irish art. A thousand
years later, the same lonely note is heard, in Maurya's monologue
in 'Riders to the Sea'.

In suggesting that the quarrel between natural and organized
religion, between instinct and restraint, is one of the major themes
of Irish literature, I am not forgetting that the early Church, the
civilization of 'the little monasteries' as Frank O'Connor called it,
had the task of transcribing that oral culture:

Now until the coming of Patrick speech was not suffered to be given in
Ireland but to three; to a historian for narration and the relating of tales:
to a poet for eulogy and satire; to a brehon lawyer for giving judgement
according to the old tradition and precedent. But after the coming of
Patrick every speech of these men is under the yoke of the white language,
that is, the scriptures.

Ancient Laws, i. 18.

This historical irony is part of the fascination of the period, for
while these monks might have been ardent Christians, they were
also increasingly conscious of being Irishmen. There are three
kinds of manuscript which contain what might be called 'the
Matter of Ireland'. The first are compilations by monks who often
left Ireland to suffer 'the white martyrdom of exile'. On the margin
of those portable libraries which they used to combat the ignorance
of the Dark Ages, a vernacular poem as delicate as a haiku will
suddenly flower:

111

> Ah, blackbird, it's well for you
> whatever bush holds your nest:
> little hermit who clinks no bell,
> your clear, sweet song brings rest.
>
> (Version: John Montague)

But the majority of the manuscripts, like The Book of the Dun Cow and The Book of Leinster, were compiled in monastic settlements, like Clonmacnoise on the banks of the Shannon, or Terryglass on Lough Derg. In both of these manuscripts one finds versions of the Great Táin, the Cattle Raid of Cooley which is the nearest thing that Irish literature has to an epic. It makes a curious picture: a monk bending his head (tonsured across the front, in the Irish fashion) to copy the scandalous deeds of some Iron Age chariot-driven head-hunter like Cu Chulainn. Sometimes this backward look produced even stranger results: what is one to make of a rag-bag of history and myth like The Book of Invasions which records with dead-pan seriousness the first orgy in Ireland, the first adultery. . . ? Whatever about their Victorianized descendants, the original Irish were not puritans.

The third group of manuscripts is medieval, historically speaking. After the Norman invasion, and the collapse of the monastic schools, the duty of preserving Irish tradition returned again to the descendants of the *fili* who had held such an important place in pre-Christian society. The Speckled Book, The Yellow Book of Lecan and The Book of Ballymote were great compendia of Irish learning compiled for the use of the leading families by their poet scholars. During the long years when their powers had been reduced by the graphic skills of the monks, the poets must often have thought of revenge. The hero of The Vision of MacConglinne is a rogue cleric, and both it and The Land of Cockaigne might be regarded as satires on the fish and watercress austerity of Irish monastic life, while in that other medieval masterpiece, The Frenzy of Sweeny (which Robert Graves regards as the prime parable of the poetic nature), the poet-king takes to the trees after being cursed by a cleric.

One constant in early Irish literature is an almost mystical feeling for nature: it is Columcille, not Patrick, who is the typical figure among the Irish saints, because he is a poet physically in love with his country, like Mad Sweeny, or the Fenians. Patrick is seen as old Tallcrook, a Romanizing bishop; the confrontation between him and Oisín, the last representative of the pagan world, is the dramatic centre of another medieval masterwork, The Dialogue of the Old Men, and of the Ossianic lays:

> Stop, stop and listen for the bough top
> Is whistling and the sun is brighter
> Than God's own shadow in the cup now!
> Forget the hour-bell. Mournful matins
> Will sound, Patric, as well at nightfall.
>
> (Version: Austin Clarke)

II

> .. were our fount of knowledge dry,
> Who could to men of rank supply
> The branches of their pedigree,
> And Gaelic genealogy?
>
> (Version: Lord Longford)

Perhaps the most difficult form of Irish poetry for us to appreciate is the strict bardic, which extends from the thirteenth to the seventeenth century. A bard was a member of the now rigid professional literary caste; he did not even speak his poems in public but designated that duty to a *reacaire*, or reciter. His aim was to serve his prince, and his training in metrics was lengthy and strenuous. Seven winters in a dark room would be one way of describing it:

Concerning the poetical Seminary or School. . . it was open only to such as were descended of Poets and reputed within their Tribes. . . The Structure was a snug, low Hut, and beds in it at convenient Distances, each within a small Apartment. . . No Windows to let in the Day, nor any Light at all us'd but that of Candles, and these brought in at a proper Season only. .. The reason of laying the Study aforesaid in the Dark was doubtless to avoid the Distraction which Light and the variety of Objects represented thereby commonly occasions.

Clanricarde Memoirs, London 1722

But feeling can shine through the chainmail of technique, and in one of the most famous of the bardic poems, we find this training supporting a classic metaphor for human existence; that of Plato's cave. According to one of the leading scholars of the period, Gofraidh Fionn O'Dalaigh's poem on the child born in prison 'appears to have been for centuries the most popular religious composition in Ireland', and its stately sententiousness represents a constant aspect of the Irish mind, to be found later in the work of the poet-priest, Geoffrey Keating. But we respond more to the few private poems the bards allowed themselves, though when Giolla Brighde MacNamee prays for a son, he is also hoping for an intellectual heir; one of the great poetic families is called Mac An Bhaird, the son of the bard (now Ward).

From a court to a courtly poetry is one graceful step. With what has been called the Norman-Gaelic love-lyric a more cosmopolitan note, ultimately traceable to the *amour courtois* of the Provençal, enters Irish poetry. It is interesting to compare poets like Gerald Fitzgerald and Pierce Ferriter (both Normans who had adopted the bardic tradition) with their English contemporaries, from Surrey to Suckling – especially when one reflects that so many of the best Elizabethan poets, like Raleigh and Sir John Davies, assisted at the destruction of a society which produced a poetry so akin to their own! But one is comparing a mature growth with a blighted: as the best modern translator of the period, the late Lord Longford (and how revealing that he, and the Englishman Robin Flower, should have felt drawn to the period) says:

If we remember that the systematic annihilation of Irish culture was in full swing before Shakespeare and Spenser began to write, there is no reason to believe that Ireland, had circumstances been favourable, might not have achieved as much in literature as the larger island. . . a unique culture, as interesting in its potentialities as in its achievements, goes down without reaching its fulfilment; and the last of the bards sing of its ruin. . .

It is this long-drawn-out death song of an order, monotonous in its intensity, like a dog howling after its master, which one finds in later bardic poetry. A detail may suggest the background – not until well into the seventeenth century have we firm dates for most of the poets: we know when Pierce Ferriter was hanged, but not when

he was born. And yet through all this strife and confusion –
Spenser's great cantos of Mutability were written in Ireland – there
never seems to have been any doubt as to who were the master
poets, despite the uniformity of their training:

> Yon spark's a poet, by my troth!
> Sprat and whale are fishes both;
> All birds build nests; so, like the rest,
> We call the tit's wee lodge a nest.
> (Version: Robin Flower)

Thus Tadgh Dall O'Huiginn, himself a Muse poet, in the Graves'
sense; like Thomas the Rhymer, he had met the Queen of Fairy-
land:

> Twice had she come. The maid with longing sore
> Wasted my cheek and scarred my brow with care.
> Twice hath she come and she will come once more
> And still I wait, for she is wondrous fair.
> (Version: Lord Longford)

By the end of the century, however, the maid of the aisling or
vision poems is a captive who is concerned with only one thing, her
freedom. But her mournful cries have to compete with a new
literature, in the language of her conqueror.

III

> Irishness is not primarily a question of birth or blood or language;
> it is the condition of being involved in the Irish situation, and
> usually of being mauled by it.
> Conor Cruise O'Brien

The growth of an Irish literature in English parallels the spread of
the language. From Spenser to Hopkins, a succession of English
poets have suffered in Ireland, but we have only an oblique claim
on them although the passage on the rivers from *The Faerie Queene*
challenges any narrow definitions of Irish poetry. The sensuous
vision of The Land of Cockaigne, however, is clearly related to
early Irish literature; I am thinking not just of loan words, like

capall, but of the goliardic spirit of the poem, so close to MacCon-glinne. The same manuscript contains 'A Satire on the People of Kildare':

> Hail be ze brewsters wip zur galuns,
> Potels and quartes ouer al pe tounes.

which like 'The Maid of the Moor' may have been one of those 'base, wordly and theatrical songs' the bishop of Ossory rebuked his clerics for singing in the fourteenth century? And did a girl from Munster not get a line in one of Shakespeare's plays (Pistol's 'Calen o custure me' is probably the opening line of an Irish song, 'I am a girl from beside the Suir')?

But until the Ulster Plantation and the Cromwellian Wars, the English language kept shrinking back to the Pale, the first significant literary product of which is Richard Stanihurst's hexameter translation of Virgil. Like a later Dubliner, James Joyce, Stanihurst suffered from logomania, and delightfully so; *bedgle* for making love, *skitop* for the roof of the sky among his compound words, *sloa* and *fats* for fates among his peculiar spellings, *petit degree* a satiric version of pedigree (one thinks of Myles's 'Paddy grees'), and a whole host of onomatapoeic words, like *chuff, clush* and *stutting* for stammering. An Elizabethan gone wrong, his alliterated and agglutinated words make him the ancestor of that verbal pedantry which dances through Irish literature.

But Stanihurst is a sport, a special case, and it is ludicrous to claim the odd writer of Irish background who strays into English like Shirley, MacFlecknoe, or Wentworth Dillon, Earl of Roscommon. Anglo-Irish literature proper does not begin until the eighteenth century. The question has often been raised by crusading nationalists, and as often dismissed, whether Swift and Goldsmith can be regarded as Irish writers. It seems to me that the claim has validity whenever a writer shows the pressure of local experience, and is regarded as a seminal influence by later writers.

Take Jonathan Swift. Born in Dublin, educated at Kilkenny and Trinity College, he kept being returned to Ireland by his ecclesiastical superiors; this confirmed him in that outsider's view of English society which may explain why so many Anglo-Irish writers have excelled in comedy and satire. There is also his powerful sense of physical disgust which some critics, thinking of

Joyce, have seen as an Irish trait. But it is the rage of the unwilling patriot which makes him our first great voice in English:

> Remove me from this land of slaves,
> Where all are fools, and all are knaves. . .

I cannot think of any modern Irish writer of quality who has not been influenced by Swift. Yeats claims him as part of his racial heritage, Clarke pays homage to him in 'A Sermon for Swift' while Joyce and Kavanagh adapt his technique of self-dramatization within a Dublin context for their own satirical verse:

> He gave the little Wealth he had
> To build a House for Fools and Mad:
> And show'd by one satiric touch,
> No Nation wanted it so much. . .

is echoed centuries later in 'Gas from a Burner':

> This lovely land that always sent
> Her writers and artists to banishment
> And in a spirit of Irish fun
> Betrayed her own leaders, one by one.

and 'The Paddiad':

> Chestertonian Paddy Frog
> Croaking nightly in the bog.
> All the Paddies having fun
> Since Yeats handed in his gun.

Goldsmith's case is less clear, although Yeats places him on his 'ancestral stair'. According to Robert Graves, 'he was offering, disguised as an essay on the break-up of English village society, a lament for the ills of Ireland, modelled on contemporary minstrel songs.' Brian Merriman was not a minstrel (he was a teacher of mathematics) but if we compare his *Midnight Court* with *The Deserted Village* we discover both that he was more Augustan than is generally allowed, and Goldsmith more Irish. It has never been pointed out, I think, that the four best long poems – I am thinking of *Laurence Bloomfield*, as well as *The Great Hunger* – by Irishmen since the late eighteenth century are all variations on the same

117

rural theme. So while the technique of *The Deserted Village* is late Augustan, its message still applies to Ireland (the ending seems especially relevant, now that we are part of the European Economic Community). And in the opening of *The Traveller*, Goldsmith analyses another of the great Hibernian themes, from Columcille to Joyce, the intellectual exile's longing for home:

> Where'er I roam, whatever realms to see,
> My heart untravell'd fondly turns to thee. . .

So in the eighteenth century the two traditions co-exist, with occasional courteous exchanges; I am thinking of Swift's translation of 'O'Rourke's Feast' and Goldsmith's essay on Carolan. And they illuminate each other; as well as the probable influence of Goldsmith on Merriman, I find it salutary to consider that Swift is contemporary with O'Rathaille and comes after O'Bruadair – three angry men, concerned in their different ways about the state of the country, and vituperating against those in power. Already at the end of the seventeenth century O'Bruadair is deploring the taste for 'gutter poetry' but before the Gaelic tradition goes underground, we hear a voice raised in aristocratic lamentation:

> So stop your weeping now
> Women of the soft, wet eyes
> And drink to Art O'Leary
> Before he enters the grave school
> Not to study wisdom and song
> But to carry earth and stone.
>
> (Version: John Montague)

IV

> The Poet launched a stately fleet: it sank.
> His fame was rescued by a single plank.
>
> William Allingham

It is only in the nineteenth century that the idea of a specifically Irish literature in English began to emerge. London was still the literary capital for writers in English but there was a subtle, historical change. Whereas Swift and Goldsmith were leading figures within the Augustan tradition, the Act of Union had the psychological effect of placing our poets in a subordinate or satellite position; as Aubrey de Vere was to Wordsworth, Moore to Byron, and Allingham to Tennyson. If one might risk a summary: our Anglicized writers did not exist in their own right and our Anglo-Irish had yet to learn how to speak for themselves.

And yet the older material began to find its way back. At first within the context of the Romantic revival; after MacPherson's garbling of the Ossianic stories, came the more spinsterly approach of Charlotte Brooke's *Reliques of Ancient Poetry* (1789):

The British Muse is not yet informed that she has an elder sister in this isle; let us introduce them to each other!. . . It is really astonishing of what various and comprehensive powers this neglected language is possessed. In the pathetic it breathes the most beautiful and affecting simplicity. . .

So the stage was set for Tom Moore, whose light charm covered a multitude of artistic sins. He appropriated the airs so strenuously gathered by Edward Bunting, without giving him the least credit, although he was being paid a hundred pounds for each of his Irish Melodies, folktunes wrought to drawing-room sweetness. He was a *petit bourgeois* snob who dearly loved a lord, but allowed the Memoirs that Byron entrusted to him to be destroyed. And yet he was the first writer of Irish Catholic background to achieve international fame, translated by Lermontov, imitated by Gérard de Nerval, adored by Goethe. He may not have the strength to sustain a theme but his plangent opening lines are as musical as Auden, who admired him:

Silent, O Moyle, be the roar of thy water. . .

or

Light sounds the harp when the combat is over

One might blame his artistic shortcomings on the company he kept, but Burns, although subject to similar pressures, remained closer to tradition. The truth is that Moore is a late Augustan, veering between the sentimental and the satiric, 'the tear and the smile'.

With Mangan we are in the presence of a real poetic temperament, as helplessly Irish as O'Rathaille. And also of that strange phenomenon I have already noted in nineteenth-century Irish poetry: like a medium, he rarely speaks in his own voice, but lets the past speak through him. These 'melancholy perversions', as he called them, while they are less translations than acts of homage, are the first real attempt to render Irish poetry in English. Flashes of exultation and desolation succeed each other, like lightning over a desert; Brian's palace is overthrown, the princes of the line of Conn die in unmourned exile, the chief of the Maguires flees through the storm, his face 'strawberry bright'. Did he influence Poe (the editor of *The Southern Literary Messenger* would have had access to the magazines where Mangan published) or vice versa? In one poem, 'Siberia', he found a metaphor for the stricken psyche, worthy of Baudelaire and, despite its rhetoric, 'The Nameless One' has real intensity.

Samuel Ferguson was a much less haunted man, but he probably knew more Irish than Mangan, and certainly more about Irish music. So while his adaptations of the saga material are dated and literary, his versions of Irish folksong ring true:

> I'd wed you without herds, without money, or rich array,
> And I'd wed you on a dewy morning at day-dawn grey;
> My bitter woe it is, love, that we are not far away
> In Cashel town, though the bare deal board were our
>   marriage-bed this day!

But soon 'my locks are turn'd to grey' and we have 'girl' rhyming with 'churl': one is reminded of 'thy mother's knee' which nearly ruins the tone of his most free-striding poem, 'Lament for the Death of Thomas Davis'. Ferguson was full of the contradictions of his period: an Ulster Unionist who married a Guinness heiress and was made a knight, he invented the Celtic Twilight:

> They're glancing through the glimmer of the quiet eve,
>   Away in milky wavings of neck and ankle bare;
> The heavy-sliding stream in its sleepy song they leave,
>   And the crags in the ghostly air. . .

'The Fairy Thorn' is also labelled 'an Ulster ballad'; it was as if his Scots blood and Irish interests led him naturally to the form.

Among the other nineteenth-century poets Darley is consumed by a melancholy which is only incidentally Irish. And I have a fondness for Thomas Caulfield Irwin who by-passed the problem by writing exactly, and often sensuously, about nature:

> Around the stalk of the hollyhock
> The yellow, long, thin-waisted wasp,
> Emitting sounds, now like a lisp
> In the dry glare, now like a rasp. . .

The most professional poet of the second half of the century was certainly Allingham, and his verse novel, *Laurence Bloomfield*, a study of Irish landlordism, deserves reprinting for both literary and historical reasons. While admitting the prolixity of nineteenth-century Irish poetry, one has to recognize that it still exercises a potent influence: Kinsella acknowledges a temperamental affinity with Mangan, the solid craftsmanship of Samuel Ferguson is continued by Richard Murphy, while John Hewitt sees himself as a descendant of Allingham.

V

> A tune is more lasting than the voice of the birds,
> A word is more lasting than the riches of the world.
> (Douglas Hyde: *Love Songs of Connacht*)

In any consideration of Irish poetry between Carolan and Yeats one comes up against the importance of folksong. As Irish declined, the poets, like Owen Roe or Raftery, moved closer to song to reach their last audience in the cabins. Almost simultaneously, Irish songs began to filter into English: in 1792, the Belfast Society of the United Irishmen sponsored the last gathering of harpers, where Bunting got the idea for his first *Collection of Ancient Irish Music* which Moore plundered. Callanan, Walsh, Ferguson all try to match the 'sweet, wild twist' of Irish versification.

At the same time, this begins to have its effect on a new growth, the ballad in English. John Holloway has argued very persuasively that these anonymous songs are the true achievement of Anglo-Irish poetry in the nineteenth century, and with their hedge-schoolmaster diction and strenuous simplicity of emotion they can be very touching. If there is nothing like the great Gaelic love-songs, the last vestige of the courtly tradition, there is a greater variety of subject, drinking songs, enlisting songs, sporting songs, political songs, springing directly from the lives of the people. 'When the Irish language was fading', says the leading authority on the subject, Colm O'Lochlainn, 'the Irish street ballad in English was the half-way house between the Irish culture and the new English way.' Nearly every Anglo-Irish poet, from Goldsmith onwards, has tried to add to this store, sometimes 'improving' an existing ballad, like Padraic Colum with 'She moved through the Fair', or writing a new one, like Donagh MacDonagh. Their influence on our two greatest modern writers, Yeats and Joyce, shows that they can be a tap-root for the most gifted.

VI

Every man everywhere is more of his age than of his nation
W. B. Yeats

Enfin, Yeats vint. His long, marvellous career illustrates how the apparent disadvantages of being Irish could all be turned into gains. He began writing during one of the worst periods of English poetry but he was saved from the aestheticism of his English contemporaries by his nationalism, and vice versa. The success of his early work led to a whole school of Irish poetry but the main achievements of AE's anthology *New Songs* (1904) may have been to provoke him to a change of style. Of those who persisted as poets, Padraic Colum practised the pastoral lyric (a mode more consistently developed by Joseph Campbell, the Ulster imagist) while Seamus O'Sullivan turned to vignettes of Georgian Dublin. Those who reacted against him did better; one thinks of Synge, of Joyce's ballads and satires, his few very personal lyrics.

But again how quickly Yeats got the point, absorbing their savagery into his own style! He escapes the stereotypes of Irish poetry, from Celtic melancholy to rapscallion masculinity, because he is at all times a professional poet, whose primary concern is the human imagination in all its complexity. So Ireland was only one of several symbols, to be defined as the need struck him, in folk or patriotic or Anglo-Irish terms; her principal value was as a backdrop. 'Behind all Irish history hangs a great tapestry, even Christianity had to accept, and be itself pictured there.'

Robert Graves follows Yeats in regarding himself as an Anglo-Irish poet, though only an occasional ballad cadence betrays the influence of his father, a minor Victorian poet and song writer, in the tradition of Father Prout. His allegiance shows itself rather in his inherited interest in Celtic literature, as documented in *The White Goddess* and elsewhere (he has written a long essay on *The Frenzy of Sweeny*) and above all, in his belief in the poet as a magician, under the rule of the Muse, a role that Yeats alone, among contemporary poets, would have recognized.

Austin Clarke's lifework can be seen as a deliberate attempt to reconcile the two traditions; he is our first completely Irish poet in English. A student of Thomas MacDonagh at University College, Dublin, he developed the idea of a distinctive Irish mode with an almost exclusive integrity. He also revived the role of the poet as satirist; his favourite *persona* is that of the straying cleric, a modern version of MacConglinne. He can be very intense, as in the closely-knit religious lyrics, and also beautifully relaxed, when he praises the city he loves so much, as in 'A Sermon for Swift'. While he may finally be seen as an autobiographical poet, his immediate historical importance is that, like MacDiarmid in Scotland, he dedicated himself to the idea of a separate Irish poetry in English, so that his work is both a rallying point and a focus for fierce reaction.

It was not surprising, therefore, that the most original poet to appear after Clarke should decide he wanted nothing to do with Irishry whatsoever. Patrick Kavanagh's magnificent but melodramatic outcry against the frustrations of rural life, *The Great Hunger* (1942), is one of the better long poems of our time, and its releasing influence on other writers, from R. S. Thomas to Seamus Heaney, has still to be estimated. And twice during his lifetime he produced lyric poetry of a high order, in simple, sensuous memories like 'Spraying the Potatoes' and in the sonnets written after his operation for lung cancer. 'I feel I have the permanent stuff in me and only need to be stirred,' he wrote once to his brother, and perhaps all the flailing anger, and the famous lawcase, were only his way of stirring the sediment; his braggadocio sheltered a talent as lonely as John Clare's.

The one thing that all these writers shared was a contempt for contemporary literature; one thinks of the jingoistic finale of 'Under Ben Bulben' and Clarke's long war against what he called 'modernism'. A poet who might have extended our view of poetry was Denis Devlin but his unwillingness to publish means that his work is still little known, and lacks a kind of primary readability. He was profoundly influenced by Spanish and French literature (even collaborating in a hare-brained scheme to translate modern French poetry into Irish) and his sequence of longer poems from 'Lough Derg' through 'The Heavenly Foreigner' to 'The Colours of Love' shows a capacity for intellectual passion as elaborate as Claudel's. Though it would be wrong to restrict his view of the world even to the European tradition: one of his best poems is about the Cambodian temple of Ank'hor Vat. The most dedicated poet of the lost generation of the Irish thirties, his work shows how an awareness of Irish literary and religious tradition can be a spring-board to the widest possible vision.

After the Irish mode of Clarke, and the comedy of Kavanagh, we have the gravity of Kinsella. His great achievement was to have restored the sense of poetry as craft; from the elegance of *Another September* to the sombre density of *Nightwalker* and *Notes from the Land of the Dead*, his strenuous dedication makes a striking contrast with Kavanagh's jauntiness. He can write with an exact fluency as in 'Chrysalides' but that is only a simple, preparatory statement compared to the pained complexity of his analysis of mutability in poems like 'Ballydavid Pier'. His work so far presents a central paradox: modern in its reliance on the integrity of the individual sensibility, it is still haunted by the mournfulness of an Irish Catholic upbringing, and despite his years in America and his overwhelming awareness of contemporary evil, he can still lapse into Parnassian metre and diction.

So, in the late fifties, Irish poets began to write, without strain, a poetry that was indisputably Irish (in the sense that it was influenced by the country they came from, its climate, history and linguistic peculiarities) but also modern. Kinsella's spearheading success encouraged others, and by the middle of the following decade Irish poets began to filter into modern anthologies, especially American, so that the critic M. L. Rosenthal could dedicate a section of his study, *The New Poets*, to Irish poetry. This wider audience did not mean any abjuring of older allegiances; Kinsella's translation of *The Táin* is a landmark in Anglo-Irish poetry's repossession of its past, while Pearse Hutchinson writes in both languages. Even in the detached music of *The Battle of Aughrim*, where Richard Murphy probes the relationship between history and the self, as it presents itself to a southern Protestant, one savours the half and internal rhymes of the older tradition:

> There was ice on the axe
> When it hacked the king's head.

The next generation of poets sprang from that forgotten and history-burdened area, the North. There has been some criticism in the Republic of the way Ulster writers tend to look to London as their literary capital, and it is true that the poems of Longley, Mahon, Heaney and Simmons share an epigrammatic neatness which shows the influence of a limiting British mode. But in other ways they are very different; Heaney is a naturally sensuous writer, very close to early Frost, while the others are more in the tradition of melancholy wit, inherited from MacNeice, who is very much a father figure for the poets of the province. What is striking in all the northern writers is how well they write, though I would hope for a more experimental approach, if they are to confront the changes in their society.

But Heaney's brooding devotion to the earth goddess, and Mahon's lithe metaphysical intelligence already place them among the most gifted Irish poets. There is not such a clearly defined generation in the South, although Michael Hartnett is the most dedicated English poet to come so far from Munster, where the tradition of Gaelic poetry was strongest. A fine translator, he extends the Irish mode, arguing that an Anglo-Irish writer should be as familiar with Gaelic metres as English. One's general impression of the younger poets is of a competing multiplicity of styles, from which only a few names separate themselves, like Richard Ryan in the South, and, above all, Paul Muldoon, again from the North. Not since early Kinsella has such an elegant and intelligent talent appeared.

An Irish poet seems to me in a richly ambiguous position, with the pressure of an incompletely discovered past behind him, and the whole modern world around. We might find parallels in the

125

way contemporary English poets, from Auden to Geoffrey Hill, have contacted the Anglo-Saxon world, but our literature is both closer to us, and more varied. A tradition, however, should not be an anachronistic defence against experience, and through our change of languages we have access to the English-speaking world – without that protective attitude an English poet might naturally feel towards his language. Stephen Spender has compared the present subordinate position of the English writer to his powerful American contemporary with that of the Anglo-Irish, who were compelled to straddle 'two different civilizations which shared a common language'. But this has been our problem for a long time, so that the Irish writer, at his best, is a natural cosmopolitan; Yeats may echo O'Rathaille in 'The Curse of Cromwell' but 'The Second Coming' is as central to his vision. And that is our best example for the future, balanced between the pastoral and the atomic age; if a poet is someone who, through words, turns psychic defeats into victories, we stand a better chance than most in the storm-driven, demon-crossed last quarter of the century:

> Growing up, I heard talk of Ulster regionalism,
> A literature for our province, a lyric Stormont.
> Coming South, I was religiously told
> Of our Irish Renaissance, a lyric Sinn Fein.
> Now both winds fail: we belong to a world.

[1974]

11

LOUIS MacNEICE : DESPAIR AND DELIGHT

When the *Collected Poems* of Louis MacNeice appeared in 1966, a strange thing happened. For years he had been taken for granted, even discounted; 'your verse half rubbish' as a minuscule contemporary avers. He was never distant like Auden, a menacing intelligence, but easily met in bars, whether The George after a BBC recording, or over in Ireland for a rugby match. To see his intelligent sheep's head disappear down a bar bench was an experience. Like everyone else who knew him slightly, I cherish a few of those occasions. Once, driving to Lansdowne Road for a match through a thick throng of supporters, he spied a small man hurrying towards us against the stream. A languid finger followed his ducking progress: 'Must be an Ulster Catholic' said that rasping, intelligent voice – this for my benefit. It seemed to count more for him that I came from Tyrone, than that I wrote poetry; a childhood servant he had loved had come from there, and names like Clogher and Augher and Fivemiletown had talismanic value for him. Used to the meanness of the Dublin literary scene, I found him disinterested, except in the serious sports of drinking and story-telling, those frail rope-ladders across the void.

When he spoke of Auden, for example, it was not as a rival but an admired friend, many of whose attitudes he could not accept. Taciturn himself, he loved word spinners like Dylan Thomas and W. R. Rodgers, a Presbyterian gone wild. He was inclined to speak deprecatingly of his own work and when I told him that Tom Kinsella had been reading *Autumn Sequel*, he said: 'I suppose he found it less good than *Autumn Journal*, like everyone else.' He was pleased to hear the reverse, but I had the impression of someone who was resigned to being partially misunderstood, but content to follow out his path. Eminently approachable but ultimately lonely, he was delighted to meet anyone who had shared a milestone with him, especially in another life. In the 'Writers Workshop' at Iowa, where we first met, we discussed Dublin; in London we discussed the North from which we both came, the France where I was living, and where he hoped to come, for some kind of mythical holiday, away from the established pattern of his life, with his last love. Only in parts of Ireland did he seem to dissolve into the warm bath of the present where myth and moment meet:

> Both myth and seismic history have been long suppressed
> Which made and unmade Hy Brasil – now an image
> For those who despise charts but find their dream's endorsement
> In certain long low islets snouting towards the west
> Like cubs that have lost their mother.
>
> ('Last before America')

And yet when he died, one's whole impression of him was shocked back into recognition. Other poets, like Roethke and Berryman, had passed through openly dialoguing with eternity, in their theatrical American way. But Louis was so casual, made so little attempt to involve us in his drama in the public sense, that the melancholy premonitions of *The Burning Perch* did not strike home until he had borne them out in his own death. In 'Goodbye to London', a lover of life says goodbye to the urban life which had sustained him, in 'The Introduction' to the love that had warmed him, in 'The Suicide' to the office which had supported him, in 'Sports Page' to the games that had amused him. And the lurking terror in his vision emerges as a reversal of the Christian promise:

> In lieu therefore of choice
> Thy Will be undone just as flowers
> Fugues, vows and hopes are undone. . .
>
> ('In Lieu')

So, stunned, one reads back, to rediscover what had always been there, under the bright plumage of his language, his professional pride in his facility, in keeping the show going. MacNeice is one of those whom melancholy had marked for her own; it had something to do with childhood and is present in the earliest poems. 'The candle in his white grave-clothes' and 'The dark blood of night-time', to take phrases from two adjacent poems, come together in those haunted nursery poems like 'Intimations of Mortality':

> Then the final darkness for eight hours
> The murderous grin of toothy flowers,
> The tick of his pulse in the pillow, the sick
> Vertigo of falling in a fanged pit.

And in 'Autobiography' we learn the age at which 'The little boy cannot go to sleep'.

> When I was five the black dreams came;
> Nothing after was quite the same. . .
>
> When my silent terror cried,
> Nobody, nobody replied.

Reading between the lines of his tight-lipped autobiography, a kind of early middle-aged exercise in personal therapy, one guesses that it has something to do with the mother, and the mongoloid brother. The latter is never mentioned in the poetry, but the mother is, in that strange poem 'Eclogue between the Motherless', where her memory is what has to be exorcised:

> I thought 'Can I find a love beyond the family
> And feed her to the bed my mother died in. . .'

And he associates his mother with that early boyhood anguish:

> Talking of ice
> I remembered my mother standing against the sky
> And saying 'Go back in the house and change your shoes'
> And I kept having dreams and kept going back in the house.
> A sense of guilt like a scent – The day I was born
> I suppose that that same hour was full of her screams. . .

We must accept that MacNeice is a poet of nightmare, only briefly allayed by love, or companionship. He has written a handful of the best love lyrics of our time, but they are also testimonies to the power of time to efface love. Love, indeed, can exist only outside time:

> Time was away and she was here
> And life no longer what it was. . .

But 'Life will have her answer'; there is no lasting escape from the tedium and the terror. The best and bravest are those who can outtalk the monster: in Dylan Thomas, MacNeice recognized a fellow conspirator, possessed by but defying death, 'he dared the passing bell/To pass him and it did'. The profound affection of Louis for anyone who could pass the time, anyone who could spin a web of words that transformed the dull earth into a magical place, even for the moment, shows in his splendid elegy for Dylan in *Autumn Sequel*.

> And so he cut his steps in the ice and rhymed
> His way up slowly, slowly by a star,
> While in his ears the bells of childhood chimed
>
> And avalanches roared beneath him far
> And the Three Kings went with him and the Three
> Gold Shoemakers of Wales, who would not mar
>
> A single stitch on a shoe, no more than he
> Would botch a verse. He made his own sea-shells
> In which to hear the voices of the sea,
>
> And knew the oldest creatures, the owl that tells
> How it has seen three forests rise and fall,
> And the great fish that plumbs the deepest wells. . .

The enemy is time and Louis dealt with it in two ways. In his early work he is excited by the details of living: circuses, Christmas shopping, driving at night, travel, anything which illuminates the ordinary, and shows that 'world is suddener than we fancy it'. This is the great attraction of *Autumn Journal*, which is a catalogue of the pleasures of being alive, even 'in an evil time'. The philosophy behind this attitude, a determination to keep going, to keep alive, in the best sense, is summed up in another poem:

And I would praise our inconceivable stamina
Who work to the clock and calendar and maintain
The equilibrium of nerves and notions,
Our mild bravado in the face of time.

('Hidden Ice')

But 'Hidden Ice' finishes by reminding us that many end in suicide and madness, despite their daily disciplines. And in his middle years, when MacNeice abjured 'the velvet image' and 'the lilting measure', the enemy appears as repetition, boring and meaningless, a Parrot mouthing a catalogue which had once been a litany of fresh delights.

The cage is ungilded, the Parrot is loose on the world
Clapping his trap with gay but meaningless wings.

(*Autumn Sequel*)

Hence his affection for anyone who could, like Thomas, 'throw the Parrot's lie/Back in its beak' and he links him with F. R. Higgins (Reilly), an Irish poet from MacNeice's ancestral background of Connacht:

and brown bogwater and blue

Hills followed him through Dublin with the same
Aura of knowing innocence, of earth
That is alchemized by light. . .   (*Autumn Sequel*)

His Irish background is relevant because it corresponds to the facets of his vision. Ulster was the setting for his early melancholy and may even have enhanced it: think of the language in the first three stanzas of 'Carrickfergus' – '*lost* sirens', 'the *blind* and *halt*', '*funeral* cry', 'a *drowning* moon' (my italics). And the West from which his father came, and to which Louis often returned on holiday, was his favourite fantasy landscape, 'his dream's endorsement'.

. . . my mother
Earth was a rocky earth with breasts uncovered
To suckle solitary intellects. . .

('Western Landscape')

And in the end it may have been an Irish quality, his easy-going character, which prevented him from being as implacable in pessimism as his great predecessor, Thomas Hardy. For it is in the company of that great master of melancholy that I would finally place him; the advocates of a lesser English tradition, linking Hardy to Larkin, seem to forget MacNeice. *The Burning Perch*, full of the sadness of an anticipated death, brings us back to the lonely sadness of the early poems, a melancholy only briefly vanquished by companionship and love. Under the delight that glitters on the surface, there is always the hidden ice.

[1974]

12

KINSELLA'S CLARKE

At his request, I called on Austin Clarke a few days before he died. He had difficulty in speaking but Nora, always brave and calm, helped him complete his sentences. He had been having dreams, frightening ones, he said. Even on the temporal level there were threats; an order for the demolition of Bridge House had just arrived. But he found the energy to be courteous, signing a copy of a little book, enquiring about our summer plans.

That last glimpse was typical of Austin, a dignified mournfulness, a courteous melancholy, a cleric turned inside out. His *Collected Poems* (1974), were to appear in a few weeks, but he would be cremated in Belfast before, a last gesture thwarting any attempt to turn him into an acceptable monument. He died as he had lived, outside all orthodoxies, except poetry.

His real monument is, if course, that great volume of nearly six hundred pages. But those crowded pages reflect too many different Clarkes, or, harsher critics would suggest, he was late in finding a distinctive contemporary voice, and often faltered, or reverted (an accusation may I remind, that is still made about Yeats).

This is Thomas Kinsella's justification for *Selected Poems* (1976): he wishes to present the essential Clarke and shears away, for example, the long poems upon which his early reputation was based. I have to bear reluctant witness that 'The Vengeance of Fionn' (1917) which brought the young Clarke, just come of age, the heady acclaim of a middle in the *TLS*, does not suit modern taste. Americans especially have no stomach for the Tennysonian literary epic. But Austin said it himself:

> The thousand tales of Ireland sink: I leave
> Unfinished what I had begun nor count
> As gain the youthful frenzy of those years. . .

By opening with 'Three Sentences', Kinsella stresses the private and the satiric Clarke (though I think he might have relented and given Clarke a more passionate start with 'O Love there is no beauty'). Then we move four years to 'Pilgrimage' (1929) most of which survives his scrutiny, poems as elaborately worked as a medieval manuscript. Too elaborate, perhaps, but the pain strikes in *Night and Morning* (nine years later, significantly with Clarke back in Dublin) over which hangs, to use Kinsella's phrase, 'the tortured darkness of apostasy'.

> But O to think, when I was younger
> And could not tell the difference,
> God lay upon this tongue.

Early Clarke reduced to twenty-four pages, Kinsella sees him as reborn in 1955 in 'sudden, full-fledged, humanitarian rage'. Catholic bourgeois Ireland now had a scourge as relentless as O'Bruadair, in one reading; 'a local complainer' (his own helpful description) if you found his clerical obsessions too narrow. This mood continues through what became *Later Poems* (1961) which brought Austin a new reputation, 'a discerning, if tiny, public' who saw his satirical directness and 'infatuation with Gaelic prosody' as parallel to modern experiment elsewhere. This late drafting of a recruit who had spent a good deal of his reviewing time in assaulting contemporary poetry had its comic aspects, but I was glad to have played my own small part in it; with the belated recognition of the mature Clarke, the existence of an Irish poetic tradition in *English*, to follow or despise, became an accomplished fact.

But for Kinsella it is *Flight to Africa* (1955) which is 'his most significant single book'. Stravinsky claimed that a man did not start to live until he had had two heart attacks, and the aged and ailing Clarke treated his juniors to an extraordinary spectacle; a yellow bittern weaving its assonantal patterns through Yugoslavia and New York. It is always fascinating to see what one craftsman thinks of another and Kinsella sees this period as 'Clarke's final escape'. He is, I know, a fairly recent convert to Clarke's work and earlier devotees may be upset to discover almost wilful absences, like 'The Lost Heifer' (probably Clarke's best-known single poem) and 'The Blackbird of Derrycairn'. One could continue the list but the important aspect of this *Selected Poems* is that it begins to pose the central problem of where, in a long career, Clarke's achievement lies.

I would agree with Kinsella that *Mnemosyne Lay in Dust* (1966) is central, although he had to wait for the vogue for confessional poetry to finish it. With *Night and Morning* it is his most anguished book, just as *Pilgrimage* and *Flight to Africa* are his showpieces as a craftsman. But I am delighted to discover that, while he scants the early poems, Kinsella emerges as a strong advocate of the last poems, 'a series of wickedly glittering narratives' culminating in the bisexual gaiety of *Tiresias* (1971). If this is true then Clarke came full circle, returning to the longer poem fuelled by his own proper obsessions, usually sex crossed with religion.

Austin's generation was one of survivors, to whom real fame came late. *The New York Times* greeted the *Collected Poems* of Robert Graves with the headline (which pleased the sixty-year-old poet) 'Famous Author Turns to Verse'. Smiling in his hospital bed, David Jones did not seem worried about a fame that would only have distracted his detailed, gentle mind. Hugh MacDiarmid weathered poverty and obscurity to emerge as a world figure in his seventies. Of these four modern masters, Austin was the most introverted, a man who had been deeply hurt by his own people. Perhaps wars are easier to survive than middle-class revolutions, but his brave and lonely spirit emerges as the conscience of our cramped and crippled southern state, during its early years. In his selection, preface and notes, Tom Kinsella, who inherits a different as well as later Dublin, seeks to expose the essence of that message in the diligent and systematic way that we have come to expect of him, though I would argue for a wider, warmer choice.

[1976]

13

PATRICK KAVANAGH:
A SPEECH FROM THE DOCK

While Patrick Kavanagh does not seem dead, his Dublin certainly has died, or changed beyond all human recognition, so that the attempt he made to transform Pembroke and Grafton Street into the slopes of Parnassus now seems historical, even Quixotic. His *pâpier maché* image by Desmond MacNamara stares forlornly down at the termite young of the present Bailey public-house who barely know his name. Where would his spirit wander now for relaxation? Much of the shoddy material that he occasionally brought to blaze has been bulldozed away and I doubt if anyone will ever be foolhardy enough again to try to make Dublin into the background for a spiritual pilgrimage; not in so public a fashion at any rate.

Now it is all over, bar the shouting, the reminiscence and comment, and the record rests: *The Green Fool, Tarry Flynn,* and the *Collected Poems* (or, better still, *The Complete Poems*). And there is the Claddagh disc, 'Almost Everything' to give a flavour of the personality. *Collected Prose* is not distinguished work but some-one may do as well for Patrick's casual prose as his brother has done for his poetry. Both in the letters as edited by 'the brother' (surely the least-dignified correspondence of any poet who achieved some greatness), and in the latter's memoirs, I come in for some black-guarding, so I would like to take this opportunity of making a brief speech from the dock, to set my part of the publishing record straight.

I admired Patrick Kavanagh but was wary of him, all the more because, coming from an Ulster farming community myself, I could recognize many of his protective – and destructive – ploys. When we met alone things went splendidly, but as soon as there was an audience his public personality intervened. Entering John Ryan's Bailey, for example, was a bit like the O.K. Corral. A glance through the door would reveal his massive presence, and I waited for the salutation: 'Montague, you're a cunt,' he would declare with satisfaction. It took me a while to discover the countersign: 'Kavanagh, you're a whure.' If the flyting worked, you were asked to sit down and allowed to buy drinks; I was even stood a round several times, in later years. I came in one day with Terence MacCaughey, Presbyterian pastor in Trinity, who asked to meet the great man. Patrick savoured the occasion, warming to an attack, all the sharper because it was a fellow northerner. 'Presbyterian – black as the riding boots of the Earl of Hell!' he announced with relish, and sat back. Terence took it in style and I left them to it.

But everyone has stories like that; maybe I merited a special edge as a younger poet whose name kept cropping up in dispatches. All of this I understood; the historical trap which meant that no one of his age and background had more than a glimmer of a chance, and that his achievement was almost all against the grain, a path scythed through the thistles of indifference, the ragwort of a new social class of post-revolutionary climbers. He was also, in a way, a casualty of the War, which interrupted whatever literary career he might have had. After he moved to Dublin in 1939 there was no way back to the small farm; and no way forward, except a claustrophobic office job. No wonder he felt hard done by!

Speaking of office jobs, my easiest time with him was when I lived and worked in the Baggot Street area, a few doors away from Brendan Behan. We would cross in Parsons Bookshop where the ladies reserved him a stool, which he managed to make into a throne, discoursing with whoever took his fancy, rising to cash a small cheque or flirt with the shopgirls. Miss O'Flaherty was a great support to him, an intensely dedicated fan. There was one splendid afternoon when I slipped out of Bord Fáilte (I worked in a cubbyhole under the stairs with a path to the Beehive pub in Delahunty's Buildings) to back a horse called Paddy's Point in the Grand National. I bet only when I am bored, as in my last year in boarding school, so I am not a true *affectionado*, to use Patrick's phrase. He shuffled into the bookies on Haddington Road and was intrigued at my choice. We sat in Mooney's, awaiting the result, and when I scored P. K. was clearly impressed. 'Fancy that, now,' he kept repeating, 'a horse with my own name and Montague wins on it.' Further balls of malt were set up, and we plunged contentedly into a rambling literary discussion, in which it was mutually agreed that while Goldsmith's *Deserted Village* had more art than *The Great Hunger*, it had less passion.

When he was at ease like that, the prickliness disappeared and he could even manage a compliment. At our first meeting in an earlier Bailey he listened to my half-stuttered rush of words: 'You're a very nervous young man, but I wouldn't be surprised if you had some merit,' he said, and I have tried to remember that kindness when dealing with the excitable young. But I never sought to become part of his circle, except in a tangential way; I was anxious to help, but not to become a sycophant. In those *Envoy* days he was determined to fulfill his public destiny, and the emphasis made me uneasy; I was well used to country law cases about rights-of-way and walls and wells, all the usual fuss between neighbours, but his upset at Iremonger's article in *The Leader* was in excess of the facts. One reading of the article convinced me that it was written in the prose style of the poetry editor of *Envoy*; the details about everyone's behaviour (including my own) showed it to be an inside job. But the essence of a lawcase is winning, and he was spectacularly ill-advised unless, as I believed, he was seeking to turn it into a public crucifixion, intent on dramatizing himself to that point where, as Yeats said, a man meets 'the greatest obstacle he can confront without despair'.

Which he came close to, and to death as well, as we know. It was in the more relaxed late fifties that we managed to talk a little. I was beginning to publish more but I didn't dare ask him what he thought of it, although when one poem, 'Like Dolmens Round my Childhood', won a small prize, I left a copy of the privately printed edition in Parsons for him. I heard he had received it, and waited for the master's comment. He halted to speak to me in the street; 'I see you got in that bag apron,' he said. You might read that both ways, but he went on to speak about authenticity, in the same terms he had when praising an early essay I wrote on Carleton. 'I never managed to get it in meself,' he offered. He was intrigued by Kinsella, whose star was rising, and secretly pleased when Tom reviewed *Kitty Stobling* warmly. 'Do you think he meant it?' he asked. Or again, looking at Kinsella's photograph in the paper, after another prize: 'The eyes,' he said, 'the eyes look inward', turning his own great horn rims towards me. It was a hallucinatory moment.

I am moving back and forward in time because my acquaintance with Kavanagh covered three periods: the *Envoy* days to before the lawcase, the more relaxed period from his convalescence to the *Collected Poems*, and afterwards. That volume was crucial in whatever relationship we managed. Some years after our leisurely occasional chats in Baggot-Street bars, the phone rang in my exile's hut in Paris. It was Timothy O'Keeffe asking if I would edit the poems of Kavanagh for MacGibbon & Kee. He had been present when Bertie Rodgers and I argued over Kavanagh's merits in The George and had carried away the idea of a collected edition, nearly half the poems being out of print for a long time. The trouble was that Patrick had decided that these poems were dreadful and would have nothing to do with them. He had given them a manuscript but it was only a hundred pages long and excluded even some of the later work.

I squirmed on the hook, only too aware of the awesome complications. What about Anthony Cronin, who was closer to Kavanagh than I had ever tried to be? I gathered that not only was he out of the country but out of favour, a name guaranteed to make Kavanagh growl. What about John Jordan? Better, but since Jordan was in Dublin, Kavanagh was more likely to find out, and the project might founder. I might not be involved with Kavanagh with the same intensity, but my respect for the man's work and my being a MacGibbon & Kee author made me the best bet to get the job done.

And there they had me, because O'Keeffe knew my basic concern for the older poet, my desire that he should receive some of the recognition he deserved before it was too late. He might scorn the public appeal of a Behan but I knew he longed for a little of it, especially outside Ireland. Comparing a review I did of *Kitty Stobling* in *Hibernia* with an anonymous encomium in the *TLS*, had he not said: 'Yours was the better review, but the other was in a better place.' With grave misgivings, as they say, I consented to help, accepting that my name should be kept out of sight. Martin

Green, with whom I was to collaborate, wrote:

Kavanagh is not the easiest man to deal with on business lines, as you will know, and I think it is fairly important at this stage to keep the selector's name out of sight. . . I would hasten to add that I don't think he has anything against you, necessarily, but he might against *anybody* who was in the position with regard to his work that you are in now.

The only person with whom I discussed my anonymous task was Tom Kinsella, who roundly declared that I was mad. 'Either get your name openly associated with the edition or don't do it,' he warned, and added prophetically. 'They don't understand disinterest; they'll attribute the worst possible motives to you.' He was right, but would the *Collected Poems* have appeared just then if I had not kept silent? Besides, the work had its own strange rewards, like discovering two copybooks of early lyrics dedicated to a girl, Anna Quinn. I could use only a few of them, or Kavanagh would have been alerted, but they established a vague link between *Ploughman* (1936) and *A Soul for Sale* (1947). Barrie Cooke had unearthed a complete file of the first *Dublin Magazine*, and copied out early poems from when Seamus O'Sullivan was one of Kavanagh's few outlets. J. Allen Clodd sent me a typescript of *Ploughman*; Martin was asked to get the Cuala edition of *The Great Hunger* copied in the British Museum, avoiding the lure of 'Skinyou's beauty parlour', a famous green herring for editors.

I remember the day I spread the results on the floor of my Paris flat. I knew it was incomplete, but time was pressing if we were to do our best by P.K. A chronological edition was out because we did not have the knowledge; or the time to gain it. To arrange it by volumes was also difficult because of the erratic nature of his career: there was only one book, *Come Dance with Kitty Stobling*, to cover fifteen years of work. With some reluctance, I tried to arrange the later poems in a pattern corresponding to what I understood of Kavanagh's progress since *A Soul for Sale* (1947) – satire, then confession, followed by acceptance. Only one reviewer, Douglas Sealy, again in *The Dublin Magazine* (but under a later editorship), understood the effort, but that was enough. I wanted to add 'From Monaghan to the Grand Canal' as preface, but Patrick came up with a few words for the occasion.

And occasion it was, with the kind of party that Patrick dreamed of, Black Velvet being served in a London mansion. I had met William Empson in Hampstead that morning and asked him to come along and he and Kavanagh got along famously. 'Hoya, Bill', was the informal greeting. Brian Higgins and I demonstrated a rugby pass with a bottle of champagne. It was on that night that I became aware of how much his future wife loved Kavanagh, for when we were treated harshly in a Henekeys pub afterwards she came firmly to his rescue. The rest we know, the featured review by Alvarez in *The Observer* ('Why wasn't I told/Of new Gallups polled?'), the general acclaim in places like *The Spectator*, *New Statesman* and *New York Times*. With three years left to live, most of his work was coming back into print.

I would like to think that things eased a little. The young adored him; he was the kingpin of new literary magazines like James Liddy's *Arena* and Brian Lynch's *The Holy Door*, the King of the Kids, as Brendan Behan amusingly described him. It is wrong, by the way, to think that Brendan did not admire Kavanagh as a writer; for him only Máirtín O' Cadháin and Myles were on the same level, and he would have been glad to settle differences if Patrick allowed. Having acted as an intermediary in passing notes between the two supposed belligerents, I can testify that Brendan, always generous when his ship was in, was prepared to make it up, and help, if he could. It was, after all, Kavanagh who had betrayed him in public, during the libel action, but Patrick, with all his talk of courtesy, could be unforgiving, even vicious, about fellow (usually Irish) writers. I came into McDaids one day with the news that Frank O'Connor was very ill after a heart attack. 'Good news, good news,' enthused Patrick. I was shocked, and told him so, and he took my rebuke seriously, agreeing that it was not a nice attitude but that I was too young to understand. It was on this occasion that he explained to me that only George Barker understood obscenity as deeply as himself, and I had a glimpse of the loneliness, frustration and rage through which he sometimes had to battle.

In addition to the *Collected Poems* I played a small part in the production of the Kavanagh record, 'Almost Everything', in my weighty capacity as (Honorary) Speech Director and founding member of Claddagh. Although it was our first speech record, I kept out of sight, for by now I was out of favour also, if I ever had been in. *Death of a Chieftain*, which appeared a few months after the

Collected Poems, had got warm reviews except for one, a swingeing performance by Patrick, more like a bull charge than a review. I briefly replied, which I probably shouldn't have done; but, worse, several people came sharply to my defence. And a deliberately provocative commentary on Irish verse for the Yeats Centenary number of an American magazine, in which I praised Patrick's 'honesty of vision' as liberating but declared that 'it has liberated us into ignorance: he has literally nothing to say', was interpreted as malice, not an attempt at truth. He put it splendidly but bleakly in one of his very last poems:

> What am I to do
> With the void growing more awful every hour?
> I lacked a classical discipline. I grew
> Uncultivated and now the soil turns sour.

He never seems to have realized that very few of his generation, anywhere, had it easy. MacNeice died before him, a release preferable to the nursery reversion of Kavanagh's idol, Auden. Even more savage was the plight of the Americans, whom Kavanagh scorned *in toto* without trying to understand (even less than he did MacNeice). Roethke passed through Dublin in the early sixties with a sheaf of marvellous nature poems, the nucleus of *The Far Field*, as wild and lovely a book as *Kitty Stobling*. He had fame and love at last, but he was shattered with drink, haunted by death which came to him in 1963. A few years later Berryman arrived in Dublin to finish the *Dream Songs*; he was eager to meet Kavanagh, but it could not be arranged, though I gather they later met in the Albert Hall. Berryman was an even greater master of the sonnet sequence as a method of spiritual exploration: they should have had much to roar about before they went down.

No, Kavanagh was not alone in his suffering and isolation: it was part of the exhausted post-War, post-Modernist atmosphere in which poets sang and died like flies, only the wily or scholarly escaping, a Barker or a Kunitz. Kavanagh was nearly alone in his poverty though, and there, I think, his reappearance in print helped. Public appearances followed, like Poetry International where he found himself among his – also dying – peers, Berryman, Neruda, Ungaretti. And there was the Arts Council award, the

British Arts Council, alas, but that would have pleased him, with his illusion that London was a centre of literary integrity. The Irish Arts Council passed over his *Collected Poems* to give the Devlin Award to a slim volume of Kinsellae, *Wormwood*. Paddy's comment showed an increasing composure about his younger contemporaries: 'Did you see that Kinsella won the Davis Cup?' You could take it both ways, but I prefer to regard it as a victory: regal indifference had won the day.

I wish it had done so earlier, for Kavanagh's erratic career, his achievement against long odds, still poses problems. The myth of the extraordinary peasant, against which he struggled so vehemently, to the point of denying his own early work, was largely his own creation, unless we are to believe that Macmillan and Michael Joseph suggested titles for his early works, *Ploughman* and *The Green Fool*. So his problem was not with the remnants of the Literary Revival, but the larger one of the peasant or small farmer who strays into literature. In accepting him as the authentic article, with roots in the soil, Dublin's literati may have been doing more for him than the Edinburgh gentry who got Burns to reform his English, or the public who played with Clare. It was Kavanagh himself who turned his back on his humble origins:

> Ashamed of what I loved
> I flung her from me and called her a ditch
> Although she was smiling at me with violets.
>
> ('Innocence')

Instead of acquiescing, Kavanagh plunged into that long, wearing quarrel with what he took to be the Irish literary establishment, forgetting that people like Clarke were, finally, as poorly circumstanced as himself in the new gombeen statelet, though for different reasons. Some of this warfare has been liberating for later writers who were forced to estimate the scene more harshly. But the irony is that, like Austin Clarke whom he attacked, or, closer in age, Fallon and Hewitt, Kavanagh's only *certain* claim to fame is within the context of Irish poetry. He did not reach the outside world like a Yeats or a MacNeice.

A stage Irishman who attacked the stage Irishman in literature, a peasant poet who refused to regard himself as one: these are the extremes between which he vacillated, both as a personality and a poet. In 'Monaghan Hills' (*The Complete Poems*) he humorously laments not having been born in Forkhill and had he been from a more secure background his passage might have been easier. A few miles can make a spiritual difference, and Kavanagh was born into no sustaining tradition, whether English or Irish, Carleton or Art Mac Cooey.

> The country of my mind
> Has a hundred little heads
> On none of which foot-room for genius.
> ('Monaghan Hills')

Deprivation (both spiritual and physical) became one of his major themes: he was a great admirer of Knut Hamsun's *Hunger*. Sometimes he sees a light on his hills, sometimes he attacks them, and here arises the crucial distinction between a country and a nature poet. Kavanagh's mysticism is still tinged with a vague Catholic spirituality. He has not the moralizing confidence of a Wordsworth. To put it another way: Wordsworth might write a poem on the plight of Clare, but the latter was too much a victim of his world to see nature as a reservoir of spiritual experiences, and could never return the compliment. It would take more detachment to organize his experience, and here I'd like to introduce a comparison between Kavanagh and a successful contemporary. Who wrote these lines?

> Of course there was talk in the parish, girls stood at their doors
> In November evenings, their glances as busy as moths
> Round that far window; and some, whom passion made bolder
> As the buds opened, lagged in the bottom meadow
> And coughed and called.

They are looking for a hero who is 'blind/to the vain hysteria of a woman's mind'. Or, to quote from another poem by the same poet:

> 'Beloved, let us love one another', the words are blown
> To pieces by the unchristened wind. . .
> Come with me, and we will go
> Back through the darkness of the vanished years
> To peer inside through the low window. . .

which ends,

> Is there no passion in Wales? There is none
> Except in the racked hearts of men like Morgan. . .

It is, of course, R. S. Thomas, a poet deeply indebted to Kavanagh, and yet far better known than him. There is a pathetic note in *Lapped Furrows* where Kavanagh declares that 'within a few months or a year the critics are about to awaken to realize the enormous influence I have had on such poets as, for instance, R. S. Thomas, who admits it'. The indebtedness is beyond doubt – Thomas was so impressed by *The Great Hunger* that he rewrote it twice in Anglo-Welsh terms (*The Airy Tomb* and *The Minister*, the two poems briefly quoted from) and Iago Prytherch may be a version, seen from the outside, of course, of Paddy Maguire. But there has been no open admission of the debt that I know of, and when Thomas's early poems were gathered, the best-selling *Song at the Year's Turning* (1955), the bland introduction by Kavanagh's pal, Betjeman, declared that Yeats seems to have been the only recent writer to have made an acknowledged impression on R. S. Thomas.

This may be unfair to Thomas who has gone on, in his later work, to explore more intensely personal subjects, his difficult dialogue with God. But it is far less unfair than he was to Kavanagh, indicating the negative lack of recognition under which Kavanagh laboured. It was to offset such injustices that I collaborated in collecting his work, though I am sure he could have done more for himself and that the 'extreme laziness' he confessed to Harold Macmillan in 1948 was as much a handicap as his poverty.

Whatever about Kavanagh's acceptance within the English-language tradition, his work can reach far beyond it. When I met the Polish poet Zbigniew Herbert, he was eager to learn more about Kavanagh and delighted when I sent him 'Almost Everything' to Warsaw. And report of a young Hungarian poet with *The Green Fool* on his shelves draws attention to the youthful Kavanagh's identification with Dostoevsky's *Idiot*; so 'that dreadful sort of stage-Irish autobiography' may be more accessible in those wide areas of the world where there is still a peasant culture, than *Tarry Flynn*, which would have to be translated into the Carpathian equivalent of the Monaghan dialect!

In every area of Kavanagh's work there are little surprises. Who else has immortalized Jack Doyle?

> Some think he might have won the crown
> That now to Brown Joe's head seems glued.
> But he got tangled in the gown
> Of Venus, waiting as she would,
> For the handsome boy who comes to town.
>
> ('On a Noted Character', 1943)

And though he could see his home-place with grimly humorous depression,

> . . . all the thin-faced parishes where hills
> Are perished noses running peaty water
>
> ('Lough Derg')

he could also suddenly transform it with caressing insight:

> Consider the grass growing
> As it grew last year and the year before,
> Cool about the ankles like summer rivers
> When we walked on a May evening through the meadows
> To watch the mare that was going to foal.
>
> (from *The Irish Press*, 1943)

Continuity, birth and growth in a single sentence, like a haiku. Can we ask for more?

[1980]

14

JOHN HEWITT:
REGIONALISM INTO RECONCILIATION

> This is my home and country. Later on
> perhaps I'll find this nation is my own. . .
>
> *Conacre* (April/May 1943)

One of the more striking characteristics of modern Irish poetry is the absence not merely of development, but even of persistence: Austin Clarke was our only real professional, whose published work correlates with the vicissitudes of his career. There are all sorts of technical reasons for this as well as our romantic acceptance of the idea of genius (the best solution to the problem of hard work ever invented) but the average Irish poet publishes fluently enough in magazines, and rarely in book form. With a writer like Kavanagh this erratic progress may not matter, but for less-assured talents the absence of outside criticism, of the pressure of comparison, has been dangerous.

Mr John Hewitt, the Ulster poet (b.1907), is an obvious example of this combination of pride and timidity. Although his poems first appeared in the *Irish Statesman* and *Adelphi* in the early thirties, the only chance we have had to examine his work in bulk has been *No Rebel Word* (London 1948). It is not that he does not write much; his well-filled notebooks have become legendary, and he has published regularly both in Irish and English magazines. In fact, if cross-Channel opinion has any relevance, one could nearly make a case for Hewitt as the Irish poet who has published most in British magazines and anthologies. But whoever wishes to read him must track him down, and we have less and less time for such courtesies.

This elusiveness may have contributed to his glaring omission from *The Oxford Book of Irish Verse*. Another factor in his neglect has been his consciously Ulster pose. To a generation slowly escaping from a morbid emphasis on nationality, Hewitt's position must often have seemed not merely reactionary but absurd. To be Irish was bad enough, but to insist on being Ulster as well seemed to drag literature to the level of a football match. But, as we shall see, Hewitt's instinct was right: the Ulster question is the only real outstanding political problem in this country: to live in the province and ignore it would be like living in Mississippi without questioning segregation. The effort toward understanding, like charity, must always begin at home.

In any case, this was a later development in his work. Hewitt's early poems were in what Geoffrey Taylor called (in an essay on him in *The Bell*, December 1941) 'the broad tradition of Nature Poetry'. Edward Thomas was an influence, with his quiet attention to natural detail:

> I saw a head, a narrow pointed head
> stirring among the brown weed-mottled grass
> as the monotonous and edgy voice
> kept up its hard complaint. . .

> ('First Corncrake')

and Frost, whose dramatic technique is openly imitated in 'The Hired Lad's Farewell':

> The sun set sharp behind the Antrim ridge,
> and there was one star over Muldersley Hill.
> I shall not be more sad at any death.

But the distance between observer and object is always greater in Hewitt: he had neither Frost's sardonic involvement, nor Thomas's pained brevity. The chief influence on these early verses, and indeed on Hewitt's work generally, was Wordsworth. The tug from description to comment demanded a larger form than the brief nature lyric and it was in 1943 that *Conacre* appeared, one of the first of those long poems which are Hewitt's peculiar method of summing up his thought at a particular time. In surprisingly neat, slow-moving couplets he analyses his ambivalent city-dweller's attitude towards nature, seeking to discover

> . . . why a man
> town-bred and timid, should attain to peace
> with outworn themes and rustic images.

I find *Conacre* more impressive than the group of long poems called *Freehold* which appeared in *Lagan* (1946) because of its relative freshness and variety: one can see why Geoffrey Grigson singled it out for his anthology *Poetry of the Present*. The structure of the poem turns on illuminations of nature, as when the poet and his wife wait for the dawn at Garron Point, a passage following Wordsworth's vision of the cliff in *The Prelude* (Book I). But there is also the sudden flash of irritation that frames such meditations in a more personal and contemporary context:

> I know my farmer and my farmer's wife,
> the squalid focus of their huxter life,
> the grime-veined fists, the thick rheumatic legs,
> the cracked voice gloating on the price of eggs,
> the miser's Bible, and the tedious aim
> to add another boggy acre to the name.

It is in the *Freehold* sequence that one comes up against Hewitt's regionalism at its most assertive. Beginning from a natural enough belief in the validity of the small community as a centre of culture (the kind of argument prevalent in the period, from Mumford to Herbert Read, and particularly attractive to someone attached to a provincial museum), it crosses Hewitt's sense that the special problems of Ulster, its different history and dialect, have rarely had their say in literature. His main thesis, that the Planter has his roots in the region as well as the Gael, is unassailable, but its expression often verges on shrillness:

> Yet we shall always ride the waters in their spite,
> who thrash and wallow to the left and right,
> drop gurgling down into the Romish pit,
> or on a melting iceberg scold at it.
>
> ('The Glittering Sod')

But this is balanced by 'The Lonely Heart' where memories of his father's kindliness lead the poet to describe a visit to a Catholic church:

> Not this my fathers' faith: their walls are bare;
> their comfort's all within, if anywhere.
> I had gone there a vacant hour to pass,
> to see the sculpture and admire the glass,
> but left as I had come, a protestant. . .
> The years since then have proved I should have stayed
> and mercy might have touched me till I prayed.

I am encouraged in my uneasiness with most of *Freehold* by the fact that the only one of the poems in the sequence which reappears in *No Rebel Word* has been reduced to a meditative pastoral lyric. Its slow-paced movement is typical of Hewitt's iambic-based metric:

> Once walking in the country of my kindred
> up the steep road to where the tower-topped mound
> still hoards their bones, that showery August day
> I walked clean out of Europe into peace. . .
>
> ('Townland of Peace')

Nevertheless, though the volume contains some of the best of his early poems, like 'The Swathe Uncut', 'Minotaur', and (a more cleanly acceptable statement of his regional position) 'Once Alien Here', *No Rebel Word* does not represent Hewitt fairly. It is the dated sadness of wartime which colours the rhetoric rather than the poet's more permanent argument with himself and his landscape. The inclusion of *Conacre*, and at least 'The Lonely Heart' from the other longer poems, might have corrected the emphasis.

One of the more important factors of book publication for a poet is that it sets his own past in perspective: if he continues in the same vein, like Frost, it will be because he knows the limits which are his strength. The chief objections to Hewitt's verse are its featurelessness, its deliberate lack of colour: *No Rebel Word* signifies not merely political but literary conservatism, 'no word leaping or tugging out of the consigned order'. In a few later poems a harder, more lonely note appears. I mean the fine lyric 'A Ram's Horn' ('I have turned to the landscape because men disappoint me') and another from about the same period in which the poet accepts his isolation:

> Because I paced my thought by the natural world,
> the earth organic, renewed with palpable seasons,
> rather than the city falling ruinous, slowly
> by weather and use, swiftly by bomb and argument,
>
> I found myself alone who had hoped for attention.
> If one listened for a moment he murmured his dissent:
> 'This is an idle game for a cowardly mind.
> The day is urgent. The sun is not on the agenda.'
>
> And some who hated the city and man's unreasoning acts
> remarked: 'He is no ally. He does not say that
> Power and Hate are the engines of human treason.
> There is no answering love in the yellowing leaf.'
>
> I should have made it plain that I stake my future
> on birds flying in and out of the schoolroom window,
> on the council of sunburnt comrades in the sun,
> and the picture carried with singing into the temple.

There was also a significant change in the direction of his thought. Whereas previously Hewitt had been concerned with asserting the planter's identification with the landscape and (almost a logical overconsequence) proclaiming an Ulster regionalism, now he begins to suggest the necessity of Planter and Gael coming to terms. In the brief parable-allegory 'The Colony' which appeared in *The Bell* (Summer 1953) a Roman settler meditates on the future of a province now that the Empire's power is broken:

> Some of us think our leases have run out
> but dig square heels in, keep the roads repaired;
> and one or two loud voices would restore
> the rack, the yellow patch, the curfewed ghetto.

But the speaker hopes for a more peaceful solution of the feud with the native tribes:

> I know no vices they monopolise,
> if we allow the forms by hunger bred,

151

> the sores of old oppression. . .
> . . . I may convince
> my people and this people we are changed
> from the raw levies which usurped the land,
> if not to kin, to co-inhabitants,
> as goat and ox may graze in the same field. . . .

The *persona* of 'The Colony' allows Hewitt more irony than he generally deploys in his semi-political poems: it also underlines the universality of the theme, more relevant now even than ten years ago, from Angola to Alabama. But the real surprise was *The Bloody Brae*, a verse-play broadcast in 1954, and later published in *Threshold*. To anyone who has been exposed to the ferocity of feeling in the North this dialogue between a Cromwellian veteran and the ghost of a Catholic neighbour he has killed is almost intolerably moving. Although the supreme taunt ('What, John? A renegade?') is hurled at his head, the old man seeks forgiveness:

> Ye'll ken no quarter from which my deed was good.
> I murdered pity when I murdered you.

It is a measure of Hewitt's honesty that while the trooper is forgiven, he cannot yet face the penance which the ghost enjoins, to go through the land 'crying for peace'.

Although there were sufficient hints in his earlier poems, like the scene I quoted from 'The Lonely Heart' (indeed, Hewitt claims to have written the first draft of *The Bloody Brae* as long ago as 1936), the direction of his later work seems to have surprised some who may have regarded him as a comfortable Surkov-like figure. In 1957 Hewitt moved to Coventry, and without unduly intruding on his privacy, one can say that he did not leave entirely at his own wish. But he seems to have found the change a release, placing him in a climate where the mild socialism which has always tinged his thought might flourish:

> A full year since, I took this eager city,
> the tolerance that laced its blatant roar,
> its famous steeples and its web of girders,
> as image of the state hope argued for. . .

Since then he has published one long poem, 'A Country Walk' (*Threshold*, Autumn/Winter 1960), more relaxed in content than any of the previous, and several short pieces like 'An Irishman in Coventry' (quoted above). But the most relevant to the aspect of Hewitt's work emphasized in this essay is 'Frontier', from the first issue of *Poetry Ireland*:

> We pass here into another allegiance,
> expect new postage stamps, new prices, manifestoes,
> and brace ourselves for the change. But the landscape
> does not alter;
> we had already entered these mountains an hour ago.

So much struggle to achieve this light detachment! One of the ironies of Hewitt's career is that his reluctance to publish has cloaked a definite step-by-step development, in theme at least: he is that rarity in our literature, a poet of sustained political thought. Without extravagant claims, one can say that, after Clarke and Kavanagh, he is one of the more serious and dedicated of our poets. His old-fashioned language, his explicitness of theme, place him at the opposite pole from someone like Devlin. (I find a curious correspondence with Patrick MacDonagh in the reliance on landscape and the iambic line.) But they are also his strength when, as in 'The Ram's Horn' and 'An Irishman in Coventry', they sustain an incongruous charge of strong emotion with dignity. In his longer works, like *Conacre*, 'The Lonely Heart' and *The Bloody Brae* we are admitted to the struggle of a stubborn, resolutely honest mind with itself: the mind of the first (and probably the last) deliberately Ulster, Protestant poet.

[1964]

15

HUGH MacDIARMID:
THE SEAMLESS GARMENT AND THE MUSE

> I turn from the poetry of beauty to the poetry of wisdom.
> ('Direadh')

Sooner or later, if one continues to write poetry, the desire grows to write a long poem or sequence, something more expansive than the lyric to which anthologies have reduced English poetry, something which is co-terminous with at least one whole aspect of one's experience. It is this latter aspect of modern poetry which is particularly irritating; that while novelists have ransacked the details of twentieth-century life (it is to *Ulysses*, not *The Waste Land*, or even *Paterson*, we must go for a contemporary equivalent of the 'felt life' in *The Canterbury Tales*), poets have limited themselves, like the castrati of the papal choir, to certain complex, asocial tones. The best relationship most of them can manage with society is chiding, chiliastic; in detecting a dissociation of sensibility within the English tradition, Eliot may have provided an excuse, as well as an explanation, for the partial absence of many twentieth-century poets from their poems.

MacDiarmid has never recognized this kind of absentee landlordism of the spirit: one of the aspects of his achievement worth stressing is the way he has got most of himself onto the page, even preoccupations one may dislike. The contemplative centre we value so much in Eliot and Edwin Muir is there, but also the coarser activity, the sparks from the rim of the wheel. Pride, humour, contrariness; patriotism, hatred, nostalgia, love, lust, longing: there is no contemporary poem more varied in mood than *A Drunk Man Looks at the Thistle* (1926). And since there is no achievement without an accompanying technique, the poem is a show-piece of MacDiarmid's early virtuosity, like *Hugh Selwyn Mauberley*, another poem in which a poet examines the civilization he is involved with. Whether this diversity of mood and skill in the early poems gets dissolved in the later is the central problem of MacDiarmid's career, as well as of Pound's; but I will come back to that.

I mentioned Chaucer, and it is clearly from medieval Scottish poetry that MacDiarmid inherits his ability to move from lyric to flyting, as well as his grasp of physical reality. In this, he is luckier than William Carlos Williams, in whose letters we can trace a baffled resentment at that aspect of modern poetics which would deny validity to the ordinary details of twentieth-century life. There is a careful recording of a pub scene in *The Waste Land*, but *A Drunk Man*, like the nighttown sequence in *Ulysses*, is written by someone for whom it is a natural backdrop. Does this adherence to a national tradition exclude MacDiarmid from the main concerns of contemporary poetry? From Anglo-American, perhaps, but his answer surely would be that he rejoins contemporary literature at a wider point on the arc, with the semi-public, racially conscious poetry of writers like Lorca and Pablo Neruda.

If the early poetry derives from a willed rediscovery of what the school-books used condescendingly to call the Scottish Chaucerians (I may seem to be riding the point but some English critics are still not prepared to pay MacDiarmid the simple courtesy of recognizing the tradition he is working in), the best of his middle poetry often springs from his fascination with the maimed Celtic tradition. I am thinking of poems like 'Island Funeral', 'Direadh' and above all, 'Lament for the Great Music':

> Fold of value in the world west from Greece
> Over whom it has been our duty to keep guard
> Have we slept on our watch; have death and dishonour
> Reached you through our neglect and left you in lasting
> sleep?

That these lines are cogged from Eoin MacNeill's translation* of Grainne's lullaby over Diarmid in the *Duanaire Finn* seems to me

* 'O fold of valour of the world west from Greece,/over whom I stay watching,/my heart will well-nigh burst,/if I see thee not at any time.' The scene is Scotland of course.

155

finally irrelevant: MacDiarmid transposes them so that they become a lament, not over a boy, but over the civilization to which he belonged, the original tradition, may it be said, of these islands. And the whole movement of the lines is changed to match the theme so that an almost naïve cry of tenderness is keyed to a Whitmanian skirl.

That MacDiarmid, with only a smattering of the language, has made some of the best translations from Scots Gaelic, is another phenomenon which links him with Pound. How much of the tradition does he manage to recreate in his own work? In the shorter poems of place, the deserted glens and cliffs whose names are the only Gaelic words current in daily speech, he can echo Duncan Bán MacIntyre's 'In Praise of Ben Dorain', but with a savager note that testifies to his sense of distance from the older poetry's ease with nature (a common note, indeed, in all the Celtic literatures, except perhaps Welsh: early Irish poetry being so full of it that it cannot be compared with anything in English but with Chinese or Japanese poetry, with the quatrain to match the haiku).

> The North Face of Liathach
> Lives in the mind like a vision.
> From the deeps of Coire ne Caime
> Sheer cliffs go up
> To spurs and pinnacles and jagged teeth.
> Its grandeur draws back the heart.

It is this sense of isolation, loss, loneliness, that dominates (since MacDiarmid is an honest man and not an official of the Gaelic League) the longer poems: 'Lost world of Gaeldom, further and further away from me/How can I follow, Albannach, how reachieve/ the unsearchable masterpiece?' There are passages in 'Lament for the Great Music' which reach the keening intensity of 'MacCrimmon's Lament', as sung by Jeannie Robertson, or that other death-cry of a civilization, Gruffudd ab yr Ynad Coch's mourning of Llywelyn, the last independent Welsh prince.

> The heart gone chill, under a rib-cage of fear,
> Lust shrivelled to dried twigs. . .
> See the oaktrees lash, the sea sting the land. . .
> Woe for my lord, unblemished falcon,
> Woe for the calamity that brought him down!

But the current of sympathy fails, and MacDiarmid's imaginative strength is overcome by the triviality of contemporary life in Scotland, 'the ultimate Incoherence'. And why not, when most of the things he speaks of, like the affinity between the *Ceol Mor* and the Indian *ragas,* and therefore the Celtic sense of form, the snake swallowing its tail in the margin of the *Book of Kells* (or *Finnegans Wake*) with oriental art, must seem outlandish to even most poetry readers? One of the troubles here is that the Celtic literatures are still the preserve of scholars obscuring 'the texts with philology', so that we have the curious compensating incongruity of poets being more familiar with the culture of the Pueblo Indians and the poetry of Basho and Li-Po than with that which most resembles them in their own countries. But a tradition which can still, at a considerable historical remove, nourish the poetry of writers like Mac-Diarmid, Austin Clarke, David Jones and even, in some aspects of his work, Robert Graves, is surely worth closer examination, especially now that the *Kulturkampf* of the Celtic Twilight can be replaced by the more exact testimony of archaeologists and textual editors.

One has to admit that MacDiarmid adds to the confusion of values in this area himself by his euphorically boundless claims for 'the Celtic Muse'. Thus his craftsman's instinct leads him to translate the eighteenth-century Voyage poem, 'The Birlinn of Clanranald', partly into the metre and mood of the Border Ballads; but when he comes to praise the author he asks that he might inherit his 'dowless spirit,/That balks at nought' ('To Alasdair MacMhaighstir Alasdair') and then speaks of him as 'a great/Gael, who like God (sic)

> . . . sees life
> As in yon michty passage in
> The Bhagavad-Gita where
> A' Nature casts its ooter skin. . .

Dauntlessness may be regarded as a quality in some Gaelic poetry, just as in Dunbar and Henryson, but whatever mysticism there is cannot be separated from a shining burden of natural detail. And here we return to the central question of MacDiarmid's career: any attempt to concentrate on an aspect of his work tends

157

to be dissipated by 'the seamless garment' of his vision, especially in the later poems. Thus *A Drunk Man* sweeps up all the lyrics and doricized reading of a particular period, but the first section of *In Memoriam James Joyce* leans back to incorporate stanzas from 'In a Caledonian Forest' *(Stony Limits)* and 'In the Shetland Islands' *(The Islands of Scotland)*, 1934 and 1937 respectively.

This is the kind of thing which annoys critics bloodhounding for development, though it may well be the clue they are looking for. The primary reason for the change, acknowledged by the poet himself, seems to have been a mystical intuition of the universe as a unity of energies. This was always latent in MacDiarmid, whose early books combine poems of marvellously coarse farmyard detail, like 'In Mysie's Bed', with glimpses of interstellar space where

> The moonbeams kilter i' the lift,
> An' Earth, the bare auld stane,
> Glitters beneath the seas o' Space,
> White as a mammoth's bane.
>
> ('Au Clair de la Lune')

But when he attempts an explicit statement, as in 'Moment of Eternity', which actually *opens* the *Collected Poems*, the language is too conventional to convince us that he has experienced Ygdrasil rather than a Shelleyan dream:

> I was a multitude of leaves
> Receiving and reflecting light. . .

Nor does he come closer in *A Drunk Man* where the visions of eternity are so locally tethered that he can use 'the mighty thistle in wha's boonds I rove' to mock the ending of the *Divina Commedia*, the one real failure of taste in MacDiarmid's masterpiece.

It was at some point afterwards, probably during his lonely sojourn in the Shetlands, that his sense of the endless pattern of the universe became overpowering. It can be expressed politically:

> I have caught a glimpse of the seamless garment
> And am blind to all else for evermore.
> The immaculate vesture, the innermost shift,
> Of high and low, of rich and poor. . .
>
> ('In the Slums of Glasgow')

as well as in the geological accumulation which is the recurrent symbol in *Stony Limits:*

> . . . We are so easily baffled by appearances
> And do not realise that these stones are one with the stars.

It can even, as we have seen, take over the Celtic muse:

> Your pibrochs that are like glimpses
> Of reality transcending all reason
> Every supreme thinker has, and spends the rest of his life
> Trying to express in terms of reason.

Compared with 'Little Gidding', however, this is a bald claim to visionary experience, and not its expression. Seamless garment or water of life, there is a force in MacDiarmid's later work which often dissipates the contrast and detail upon which, line by line, poetry must depend. And here perhaps one should enter the dangerous but necessary ground of poetic psychology; for the Universe of Light, the poetic equivalent of the Burning Bush seen by Moses in the Old Testament, is only one of the two primary poetic experiences. There is also the Muse, who, even through the medium of someone else's translation doctored into doric, dominates the variety of *A Drunk Man:*

> I ha'e forkent ye! O I ha'e forkent.
> The years forecast your face afore they went.
> A licht I canna thole is in the lift.
> I bide in silence your slow-comin' pace.
> The ends o' space are bricht. . .

She had appeared even earlier in the already quoted sequence 'Au Clair de la Lune', where he sees the huntress crossing the skies

> Oot owre the thunner-wa'
> She haiks her shinin' breists,
> While th' oceans to her heels
> Slink in like bidden beasts.

and speaks of himself as 'moonstruck':

She's seen me – she's seen me – and straucht
Loupit clean on the quick o' my hert.
The quhither o' cauld gowd's fairly
Gi'en me stert.

An' the roarin' o' oceans noo'
Is peerieweerie to me:
Thunner's a tinklin' bell: an' Time
Whuds like a flee.

This last stanza may seem akin to the later poetry, but there is less monotony in the metre, and more energy, even humour, in the images. But these are qualities to which the later poetry only rarely aspires: what I want to define here is a change of allegiances which removed MacDiarmid's poetry from the realm of the personal. That it was conscious one can hardly doubt since in his essay on Ezra Pound (*The Company I've Kept*) he goes out of his way to praise *The Cantos* (mistakenly, I think) for ignoring the pre-scientific occult tradition of poetry.

But the Muse is entitled to her revenge, and she refuses to wear a seamless garment, or else she loses her female shape; the reference to the great Irish poet Aodhagan O'Rathaille's aisling or vision poem 'Gile na Gile' in *In Memoriam James Joyce* is tepid, compared to the original:

Brightness of Brightness, I met on the way in loneliness,
Crystal of Crystals, in her grey-flecked eye;
Sweetness of Sweetness, in a voice without complaining,
Red and white blended in her bright cheek's dye.

The combination of grotesquerie and tenderness which marks a poem like 'Tragic Tryst' ('It's a queer thing to tryst wi' a wumman/ When the boss o' her body's gane') or the comic extravagance which sees the Thistle looping out, 'rootless and radiant', into the infinite, like a Doric space-craft (both from *A Drunk Man*), seems absent from *In Memoriam James Joyce*, to be replaced by, at its best, a cerebral intensity, at its worst, a cataloguing insistence which recalls neither Gaelic nor Scots, but the tradition of compulsive Scottish pedantry. Then, abruptly, the roll-call stops, and we have one of these arias which, as in *The Pisan Cantos*, restore one's faith in the whole enterprise.

So I think of you, Joyce, and of Yeats and others who are dead
As I walk this Autumn and observe
The birch tremulously pendulous in jewels of cairngorm,
The sauch, the osier, and the crack-willow
Of the beaten gold of Australia:
The sycamore in rich straw-gold;
The elm bowered in saffron;
The oak in flecks of salmon gold:
The beeches huge torches of living orange.

I keep coming back to Pound, but the difference between this passage and

but old William was right in contending
        that the crumbling of a fine house
profits no one
        (Celtic or otherwise)
nor under Gesell would it happen

As Mabel's red head was a fine sight
worthy his minstrelsy
a tongue to the sea-cliffs or 'Sligo in Heaven'

is surely also technical: Pound's method of association, suppressing the connecting links so as to convey all through the juxtaposition of images enables him to retain the variety of mood in his early poems. Superficially he and MacDiarmid are ambitious and obsessed in the same polyglot way: the difference is that while it is a measure of Pound's commitment that (except for the translations) he has not written any shorter poems since beginning 'that great forty year epic', *The Cantos*, MacDiarmid's procedure tends to be the reverse; everything he writes after a certain point in his career can be assembled into larger units like *In Memoriam James Joyce* but may first exist as a separate poem.

Certainly he has been for many years the most interesting of what John Berryman once described as 'the outriders' in contemporary poetry, the only one who has sought to reconcile defiant adoption of a local or special tradition with the international claims of modern poetry. When I first discovered *Stony Limits* in the darker shelves of a Dublin library I was dazzled by its variety and energy, and although I think Austin Clarke has transferred more

161

of the skills of Gaelic poetry into English, and that MacDiarmid's later poetry might be more successful if he had learnt, like David Jones, to break the line for emphasis, his *Collected Poems* makes most contemporary work seem thin-blooded. His aggressive masculine pose may seem inimical to intimacy, but it is close to the concept of *duende* in Lorca's essay or to Wyndham Lewis's famous prescription for modern poetry: one knows that it is a man singing, and not a bird.

[1967-68]

SCOTIA

In memory of Hugh MacDiarmid

We have come so far North,
farther than we have ever been
to where gales strip everything
and the names ring guttural
syllables of old Norse:
Thurso, Scrabster, Laxdale,
names clang like a battle-axe.

Then farther West. There beauty
softens, a darkening estuary,
Farr or Borgie or Skerray where
waist-high in shallow waters
silent shadows cast at night
to lasso the lazily feeding trout
to gleam upon our hotel plate.

Still farther, mountains gather,
blue peak lifting beyond blue peak,
Ben Loyal and then Ben Hope,
noble, distant as the Twelve Bens
or Brandon; single-tracks on
endless moors, or threading along
the flanks of melancholy lochs.

Loch Loyal and Loch Naver,
where Alpine flowers blossom,
the wilderness's blessing;
as MacDiarmid will proudly remark

in our last, rambling conversation,
'strange, lovely things grow up there,
ecologically, *vairy* inter-resting.'

By such roads, only sheep prosper,
bending to crop the long acre, or
whiten the heather, like bog cotton.
The name of this county, Sutherland,
synonym for burnings, clearances,
the black aura of Castle Dunrobbin,
stone cottages broken, like Auburn.

We are not Thirties aesthetes, leaving
on impulse 'for Cape Wrath tonight'
but fellow Gaels, who have come
as far as the Kyle of Tongue
to see a sister country, Scotland,
or what is left of it, before
Scotia, like Wallia, is plundered.

Along the new motorway, trucks
and trailers strain, an invasion
grinding from England, the Grampians
pushed aside, in search of wealth;
the North Sea's blackening pulse,
the rigs towed from Moray Firth
to prop a fading imperial strength.

Beyond Tongue, still rises Ben Hope
and that star of mountains, Suilven,
that beckons to an intent fisherman,
 MacCaig, with whom I share a patronym.
His unswerving eye and stylish line
pierce through flesh to dying bone.
May Scotland always have such fishermen

Nourishing a lonely dream of how
this desolate country might have been!
The rightful arrogance of MacDiarmid's
calling together of Clann Albann,
or the surging lamentations of MacLean,
the sound of his echoing Gaelic
a fierce pibroch crying on the wind.

III

16

THE YOUNG IRISH WRITER AND *THE BELL*

Part of the function of *The Bell* in the past, and I hope in the future, has been to catch the signs of controversy as they began to crackle in the air, to try and uncover the uneasy current of suspicion and failure and distrust under the seemingly prosperous surface of modern Irish life. In this the Editor was playing the part of a surgeon who did not shrink from tackling an unpleasant but necessary operation – trying, in fact, to draw off the bile or unhealthy matter before it localized into some ugly and undefeatable shape. Thus, besides publishing the work of young Irish writers the magazine tried to give coherent expression to the view of the more intelligent members of the community, and in that work it approximated to the tradition of AE in the *Irish Statesman* where it was often and truly said that what the Ireland of the post-civil-war period wanted was, not more policies or ex-revolutionary politicians with the memories of the proverbial elephant, but more intelligence. 'Intelligence is more important than policy', wrote AE. 'Countries with intelligent and educated citizens can be prosperous with, or without, politicians or protection, but they cannot be prosperous under any system conducted without intelligence.'

In this important work *The Bell* has gained its own audience, mainly among the educated *petit bourgeoisie* in the professions, the Civil Service and the business world: the growing and very important audience created by the overflowing universities, people who are glad to see intelligence sharpening itself on the old weary problems of the politicians and are, or should be, hungry for some kind of genuine political and social thinking. Gaining the ear of the few, *The Bell* has incurred the dislike of the many, or rather of those journalists, politicians and preachers who take it upon themselves to express the indignation of the decent community, especially when some of their ideas have been examined, and found, in all justice and charity, to be mere shibboleths of pious memory. What I am trying to show is that literature has suffered by having to appear beside this work of mainly social emphasis and reference, that the young writers nurtured by *The Bell* have tended towards a uniform pattern, perhaps more harmful than helpful in any final analysis. Such social criticism has, on the other hand, directed a steady spotlight on certain flaws and dragging ailments in the present situation which have tended to check creative activity. But under savage pressure from the sort of people responsible for the Censorship Board, and the atrophy of the Abbey Theatre, *The Bell* has developed an argumentative complex, and by constantly keeping in mind the social angle or problem has tended to lead writing away from its real purpose at the present time, the imaginative and honest expression of the writer's own problems, not those of his sickening community, though the one will indirectly be reflected in the other. In this approach *The Bell* has approximated to the reportage approach of *New Writing*, or perhaps rather the much older tradition of close natural description and poetic undertones, as exemplified by a whole school of writers under the guidance of Edward Garnett. In England, this school – H. E. Bates, Manhood, Hudson, etc. – has been by-passed and partly forgotten, but in Ireland it has attained a certain fixity as the Irish school of writing. I feel, in some way, that writers using this approach to material are not moving on new ground but recovering old, that in some way they are speaking for an Ireland that no longer exists. Such writers as follow them, without rethinking their problems as a completely different generation, seem to hanker after the easy give and take of village life, still carry the mind of the smaller community around with them, and would rarely, for instance, write a story about a tractor, a cinema, a fight in a dance-hall, or a carload of drunken young men riding to a seaside resort. They miss the point of Ezra Pound's remark that there is only one artistic sin: doing something again which somebody else has done better. Ireland is at present in the awkward semi-stage between provincialism and urbanization, and the writing that will best serve should deal with the problems of the individual against this uneasy, semi-urban setting.

It would appear then that Ireland needs a contemporary litera-ture, that any attempt to develop any past tradition of writing, beyond insisting on a basis of observation and some sense of the line of past achievement, is harmful: that the older writers, like Sean O'Faolain, have tried to rationalize their failure to come to grips with contemporary life in Ireland, and that though it may be a long time before young writers appear who are equal to this kind of writing (in fact approach it so naturally that there is no need to argue) the future is in their hands and no attempt should be made to turn negative criticism on their first attempts.

This controversy is in fact no more than another version of a very old division between the anxious elder generation, like O'Connor, O'Faolain, and successive generations of not very successful young writers, some losing themselves in the Irish tradition or the Gogarty wineglass tradition of the eighteenth century, some writing small-town short stories, some, confused by the muddle of traditions and methods, just petering out ineptly or giving the matter up as a bad job. *The Bell* has always had the best intentions and been anxious to discover and encourage new writers, but it has never been satisfied with those that God gave it, and when they, in their turn, faded away without any substantial achievement, the old gloomy cry arose (John V. Kelleher, O'Con-nor in *Horizon*, O'Faolain in the *Month*), 'there are no young men appearing'. Which is practically true, since we have had no group of young writers comparable in influence and *esprit* to the Auden group in England, and when *Envoy* arrived as platform for all the eager young men it found there was none, and degenerated into a kind of anarchic aestheticism. The successive generations of young men recruited by *The Bell* served as intelligent commentators and spokesmen for the particular ideas in the air at the time; disbanded, they retain varying force as critics, and poets and journalists, some of them marked by that well-educated peevishness which seems the only real distinguishing mark of the dissatisfied young Irish intellectual. It is a pity that there has been so much side-tracking of talents, due to lack of real direction, and that so many young men have learnt the lesson of bitterness, or become truant intellectuals, who specialize in a kind of incestuous mutual criticism. What appears to have happened is that on one side we have had a failure of talent among the younger writers, and on the other a decline in the creativity of the elder; both, however, gain very little attention in the English critical press. This failure would certainly appear to indicate some general *malaise*, accentuated perhaps by our isolation in the recent War. In purely literary terms it seems to be the aftermath of a conscious attempt to create a specifically Irish literature – the tradition of the Revival exhausted, we find ourselves cut off from contemporary European literature, with little or no audience in England, since our national preoccupations have left us miles behind in the race. Therefore the natural attempt to evaluate past work, to see how much of it will help in the future, since Irish literature has rarely had to undergo real criticism. 'It does not do to leave corpses lying by the roadside,' said Gerard Hauptmann, 'you must bury them.' This same ostrich attitude is apparent in the Irish theatre, particularly the Abbey, which regularly protests its fidelity to young playwrights but would not dream of transferring the theatre into younger and more lively hands. It has in fact become a kind of National Repertory Company, and not a living theatre, which we will not have until we have a few young men with playwright ability, and another small theatre with a few actors and a good deal of enthusiasm. How can a young man be expected to tackle a play on a modern subject – which he must do or repeat *ad infinitum* – when he is cut off from the whole modern theatre? Is he to learn his trade only by worshipping at innumerable kitchen dramas or occasional revivals of the two great tragedies of the exiled Joxer?

One would naturally anticipate some kind of 'Catholic' literature in Ireland, in the continental sense of a Mauriac or a Bernanos or a metaphysician like Gabriel Marcel, but Irish Catholicism seems to pride itself on simple piety and hostility to the questing or unusual mind. In a small and almost completely Catholic community, where thought never seems to go far beyond text-book Thomism, the pressure is so great that it either drives the writer into savage reaction, like Joyce, or teaches him to avoid bringing his religion into his work, though how this can be done if one is a serious Catholic is hard to see. This emphasis on writing on the lowest level of pious journalism, and the almost complete refusal of professors and priests to declare some sympathy for the ordinary intellectual graces of Catholicism, is very hard to understand. It is probable that to be a 'Catholic' writer is only possible in a country where the religion is an active and more intelligent minority, and has to learn charity and understanding in facing a rational opposition. One could imagine the conspiracy of silence and outrage that would surround an Irish Simone Weil or Leon Bloy.

Ireland then appears to share the mood of apathy and intellectual weariness that is more apparent in post-War France than anywhere else. I think one is justified in calling it an 'existentialist' feeling, and it is more common among the growing numbers of clever young men than among any other class, though the recent apathy in the elections here would indicate that disinterest is general. The people are no longer deceived by the pointless mock-wars of politicians, and the best silent indictment of the whole situation is the stream of exiles, some going because they feel a little less unhappy in an industrialized country like England, the majority because Ireland has been too absorbed in its political and religious catch cries and witch-hunts to plan the country its young men need. One knows only too well that the louder the wail of paper or politician, the greater the sense of guilt. In literature this mood leads to an excess of negative criticism, the failed or faded writer taking it out on his more successful contemporaries. One is no longer amused when one reads what purports to be a review and discovers a paragraph of spiteful reference; in Ireland at present the mocker will bear no brother near the throne, and sells the best work for a laugh from the gallery. Reading such, one wonders if the critic has really any love for his subject at all, or if he is concerned only about keeping his place at the table. But there has always been the truant intellectual, as witness Flaubert writing to George Sand: 'When will critics be artists, only artists, but really artists? Where do you know a criticism? Who is there who is anxious about the work itself – in an intense way?'

In such a situation it is difficult to check the good man from lifting the besom and going for the cobwebs. As Eliot said about Matthew Arnold, he may never resume his real work again, exhausting his energies in his job of spring-cleaning. It is a pity that Sean O'Faolain has had to turn from being our best novelist to polemical writing, and that Patrick Kavanagh feels himself impossibly goaded by the little stupidities and deceptions and assumed attitudes that seem so much a part of Irish life. Perhaps Ireland needs one fearless critical writer and satirist, another Swift, though preferably a Catholic, to clear this apathy from the air; his only reward, however, for his single-mindedness would probably be humiliation, the kind of humiliation which Newman suffered in the boasted Catholic atmosphere of Ireland. And yet one feels that the ordinary people have nothing to do with this, that they are instinctively on the side of the good; it is rather the work of the half-educated.

The serious young writer will inevitably have to face the problem of exile, for as Anthony Cronin argues he may be quite justified in taking his possible gifts away with him; it is difficult to feel that Ireland, in her present shape, has any real claim on him. The age of the melodramatic gesture is past, however, and he would choose to leave because he could work better in another country, or live more simply, and the choice would seem to be between some form of compromise in Ireland or living more simply abroad. Exile is therefore a personal decision and will depend on the ability of the writer to carry his country or his city with him in his heart – there is a fine poem by the Greek poet Cavafy which explains how the writer can never really become an exile, his early impressions are too strong:

> You'll find no other places, no new seas in all your wandering,
> The town will follow you about. You'll range
> In the same streets. In the same suburbs change
> From youth to age; in this same house grow white.

Some writers, like O'Casey in Devon, or Lorca in America, appear to have gone away in sudden rage and despair, without the natural preparation which renders exile not an escape but another stage in a personal journey. In making this decision we can do no more than help the writer to clarify his grounds of distrust.

There are a great many things in Irish life that the young writer may feel strongly opposed to, but it would be dangerous for him to attempt a rationalization of his possible failure, or to expend his energy in ragged attempts to clear up the mess, more than likely alienating many who would otherwise feel kindly disposed towards him. The present, almost palpable air of distrust and ineffectuality is not something that can easily be shrugged; it is, in fact, one of the things that will demand expression by the serious writer, and nothing is more difficult to achieve than a satisfactory statement of things like rancour, disgust, tiredness and aimlessness. If anyone thinks I am exaggerating the mild horror of it, let him observe the heavy, almost neurotic shadows that lie over the best Irish writing of the last fifteen years: *Dutch Interior*, for instance, or *Watergate*, or *Tarry Flynn*, or *Bird Alone*, all good work that we have no reason to be ashamed of, but almost always on the single theme of frustration, the sensitive striving to exist within an unsatisfactory society, where the intellect and the flesh are almost regarded as ancient heresies. The average Irish novel of sensibility in the period ends in some kind of uneasy stasis or accepted defeat, or some *deus ex machina* gesture of emancipation. Mervyn Wall alone, in two amusing though clumsily constructed satirical chronicles of medieval Ireland, has taken the chance for objective satire, though again the attempt can be little more than a diverting sideshow, apart from the natural trend of future literature. It would almost be fair to trace this canker as far back as the post-civil-war period, to the work of that embittered and brilliant young man, Eimar O'Duffy, prototype of all later disillusion. It may be that *Ulysses* was the first and last statement of all these themes of disgust and alienation, and that Joyce laid waste a whole vast area of experience for future writers in Ireland. But in the end the only real answer to any controversy of this kind is proof of actual achievement, a section of the work in progress. For anyone engaged in honest-to-god writing and not mere concern for his local reputation as an authority in matters literary, questions like these are a mere deflection and hindrance. What matters is that the young writer should be able to estimate his heritage without hastiness or bias, and having understood the present confusion and depression, move on to fresh and original work. For what it is worth, I would suggest that the young writer avoid wrangling with his elders and concentrate on the actual work, whether it be a novel, poetry or a play, though there is considerable room for genuine criticism. It would appear that to write well in Ireland requires greater courage and clarity of purpose and dedication than ever before; no complete rejection of the past will suffice but a ruthless severing of dead branches that black out the sunlight. And there are many subjects for the courageous satirist – providing he has an independent income.   [1951]

173

17

FELLOW TRAVELLING WITH AMERICA

In the early summer of 1950 I travelled all the way to Schloss Leopoldskron, Salzburg, Austria, to join a seminar in American literature and philosophy. It was, in a minor way, a close-up of the whole
general intellectual tug-of-war in Europe today. This time it was
not capitalists or economic physicians injecting doses of Marshall
Aid, but a few sensitive Americans living by literature whether as
poets, novelists or just professors; poor as Americans go and
awkward at foreign languages, but eager to prove to a critical group
of continental students that American literature is very much
alive, and equal to or perhaps more vital than any European
modern literature; sympathetic, eager to help by pulling on the silk
rope of intellectual appeal, and claiming with some reason to
represent the real America, the better half behind the bullying
façade. And facing them, a new phenomenon in Europe, 'the
American generation', young students who are shrewd, alive to
their own country's heritage and quick to sense any kitsch culture
or jingoism, but plainly drawn to interest in the New World of
opportunity and strength. In a way a parable or caricature of all
that's going on in Europe: part of the elaborate duel for the minds
of the people waged on radio wavelength, in the mushroom growth
of information centres, and in summer schools, the new and more
discreet form of cultural megaphone.

One might, of course, view this journey from another angle,
equally exciting in analysis. Matching myself against European
graduates, comparing their training with mine, how did the Irishman come off? Pretty badly, I'll admit: for the average Irish student,

as produced by our universities, is far behind in fluency of languages, humility before achievement, or just plain *savoir vivre*. He is gauche, eager perhaps, but more arrogant and precious than his counterparts abroad. His faults are reflected in the cultural atmosphere of a country: there is no active sense of European culture, but a kind of self-conscious, isolated bravado with the artist in the invidious position of spiritual director to the intelligentsia. Literary criticism is more by gossip and instinct than rule: beyond conscientious Austin Clarke and an odd straight word from John V. Kelleher, have we had a critic worth his salt since Ernest A. Boyd or since Yeats forced merit on shrinking, shrewd John Eglinton? Without general principles to refer to or break violently from, arrogance replaces knowledge, instinct, bellowing well, is better than reason. Joyce avoided the university, made do with his scraps of Aquinas. And today they are still culpable, for however doubtful any creative writer feels about the benefits of a higher education, universities should provide an intellectual background for good writing, estimating past achievements, keeping the lines clear, a constant centre to react against, if it were no more than that.

Schloss Leopoldskron is a pleasant place; an over-ornamented mastadon of a building on the edge of an artificial lake and facing snow-capped mountains. Before a group of idealistic Harvard graduates got the idea of showing Europe that America was not the blatant industrial mammoth she appeared to be – in fact, an intelligent Big Bad Wolf, if wolf at all – this house was famous as the home of Max Reinhardt, the flamboyant theatrical producer. When you come to think of it, the tasteless, overblown, baroque architecture, the big rooms with painted ceilings and the over-decorated woodwork of the library, all were appropriate for housing the new spiritual message of William James, Thomas Wolfe, Margaret Mead, *Partisan Review* and George Washington. Critics have noticed before the affinity between baroque architecture gone to seed and the American ideal of country or suburban mansion, large, roomy, pretentious.

I was not the first Irish student to go to Salzburg, and many have since followed. Only in June last, Shelagh Richards and four young Irish players from the Abbey attended Eric Bentley's International Theatre Month and performed Synge's *Tinker's Wedding* on Reinhardt's open-air theatre. That picture makes us think a little: the one play of Synge's scarcely performed in Ireland, played on a broad, tree-sheltered stage in Austria by a few young Irish actors, under the auspices of a Seminar in American studies, and the egregious cosmopolitan guidance of Eric Bentley, for the benefit of a mixed audience of Austrians, Italians, Germans, French, Americans, and God knows what occasional nationalities. I remember chatting to one of the Seminar staff about the ignorance concerning Irish writers abroad, except Yeats and Joyce, comfortably annexed by continental and American criticism. 'What you people want', he said seriously, 'is a publicity agent.' I thought maliciously of the Joyce industry which gives so many American critics, professors, students their little slice of art and literary kudos. And so we get the comedy of professors who speak only broken German or French with a nasal twang, explaining literature to an alert body of continental students bred on Goethe, Thomas Mann, Dante and Baudelaire. But the anomaly is not all one sided: the students speak fluent English with an American accent and smoke Camel cigarettes. Many of them work in American Embassies or offices, borrow their books from the nearest United States Information Centre, hope for scholarships to American Universities. They even sing cowboy songs, and can jitterbug with true abandon.

Being an American born – I came to Ireland at the age of four – a good leaven of sentiment for my sprawling, hydra-headed patria kept tugging my attention to American books and reviews. Later I was to realize from contact with these other European students and young writers that this interest was general: Sartre, Vittorini, Silone and others had openly acknowledged their debt to American authors, Vittorini to Hemingway, Sartre, in his famous article on American literature, to Dos Passos, Hemingway, Caldwell, Faulkner, nearly every one, good or bad. There was a strong feeling that American writers had energy, technical excellence, qualities impossible in a shattered Europe: German and Austrian bookshops stocked bulky translations and originals of the novels of Thomas Wolfe, and Eliot drew attentive crowds in his lecture tour of German universities. It was perhaps the same impulse, in miniature, that drew my interest to American books on public library shelves: to a young man reared on Keats and King Lear in secondary school and university, Oscar Williams, Ezra Pound, E. E. Cummings, had the fascination of the unusual, the bizarre, the blatantly contemporary. I was amazed by their daring freedom in metrics, but doubtful if such liberties were possible in either English or Irish poetry. The question implicit then in the whole Seminar was – has America a moral and intellectual power, reflected in an unruly and active literature, to match her present dominance in politics and technological warfare? There was always the caustic scepticism of the young Italian girl student from the Free City of Trieste who wrote on her application form: 'Didn't know you had a culture. Where did you buy it?' She was immediately accepted.

Intelligent ideas like the Salzburg Seminar were not part of an official American Government policy: in fact, it came for a while under government suspicion. F. O. Mattheissen, one of the most readable of American critics, was the first guest professor of literature. He left a record of that last visit to Austria and his joy at the work of the Seminar in *From the Heart of Europe*. And Mattheissen was a well-known fellow-traveller and no jingoist using an opportunity to indoctrinate. He believed that American literature could provide the necessary stimulus for renewed zest in European writing and that the exchange would not be bad for the Americans concerned either. Randall Jarrell, the American poet, took another session of students. There were seminars in music with composers like Dave Diamond in charge, seminars in theatre with Eric Bentley, spiritual descendant of Max Reinhardt and the Keystone Cops, seminars in sociology, labour problems, politics, all the democratic apparatus of electoral systems, Gallup polls and congresses. Baseball, ping-pong, jazz records and concerts in the Mozarteum in Salzburg provided recreation.

Candidates were chosen with an eye on their possible future influence in preaching the gospel of American culture. Actual social workers, actors, lecturers, teachers, journalists, young critics and aspiring writers, workers in the radio, theatre, cinema. A photograph was required, a special article or interview, proof of at least graduate status and ability, evidence of published writings. It was no unusual thing to have three or four quite well-known minor novelists amongst the group. Emphasis was on 'the need for participating in the group activity', the old English slang phrase of slacker given an ominous American turn. Individualism was at a discount, zeal at a premium: each student was expected to prepare a paper on something or other, to act in readings of various plays, to make himself more and more useful every day. If you had a musical instrument you were expected to bring it along; a short-cropped Danish journalist in jeans and American jacket lugged along his banjo and strummed nostalgic cowboy ditties on the verandah. Richard, a talkative, brilliant French student, brought a tiny wooden flute, as well as beautiful copies of St Jean de la Croix and Baudelaire. Sometimes late at night, when the air was close and the frogs croaked like old men in the marshes at the edge of the lake, he sat at the window and played, the sound reedy and thin and infinitely melancholy. An Austrian brought a zither and the complete works of Sigmund Freud, and repeatedly plucked out the Harry Lime Theme as well as sentimental fox-trot tunes. There were two excellent violinists, both German, and innumerable pianists. Naturally, being an Irishman, I was not very gifted musically and left my ninepenny fiddle at home.

In my quickly compiled dossier I listed myself as a graduate student in literature, a potential poet (a rather magnanimous forecast on the strength of a few published poems) and an actual film critic (specimens enclosed with clip). It is remarkable how impressive one's own achievements can be made to appear when you compile them for an authority a thousand miles away: anyway, I was the only Irish applicant and would have no one to belie my gargantuan fame, once I had attained my point and got as far as Salzburg. The special article was a little more difficult. Flicking through the pages of Louis Untermeyer's anthology and some reference book on the American novel I could not discover anything that was not either hackneyed or dangerously beyond the power of my scattered reading. By chance, two articles on a rather less known American poet, Hart Crane, fell into my hands at the same time and attracted by his garish, sensitive rhetoric, I produced a fervid essay on Crane with suitable reference at intervals to dignitaries like Melville, Whitman, Emily Dickinson and the Book of Job. The essay was rhetorical and evasive, side-stepping exact knowledge as the mouse does the trap, and in a moment of levity (maybe also a congenital Irish distaste for scientific literary criticism) I added that I was working on a verse-play, 'Hamlet and the Leprechaun'. No one, I discovered later, questioned my integrity in choosing this remarkable subject. I was asked quite seriously on several occasions how the verse and the play were getting on and would I use the cadences of ordinary speech as in *The Cocktail Party?*

I received no acknowledgment of my application until one night at about 10.30 a telegram came for me: I had been chosen. Could I come. Particulars following later. That was two weeks before the Seminar began. I gave up my job, packed my bag and on April 3rd I dropped off the train from Paris to Vienna at Salzburg. I had shared a compartment with a gay party of French students on a skiing holiday. (They sang lustily while I tried to sleep on the luggage rack.) There were a few wealthy American lady tourists looking for a taxi and several GIs slouching at the entrance to the station. I asked them the way to the American Seminar.

'Sorry brother, I never heard of it. Don't know much about this town 'cept the camp and a few streets. Ain't no Yankee Seminar out here as I ever heard of.'

Schloss Leopoldskron was on the edge of the town – actually a few hundred yards away from the army barracks and parade ground. Occasionally we heard the howls of the soldiers during a game of baseball or a bugle sounding or a neat little jeep shooting along the winding lane, past old women with their dog carts. In the centre of the town was God's gift to the Austrian people: an ornamented Coca-Cola fountain, not far from the cathedral with its famous baroque belfry and bells. The army's special pub was only a short distance from the house where Mozart had been born. An American flag hung limply in the square from a high flag-pole with the American Express facing it on one side and on the other an army office or barracks. Heavy army lorries lumbered through the streets. A huge medieval castle on a steep cliff-face overlooked the entire town.

It took a few days to get settled down to the routine of the Seminar: students and professors had to get used to each other and the hostility of national groups had to be soothed over. Not that resentment was ever vocalized; occasionally a French student (ex-member of de Gaulle's Free French) would shrug his shoulders and say, 'These Italians. . . O yes, charming, amusing. . . playing at war.' This was directed at Aristide (called Harry for short) from Salerno, a cheery, garrulous, spruce little commercial traveller, an ex-captain of the Italian army, who constituted himself Court

Jester. Harry smiled and joked for us all day and spent hours in the bathroom or dormitory, combing his sleek black hair, washing and changing his perfect suits three or four times, settling his little black moustache in the mirror. In argument or a discussion of T. S. Eliot, he would switch over to intent seriousness, quoting Dante or Croce or expounding a highly involved theory of aesthetics. In a way, like the modern Italian writers, Moravia, Pratolini, Marotta: volatile, sunny, suddenly intense. The Germans kept mostly to themselves, a little doubtful and shabby and slow to push themselves forward. Before the real work commenced there was a dance in the library with the thick carpets rolled up and weak coffee, cider and doughnuts as refreshments. Here national differences came out again, the Germans dancing stiffly and stolidly like puppets, Harry twirling extravagantly like a pudgy ballerina, others jitterbugging recklessly with still a trace of the staid old-time waltz in their steps. Our poet-professor, a quiet aristocratic southern gentleman, who taught in a college in New England, preferred polkas and quadrilles. Saul Bellow the novelist just sat and looked on, smiling wryly.

James Thurber could make good fun out of the American practice of the Seminar – Seminars in Sociology, Seminars in Industrial Relations, Seminars in Poetry and the Psychology of the Adolescent. After a brief pep-talk about the need for each one playing his part, the general good, miniature League of Nations, we began our programme with one or two one-and-a-half-hour Seminars a day, with lectures on Whitman, Emerson, Henry James, etc., and discussion groups. It was beginning to get warm about this time of the year: there were moody showers of rain and hours of dull, foggy heat. In short sleeves or jackets or light frocks, squatting on the carpet or curled up on chairs or sofas, smoking the inevitable Camels or Chesterfields, we encircled the professor in charge of the Seminar. The idea was that all should contribute, the professor only keeping the discussion on the right lines by sympathetic interjections. Sometimes this wasn't easy – Theodore Dreiser held as much excitement for most of us as a Temperance Tract, though the Germans appreciated his length. Discussion was haphazard and fitful, glances strayed to the sunshine outside or the mountains in their cool perennial snow. The calm tinkling of the cow-bells drew a sharp line of silence under these lulls.

Emotions alternated between the idealistic, the excited and a general distrust and uncertainty. At first everyone was talkative, stimulated by the presence of people of their own kind from other countries, especially former enemies. A single conversation might touch on a hundred things that fascinated these young intellectuals: starting with the subjective element of modern German theology, Karl Barth, Heidegger, going on by way of St John of the Cross, William James's *Varieties of Religious Experience*, André Malraux and the religion of art, Simone Weil and the mysticism of suffering, to end up in a violent conflict over Trotsky, Proudhon and Lenin. Would such a discussion ever have been possible in an Irish university where jeers rather than theories are the expression of most students?

The Germans and Austrians took work very seriously, tabulating, filling up great black-backed notebooks and index cards, reading through all the books prescribed, whether Sherwood Anderson's *Triumph of the Egg* or Eliot's *Waste Land*. A Danish student was making a translation of *J. Alfred Prufrock* and I found myself dragged in to help, I providing English alternatives, he trying and discarding the different Danish words. Hardest worker of all was a little Italian girl, a friend of Vittorini and of Stephen Spender, who kept all the books the others were looking for stored away in a little cubby-hole of her own. Harry obviously disapproved of serious Italian girls: he whispered to me one day, when she was relating Jung to the poetry of Eliot, 'An intellectual woman is bad enough, but an intellectual girl is a monstrosity, an affront to God and to any man with normal appetites.' Between myself and the others I found a gulf that was at times hard to bridge: they knew little about Ireland, some even thinking that Joyce was an American, and they had shared, even if on opposite sides, the common experience of war.

Gratitude compels me to say that I learnt more in those four or five weeks chatting and reading with my European contemporaries, and firing questions at an agreeable professor, than in three or four years at an Irish university. The man to man atmosphere pitches interest high; you have to hold your own against the others and you really get under the skin of the work being read. For our professors ate and drank and smoked with us: they were writers themselves (Bellow, a better novelist than any writing in Ireland today) and they tackled literature as something essential, alive, written by a man facing the same problems as ourselves, only different in depth of feeling and articulacy. We read Eliot slowly together; the professor with all the sensitivity of a suppressed poet, reading gently and with a likeable humility, ready to accept the promptings of different students who quoted parallel passages in Rimbaud, Dante, Rilke. Watching the general interest in Eliot I knew for the first time to what extent he was a European poet, working in the great historical tradition. At home Auden and MacNeice were closer to my daily needs, more immediately relevant – here they were barely mentioned.

As days passed and enthusiasm cooled, criticism grew stronger, gained form, dislike of certain neurotic trends in American writing became more plain. Lying at night talking in the dormitory or drinking mugs of beer and eating thin spiced German sausages in the Weinstube we argued incessantly about the mushy core of much of this American writing, the bad dreams and formlessness of writers like Faulkner, Kenneth Patchen and Henry Miller. Richard, who was a spiritual Marxist (a combination possible in France where idealism and a youthful realism jostle each other), led the assault on E. E. Cummings, his chopped-up perverse little *avant garde* poems and his *Enormous Room*, a truly egotistical piece of American aestheticism. ('An *enfant terrible* fed on Coca-Cola,' said Richard to me after one furious discussion. 'Every sensible writer got over that stage so long ago, it's so backward an attitude.')

At times working in the library the atmosphere of American thought drove one frantic: the purely pragmatic approach, the facts and statistics on the paper, the theory not an inch beyond reason, technology clamping its artificial structure on creative effort. Bookshelves lined with the complete works of James, Dewey, Farrington, Emerson, biographies of Lincoln and Roosevelt, studies in industrial organization and all the pseudo-sciences of a depersonalized bureaucratization of life. A strident modern art, piles of critical reviews edited by poets turned professors and their student writers, top-heavy with a critical jargon that aped all the semi-abstract technical terms of psychology. Book after book on individual psychology, social psychology, racial psychology, group dynamics, anthropological studies of South Sea islanders and citizens of Chicago; man, the machine, ticking to order on every shelf. From time to time I watched a long-legged, lonely Swiss student puzzle over these shelves. He was writing a doctorate on 'The Philosophy of Loneliness', and was only interested in Heidegger, Kierkegaard, Gabriel Marcel. He came to a few lectures and sat silently in the corner. Emerson interested him slightly, Thoreau had spots of intelligence. Eventually he stopped attending and sat in the sun reading odd books, Margaret Mead's *Male and Female*, Ruth Benedict's *Patterns of Culture*, the Kinsey Report on the Sexual Behaviour of the American Male. I sat talking to him one day while the American staff and a few others were playing baseball under the shadow of the trees. 'This anthropology', he said, 'is just their sort of science. They list philosophers, like race horses according to their form, and then they stratify us all in layers like geology. Spengler, Freud, Toynbee, Sartre, Jung, the sacred names of the reviews. And then comes the offspring of imitation, a new Movement, New Directions.' And the omnibus complete volumes, big print and black lettering, the whole man on your shelf for a few dollars, or delivered at your door, while in Ireland we scrounge the bookshops for second-hand single copies.

The American system of teaching literature was new to nearly all the students, but they approved of it and indications are that it will be adopted in many European universities. They revolted, however, against its product, the diagrams of plots and sub-plots, climaxes and characters, the jargon of the reviews, the competitive newness in poetry. There was this constant war of critical intellect against creative imagination, Yvor Winters, Harry Levin, Elizabeth Drew, Kenneth Burke, William Van O'Connor, Joseph Warren Beach and a hundred others getting a complicated revenge on the writer by strait-jacketing him within all kinds of methodological and psychological criticism. This university stranglehold on literature is the principal and most disturbing phenomenon, but has its good points: Robert Penn Warren, Robert Lowell, Allen Tate, Randall Jarrell, were all pupils of John Crowe Ransom, who is professor of poetry at Kenyon College and has his own review – *Kenyon Review*. Shortly before we arrived in Salzburg news of Matthiessen's suicide had arrived: naturally some of us asked questions. Saul Bellow shrugged and quoted softly a poem of Edwin Arlington Robinson's:

And he was rich – yes, richer than a king –
And admirably schooled in every grace:
In fine, we thought that he was everything
To make us wish that we were in his place.

So on we worked, and waited for the light,
And went without the meat, and cursed the bread;
And Richard Cory, one calm summer night,
Went home and put a bullet through his head.

What then was the snag? Beyond the natural antipathy of the French to any writing that was not done in good taste: I remember, for instance, that Richard had partly translated Djuna Barnes. And the Germans, revelling in the blind bull mysticism of Thomas Wolfe, got a pretty shock when his name was never mentioned except in disparagement. This is the American century, and Wolfe seemed the epitome of America in all its volcanic misdirected energy. Anyone living in the north of Ireland during the War knows the changes American occupation can bring, the general uniform craze for jazz bands, blaring technicoloured films and other better, simpler things like jeeps. Still, even for an Irishman on a short leave of absence from his national duck-pond, there is a sense of hurt in seeing an American Information Centre in Vienna's famous fashion street Kärntnerstrasse, or hearing an audience howl for 'The Count of Castille' in one of the back streets of Venice. We know that they are not to blame; maybe, God knows, there is more altruism than opportunism in their plans of aid and occupation – but no one with a sense of tradition can count it as a cultural advance, only the hasty propping-up of the butt-end of an endangered civilization.

Berdyaev prophesied a Russian century, a grandiose and perhaps naïve speculation; the nineteenth century was presumably the hey-day of English and French imperialism. Certainly culture has shrunk to the size of a traveller's ego; and a man like Eric Bentley can take Shaw, Yeats, Bertolt Brecht and Broadway in his stride and demonstrate the great international linking up. But literature still seems to the writer himself a matter of patience, imagination, great and cultivated skill, for which qualities no amount of cultural globe-trotting is substitute. (Gide said: 'Let the idea take flesh and grow.') Eating canned food prepared by Slav cooks, and hearing

'Shorty', the Danish journalist, talk in his resonant twang, there was the half-conscious instinct to revolt against this great Standardization. We even resented at times the too easy and fluent references to our own literatures: Rilke, Malraux, Yeats. They took what they wanted, the cream of our cow, and bound it in a big, bright book: but that in itself wasn't criminal, and looking up at my own bookshelves at this moment I find the lie thrown in my face, fair exchange in writers like Pound, Melville, Henry James, Thornton Wilder, Faulkner, Edmund Wilson, J. F. Powers, Delmore Schwartz, etc. Only the few on one man's shelf and yet balancing the French, dwarfing recent English poetry and fiction. Then the argument that we raised against them day after day: the truancy of James, Pound, Eliot, Djuna Barnes, Hemingway, Kay Boyle. These writers had felt the restless dispossessed atmosphere of a big industrial country, without tradition or heritage of grace in speech and word: had emigrated wholesale; Eliot, for example, being European, only American by accident of birth. Where was their Negro literature? Sherwood Anderson makes the big buck-nigger say: 'Would white poet ever know why my people walk so softly and laugh at sunrise?'

But that is a dangerous approach for an Irishman: do we cherish our own writers? And could these others have come from any place except America? Pound, in his cape and big red beard, storming literary Europe, capturing its whole culture single-handed, swaggering through Fascist Rome. Cyril Connolly complained that all the good young writers came from America: the new and odd generation of Truman Capote, Paul Goodman, Lionel Trilling, Saul Bellow, too many to mention. But in Salzburg desertion from the various seminars increased: many preferred to row or splash about on the lake, climb the peak opposite, hitch to Linz on the Danube. But that might be only youth, and any writer or reader worth his salt prefers sunlight to a study dark with books.

Why, then, did Richard say to me three months later in Paris: 'I doubt if I could stick it all again'? Was it merely the defence mechanism of underdog nations? For myself, the journey did a lot of good: but there was a feeling that all this listing and correlating had very little to do with literature. Melville said: 'A whale boat was my Yale and Harvard.' Scott Fitzgerald wrote to his daughter: 'I hate to see you spend your money on a course like English prose since 1800. I don't know how clever the other professor is, one can't raise a discussion on modern prose to anything but tea-table level . . . anyone that can't read modern English prose by themselves is abnormal, and you know it.' Or was it the sense of pain and incongruity in seeing French and German students swing into the rhythm of 'Under the Bam, Under the Boo, Under the Bam-boo Tree', or construing this lyric of E .E. Cummings with its pleasant little home truth for themselves:

LISN bud LISN

    dem
    gud
    am

    lidl yelluh bas
    tuds weer goin

duhSIVILEYE zum

Behind all this fostered persuasive vision of American writers, spawning healthily, bulked the ignored shadow of the pseudo-arts, the blaring commercial films, the glossy magazine story, the whole American industry of entertainment falsifying the lives of an entire people. Power fantasies and sadism and at another time the good dream of simple-hearted GI Joe, bringing joy and equality to quarrelling Europe. And this was, perhaps, the falsity at the heart of the Seminar: why we questioned and doubted and lapsed into reading odd volumes of our own literature. Dos Passos was big, powerful, shining, a writer like a Chrysler car, featuring on his main bill what J. B. Priestley has called 'the American Rhapsody, with the strings celebrating the dream and the brass thundering the way of life': Mickey Rooney quoting Thomas Jefferson at Eton and the great new Land, 'the real America that Jefferson, Lincoln, Whitman and Mark Twain meant, smaller, simpler, clearer, the light of morning still gilding it, where men knew they have been created equal, have broken forever with the tyrannical Old World and see the frontiers of the West glittering with a gold that had nothing to do with Bretton Woods'. But to see that dream you had to be perpetually drunk, or celebrating Thanksgiving Day. And so a great new industry of entertainment had come into being, the dream-made-noise, flawless hero and heroine, dispensing joy from a thousand screens.

No one ventured to explain to us the suicide of Hart Crane, the maniac's dream of Kenneth Patchen's *Journal of Albion Moonlight*. Sense guttering low, the slobbering that made mush of Saroyan's instinct for the true and the good, the whole magnificent noise and strain drowning a nightmare. Scott Fitzgerald's 'The Crack-up', *The Air-Conditioned Nightmare* of Henry Miller: the frightened vision of these few serious writers was not fit subject for a Seminar.

The night before we left we all gathered in the local Weinstube and sang folksongs, pounding beer mugs on the table. Saul and the others sang bawdy little American ditties with a deft lilt, the French sang their countless folksongs with a doubtful harmonizing, even Shorty sang a boisterous Danish rowing song. Being joyously drunk I raised the roof with six verses of 'Ag Uirchill an Chreagáin' remembered from my schooldays. Though few knew what the others were singing about, it was the most successful night of the whole Seminar.

[1951]

18

AMERICAN PEGASUS

Granted the usual unsympathetic image of American culture, it is rather a shock to realize the extent of its achievement in contemporary poetry. For American verse has, finally, come of age, with an impressive terracing of generations, from living masters – like Frost, Williams, and Pound – to the newest, brightest recruit from Harvard, Iowa or San Francisco. In 1959 the European pilgrimage is no longer a necessity, except as a brief, leisurely interlude, probably on a travelling fellowship. In a world dominated by American-type modernity, expatriation is the problem of the European artist; influence, the prerogative of the American.

It is a pity, therefore, that our view of American poetry, this side of the Atlantic, is still radically incomplete. Criticism, of course, is partly to blame for this situation: it is almost impossible to get a book on a contemporary poet which is not based on a sort of elaborate *petitio principii*; assuming his author's ultimate importance, the critic creates a superstructure of interest only to fellow Martians. The publishers are also to blame: there are no editions of Crane, Cummings, Williams, or John Peale Bishop available, to name only the obvious. Even Wallace Stevens, probably the finest American poet of the century, only received belated recognition in England with a *Selected Poems* (Faber & Faber 1953), although he had been publishing steadily in America since *Harmonium* (1923). Only one British publishing house, Faber & Faber, has made a consistent effort to present American poetry, and even their lists show curious omissions and alterations. (Contributing to a Wallace Stevens special issue of the Harvard Advocate a few years ago, Eliot remarked with typical blandness that he had always taken for granted that Stevens had a British publisher: a marvellously politic oversight!)

Four recently published volumes* may be taken to illustrate the diversity of American poetry, its daring directness in pursuit of a language to accommodate modern experience. The American works closer to experience and natural speech that his British contemporary: he can tackle a subject frontally without that horror of naïvety which forces the average Oxbridge talent into defensive literary reflexes. He is also, generally, much more trained in the tradition, even if it is only to discard it; witness William Carlos Williams. This double seriousness of craft and subject means that while American poets are not always automatically good, they are almost always readable. Between the polarities of Eliot's purified line and William's 'new measure' based on the American vernacular, lies a variety of talents, a variety of solutions to the Wordsworthian problem of natural language.

John Berryman first (*Homage to Mistress Bradstreet*) since in many ways he is the most baffling, the most exclusive of the four; a fiercely contemporary intelligence. Born in 1914, he came of age during that period when the Spanish Civil War gradually widened into world conflict. His early poetry represents a struggle towards a post-Auden rhetoric of endured despair, appropriate to the time:

> When we dream, paraphrase, analysis
> Exhaust the crannies of the night. We stare,
> Fresh sweat upon our foreheads, as they fade:
> The melancholy and terror of avenues
> Where long no single man has moved, but play
> Under the arc-light gangs of the grey dead
> Running directionless. That bright blank place
> Advances with us into fearful day,
> Heady and insuppressible.
> ('Desire Is a World by Night')

The dangers are obvious: a desire for full integrity can often end as a kind of compulsive chic, an induced pessimism. But a poem like

*A review of *Homage to Mistress Bradstreet* by John Berryman, *Life Studies* by Robert Lowell, *Promises* by Robert Penn Warren and *In Defence of the Earth* by Kenneth Rexroth (all London 1959).

'World Telegram' illuminates an aspect of modern experience in a way I have not seen elsewhere:

> All this on the front page. Inside, penguins.
> The approaching television of baseball.
> The King approaching Quebec. Cotton down.
> Skirts up. Four persons shot. Advertisements.
> Twenty six policemen are decorated.
> Mother's Day repercussions. A film star
> Hopes marriage will preserve him from his fans.
>
> News of one day, one afternoon, one time.
> If it were possible to take these things
> Quite seriously, I believe they might
> Curry disorders in the strongest brain,
> Immobilize the most resilient will,
> Stop trains, break up the city's food supply,
> And perfectly demoralize the nation.

Berryman's later work shows more variety, including a very beautiful epithalamion, 'Canto Amor', and a very intelligent extension of the technique of Yeats's 'Crazy Jane' poems into a series of 'Nervous Songs'. His major work, however, is *Homage to Mistress Bradstreet*, a long poem first published in *Partisan Review* in 1953, and hailed by Edmund Wilson as 'the most distinguished long poem by an American since *The Waste Land*'. What is one to say of this mysterious dialogue between the author and the conjured ghost of a New England poetess? Anne Bradstreet crossed to New England on the *Arbella* in 1630, under Governor Winthrop. She reared a large family in the New World and yet found time to publish a collection of 'abstract, didactic rime', imitations of Quarles and Sylvester's Du Bartas. Across the centuries, Berryman invokes her spirit as the first American poet, alienated, like him, from a negative, constricted culture:

> Outside the New World winters in grand dark
> white air lashing high thro' the virgin stands
> foxes down foxholes sigh,
> surely the English heart quails, stunned.
> I doubt if Simon than this blast, that sea,
> spares from his rigour for your poetry
> more. We are on each other's hands
> who care. Both of our worlds unhanded us. . .

The privations of pioneer life, childbirth, harsh theological feuds which separate friend from friend, the sadness of maturity, the sicknesses of old age; the poem works closer to the root of living than any I have read for a long time. The spirits of the two poets touch, hers in feminine loneliness, his in modern despair; there is a suggestion of ghostly passion which savours slightly of demonology. It is the poet as medium: an impressive but rather frightening technique.

I doubt if *Homage to Mistress Bradstreet* will ever become widely popular; there is something antagonistic and posturing in Berryman's approach, a deliberate slurring of language through inversion, strained images, recherché words. In the childbed scene, these tricks of language succeed astoundingly; elsewhere, they annoy and detract. Nevertheless I am deeply impressed by the almost manic intensity of the poem, the relentless seriousness which drives it towards the limits of communication. One cannot, after all, penetrate the secret and total meaning of another's life, but this is a fierce and honourable attempt.

> So squeezed, wince you scream? I love you & hate
> off with you. Ages! *Useless.* Below my waist
> he has me in Hell's vise.
> Stalling. He let go. Come back: brace
> me somewhere. No. No. Yes! everything down
> hardens I press with horrible joy down
> my back cracks like a wrist
> shame I am voiding oh behind it is too late
>
> hide me forever I work thrust I must free
> now I all muscles & bones concentrate
> what is living from dying?
> Simon I must leave you so untidy
> Monster you are killing me Be sure
> I'll have you later Women do endure
> I can *can* no longer
> and it passes the wretched trap whelming and I am me
>
> drencht & powerful, I did it with my body!
> One proud tug greens Heaven. Marvellous,
> unforbidding Majesty.
> Swell, imperious bells. I fly.
> Mountainous, woman not breaks and will bend:

sways God nearby: anguish comes to an end.
Blossomed Sarah, and I
blossom. Is that thing alive? I hear a famisht howl.*

Robert Lowell's new book of poems (*Life Studies*) is his first since his rather unsuccessful attempt at a long narrative poem, *The Mill of the Kavanaughs* (Harcourt & Brace 1952 – unpublished in England). It comes to us shorn of the long autobiographical essay which prefaced the American edition: was it considered too daring an innovation for the Faber series, or irrelevant for an English audience? Nevertheless, despite this omission and the fact that the opening poems in the volume are substantially in Lowell's earlier manner, one senses all the drama of a change of style, of approach.

> These are the tranquillized *Fifties*,
> and I am forty. Ought I to regret my seedtime?
> I was a fire-breathing Catholic C.O.,
> and made my manic statement,
> telling off the state and president, and then
> sat waiting sentence in the bull pen
> beside a Negro boy with curlicues
> of marijuana in his hair.
>
> ('Memories of West Street and Lepke')

Lowell's problem has been to break the mould of his success in *Lord Weary's Castle* (Harcourt & Brace 1946), the best book of poems since the war and the first to show a genuine post-modern sensibility, a return to traditional techniques with all the freshness of assimilated experimentation. Learned, savage, exhilarating, *Lord Weary's Castle* seemed more an end-product than a beginning.

> Christ walks on the black water. In Black Mud
> Darts the kingfisher. On Corpus Christi, heart,
> Over the drum-beat of St Stephen's choir
> I hear him, *Stupor Mundi*, and the mud
> Flies from his hunching wings and beak – my heart,
> The blue kingfisher dives on you in fire.
>
> ('Colloquy in Black Rock')

* When this piece was originally published in the Jesuit journal *Studies* I omitted this quotation.

In poem after poem, the militant Catholicism of the convert was used to batter the inertia of Boston, the Puritan constrictedness of his ancestors: 'in Boston serpents whistle at the cold'. With the generosity poets often show to portents in their own generation, John Berryman described Lowell as 'the most powerful poet who has appeared in England or America for some years, master of a freedom in the Catholic subject without peer since Hopkins. . . a talent whose ceiling is invisible'.

Some critics had reservations, however: Blackmur and Marius Bewley, for example. There was the wilful and gritty obscurity of many passages. In a few very beautiful later poems, like 'Mother Marie Thérèse' and 'Falling asleep over the Aeneid', Lowell developed his talent for the dramatic monologue; despite their clearer organization and logic, however, these successes were implicit in the earlier work; and despite the bravery of the attempt, the long poem *The Mill of the Kavanaughs* seemed largely an anthology of favourite Lowell effects.

The first two sections of *Life Studies* bring no surprise. The approach is softer, perhaps:

> Your great nerve gone, Sire, sleep without a care.
> No Hapsburg galleon coasts off Finisterre
> with bars of bullion now to subsidize
> the pilfering, pillaging democracies. . .
>
> ('The Banker's Daughter')

A series of poems in homage, 'Ford Madox Ford', 'For George Santayana', 'Words for Hart Crane', show an unexpected humanity; the Santayana poem, in particular, celebrates a *non-conversion*, a deliberately pagan death. And that is our first hint. . .

> Lying outside the consecrated ground
> forever now, you smile
> like Ser Brunetto running for the green
> cloth at Verona – not like one
> who loses, but like one who'd won. . .
> as if your long pursuit of Socrates'
> demon, man-slaying Alcibiades,
> the demon of philosophy, at last had changed
> those fleeting virgins into friendly laurel trees
> at *Santo Stefano Rotondo*, when you died

near ninety,
still unbelieving, unconfessed and unreceived,
true to your boyish shyness of the Bride.

The final group of autobiographical poems, which constitute
the bulk of the volume, present a new Lowell, quieter, more
sympathetic, distinctly tender. The fiery objurgations of *Lord
Weary's Castle* are gone, and with the change in tone and subject
comes also a change in technique, from strict metres to free verse,
with echoes of William Carlos Williams's dictates and practice.
My impression is that the earlier poems in *Life Studies* represent
scattered efforts, and that when Lowell began working on a prose
autobiography, he suddenly found the material changing into a
portrait gallery of poems. One can underline Lowell's luck in being
born into a family both branches of which enshrine a culture, but
cannot deny the jagged tenderness of these portraits, from Grandfather Winslow who found 'his grandchild's fogbound solitudes
sweeter than human society' to the poet's baby daughter in her
'flame-flamingo infant's wear'. Quotation is difficult, since the
poems depend on a seemingly casual build-up of detail; on first
reading, they seem clumsy, embarrassing, pointless; then, suddenly, they seem exactly right, moving almost to the point of tears.

Although there are fewer quotable tours de force, *Life Studies* is
as impressive, in its more subdued way, as *Lord Weary's Castle*.
And, unlike the earlier book, the poems open out onto life with
appreciation and a kind of perplexed humility and love. That this
change has not been achieved without 'an expense of spirit' is
shown by certain poems on mental illness; the sequence itself is a
form of therapy, distilling something of the poised uneasiness of an
'adjustment' to reality.

Robert Penn Warren (b. 1905), poet, novelist and critic, is one
of the most formidably gifted writers on the American scene. The
general reader will probably know one or two of his novels: *Night
Rider*, *All the King's Men*, *World Enough and Time*, *Band of Angels*.
His poetry is not so well known, although his long poem, *Brother
to Dragons*, published in 1953, was as colourful and violent as an
historical novel. Warren's technique, indeed, is often to take a
popular form, like the historical romance, and recover it for
orthodox literary purpose; rather in the way Graham Greene

employs the conventions of the modern thriller. This is easier to do with fiction, of course, although poems like *Brother to Dragons* and 'The Ballad of Billie Potts' make use of the thump and clatter of the Kentucky mountain ballad:

> Big Billie Potts was big and stout
> In the land between the rivers.
> His shoulders were wide and his gut stuck out
> Like a croker of nubbins and his holler and shout
> Made the bob-cat shiver and the black-jack leaves shake
> In the section between the rivers.

The theme of this poem is the same as Camus's *Le Malentendu* (the returned son murdered by his parents), but the technique is that of a rural ballad describing a brawl at a football match.

This deliberate hillbilly roughness is represented in his new volume *Promises* by poems like the following, based on a local tragedy where a poor farmer massacred his entire family with an ice-pick:

> They weren't so bright, or clean, or clever,
> And their noses were sometimes imperfectly blown,
> But they always got to school the weather whatever,
> With old lard pail full of fried pie, smoked ham, and corn pone.
> It was good six miles to the Gillum place,
> Back where the cedar and hoot owl consorted
> And the snapping turtle snoozed in his carapace
> And the whang-doodle whooped and the dang-whoodle snorted.

The excuse for this titbit of rural sensationalism lies in the thematic structure of *Promises*. The long section in which such poems occur is dedicated to his son, Gabriel; they represent Warren's honest attempt to retell, re-evaluate incidents from his own Kentucky mountain childhood. To pass on a felt heritage, however rudimentary, as he in the past had received his:

> Some were given to study, read Greek in the forest, and these
> Longed for an epic to do their own deeds right honor:
> Were Nestor by pigpen, in some tavern brawl played Achilles.
> In the ring of Sam Houston they found, when he died, one
>   word engraved: Honor.
> ('Founding Fathers, Nineteenth Century Style, South East U.S.A.')

But Warren has another poetic mood, romantic, cosmopolitan, the great clauses swinging like hinges in the construction of an elaborate metaphysical conceit: 'Love's Parable', for instance, in the *Selected Poems*. Here we have 'To a Little Girl, One Year Old, In a Ruined Fortress', the opening poem, dedicated to his daughter:

> To a place of ruined stone we brought you, and sea-reaches.
> *Rocca*: fortress, hawk-heel, lion-paw, clamped on a hill.
> A hill, no. On a sea-cliff, and crag-cocked, the embrasures
>   commanding the beaches,
> Range easy, with most fastidious mathematic and skill.
>
> *Philipus me fecit*: he of Spain, the black-browed, the anguished,
> For whom nothing prospered, though he loved God.
> His arms, a great scutcheon of stone, once over the drawbridge,
>   have languished
> Now long in the moat, under garbage; at moat-brink, rosemary
>   with blue, thistle with gold bloom, nod.

The enigma of Warren's extraordinary talent remains. Some will be excited by the rough stoicism, the bathos, the preoccupation with images of sordid violence; others repelled. If a man's life-work can be seen as a pattern, with individual works existing not so much in themselves but as part of a total elaboration and investigation of themes (Eliot's view of Shakespeare), then Warren may be as massive an artist as Melville (whose poetry so much resembles his own in purpose and manner). Conversely, it might be argued that Warren, with his great training (he is a Rhodes Scholar, and, up to recently, a university professor) has made less of his southern background than William Faulkner with his purely instinctive craftsman's intelligence; the moral: stay at home, trust in God, and don't read too many books.

Warren's pursuit of the colloquial line, his Kentucky modernism, is paralleled by Kenneth Rexroth's casual Californian toughness:

> At sixteen I came West, riding
> Freights on the Chicago, Milwaukee
> And St. Paul, the great Northern,
> The Northern Pacific. I got

A job as helper to a man
Who gathered wild horses in the
Mass drives in the Okanogan
And Horse Heaven country. . .

('A Living Pearl')

Despite all the recent Beat Generation publicity, Rexroth (b. 1906) is an interesting poet, learned and serious in his craft. His *The Dragon and the Unicorn* (New Directions, 1952) is an impressive solution to the problem of the long modern poem. The form is that of the Victorian travel poem (Samuel Rogers or Arthur Hugh Clough) but on the thread of a year's travel in Europe he hangs meditations on politics, on art, on the nature of love.

Chaumont, brilliant in the sun,
The working of a consistent
Principle, the best of the
Big Châteaux. Amboise dull and
Hot in August midafternoon,
And then a cool hand, over
The chapel doorway the high
Relief of St. Eustace and
The cruciferous stag, almost
As touching as Pisanello's.

The present collection, *In Defence of Life*, consists mainly of shorter pieces, apart from one gruesome mistake ('Thou Shalt Not Kill', a memorial poem for Dylan Thomas). Like most West Coast poetry it plays it cool, dispensing with the usual tensions and dialectic of verse and the corresponding complexities of structure (Rexroth always uses a simple syllabic prosody with a counterpoint of ideas tracing larger units of form; rarely stanzas). The geographical analogy is obvious, for in California one experiences the discomforts of the garden of Eden; perfect landscapes, perfect climate. The drama of the seasons is replaced by an extravagance of natural phenomena:

. . the illimitable
And inhuman waste places
Of the Far West, where the mind finds
Again the forms Pythagoras

> Sought, the organic relations
> Of stone and cloud and flower
> And moving planet and falling
> Water. . .
>
> ('A Living Pearl')

Man, in a marvellous setting, achieves a kind of ecstasy of solitary contemplation, akin to the spiritual intuitions of the East towards which California faces.

> . . . The late
> Afternoon sun behind it
> Fills its leaves with light like
> A gem tree, like the wishing
> Tree of jewels in the Eastern
> Stories. Below it the cliff
> Falls sheer away five hundred
> Feet to a single burnt pine. . . .
>
> ('Time is the Mercy of Eternity')

These four talents, intelligent, energetic, various, indicate the level of current American production in poetry. Of the four, only Lowell, perhaps, is of first rank, but how much better even the worst of the others is than the average British effort! As we move towards the sixties, the achievements of the first half of our century become clearer; already the received or textbook picture of modern verse, with its Eliot-Pound axis, is crumbling. The orthodoxy of the various pioneer anthologies and studies is dissolving in favour of a wider and more fluid view, hospitable to the independent talent, like Stevens or Williams or Robert Graves. The full range of Anglo-American activity can no longer be interpreted in terms of one tradition, like a vast historical umbrella: the individual poet chooses, creates his tradition from the living elements in his background, whether Californian or Bostonian or Admass American. The integrity of his achievement lies in his ability, like a diviner, to find where, in darkness and noise, the living water flows.

All this is much better understood in America than here. It is why William Carlos Williams's brilliant book, *In the American Grain*, has become almost a Bible for younger American poets. The tradition it posits in its investigation of the American past, is, paradoxically, wider than Eliot's, because it acknowledges more than American Protestant experience: there is also, after all, pre-Columbian America, Indian America, Spanish America, even for a brief moment Russian America (their trading posts came as far south as Monterey). There are the traditions of the various emigrant groups. Similarly, Wallace Stevens's quiet refusal to appeal to any orthodoxy, whether High Church or Communism, his reliance on the creative imagination as a means of satisfaction and knowledge, is much admired by younger writers. A secular aesthetic may represent an almost religious honesty if the social context offers nothing more: look, no hands, no feet, no solid ground! In the inevitable rewriting of recent literary history Eliot may yet be cast as the villain of the piece.

[1959]

19

JOHN BERRYMAN: HENRY IN DUBLIN

Few people realise that *The Dream Songs* were completed in Ireland, and since I was in attendance, a few notes on that difficult delivery might be in order, especially since I already knew Berryman.

The first background against which I saw John Berryman was in the State University of Iowa, 'dreadful state' as he mutters in one of *The Dream Songs*. I think I know why he says that, from my acquaintance with him that year ending with a quick exit and a banging door. And the man whom I met in Dublin twelve years later was a very different and much less touchy man.

I met him at the house of the professor in charge of the writing programme. I was coming as a junior lecturer in charge of a course called 'Understanding Poetry' based on the Brooks and Warren textbook of that name. He was ostentatiously shunning poetry, teaching a course on the short story, and sharing the Fiction Workshop: I had the impression that he was determined to bring the talent glimpsed in his short story, 'The Imaginary Jew', to fulfilment. In any case, he ignored me all evening except to point out that I should not speak about American football if I knew nothing about it (the season was just beginning and the Hawkeyes had a good team) and that I had no right to enquire about *his* friend's health (this, in answer to a tentative question about Lowell, who was rumoured to be sick again). Our host was partly to blame himself, I gathered, both for raising such topics and inviting a naïve outsider like myself along. Not a promising beginning. . .

I saw another side of him a few days later, when having set us a class theme on Isaac Babel he chose my essay to read out as an example of good writing. It was done in such a polite and elaborate way that it sounded like a public version of a private apology. Things became even more complicated when, at the first Fiction Workshop meeting, he came under very heavy fire indeed for a story he had read by one of his East Coast students, which was taken as an insult to women by the lady novelist with whom he was sharing the platform. In the anti-Berryman barrage that followed I found myself coming in on Berryman's side, declaring that while Shakespeare had written about whores and bitches this did not necessarily mean he was prejudiced against women or the lower classes. It was a nervous, fractious discussion, linked more with the personalities involved than literature, but Berryman was clearly uncomfortable. When it was over he whisked over to thank me tersely for my few words, and asked me if I needed an Assistantship in the Department. I had gained his confidence, but perhaps lost the support of a whole department.

Next, the banging door. It was very noticeable that Berryman was alone: one saw him eating in the local hotel, or coming with a book under his arm into the cinema (significantly, it was *The Caine Mutiny*, with Bogart as the Captain who loses his self-control). And in the evenings he was in a bar near the university, hunched up on a stool, the book open before him, forbidding conversation. And it was there that whatever kind of confrontation that was involved took place one autumn evening in that second week of term; Berryman hit or at least scuffled with someone and was landed in the town jail.

That in itself is not unusual among writers, but they are usually not attached to universities, and do not find themselves exposed on the morning news ('Professor Strikes Student' was, I think, the headline). Since I was now accepted by Berryman I found myself involved with the rescue party that came to bail him out: Gertrude Buckman, the first wife of his beloved friend Delmore Schwartz; Emma Swan, a poet from the East, who was both discreet and helpful. Berryman was in a very grim mood, complaining that he had been baited and humiliated by the cops, who had taken away his glasses (which is standard practice in most jails, to prevent a suicide attempt). But I was still surprised when he did not show up for class: our youthful hero-worship of writers did not make any allowance for how very differently the administration of an institution might see such behaviour. Whether Berryman was fired or resigned before any pressure was brought to bear upon him, the result was the same: he left Iowa for Minnesota, where his friend Allen Tate 'would welcome him properly'. There was a tense farewell dinner where very little was said directly about the incident, and then he was gone.

All this would have little relevance if the incident had not helped to trigger off some kind of change in Berryman himself; or so it seemed to me. For the man I was beginning to meet in Iowa was nervous, taut, arrogant, uneasy; very nearly a caricature of the over-trained, fiercely cerebral, academic poet of the fifties; a man hair-triggered for insult, and quite capable of getting angry with a student. The man I was to meet in the Majestic Hotel in Dublin was very nearly the reverse – enthusiastic, hilarious, drunken, as splendid and generous a man as one might meet, who fitted into the roar of Dublin pub life with ease. Or rather for whom it was a natural backdrop, not for reading but for writing. There were other reasons for this change, but I could not be expected to know them. I mainly want to convey my delight in the man I met who radiated a kind of wild benignity. He had written to me from Minnesota asking if I could find him a house, and since I happened to be back in Paris at the time I suggested that he stay in the Majestic Hotel on Baggot Street for a while, and get Liam Miller of the Dolmen Press to help him to find a place. For a few months he stayed in the Majestic, and the lounge there was the scene for many memorable conversations, well fuelled with a variety of drinks. And then he found his own place, a semi-detached behind Northumberland Road with an excellent, old-fashioned pub nearby into which he could slip to work.

This is something I want to make clear: Berryman is the only writer I have ever seen for whom drink seemed to be a positive stimulus. He drank enormously and smoked heavily, but it seemed to be part of a pattern of work, a crashing of the brain barriers as he raced towards the completion of the *Dream Songs*. For he seemed to me positively happy, a man who was engaged in completing his life's work, with a wife and child he adored. He had come into his own and radiated the psychic electricity of genius. He delighted to talk about literature, which he clearly loved with an all-absorbing passion; he would cry as he recited the Paolo and Francesca episode from the *Inferno* or suddenly leap up to shake the hands of someone who agreed with him about the merits of a Henry James story. He no longer cared, he was no longer concerned with appearances, as his long, hacking coughs halted his conversation or an elbow sent a glass flying. He could be wildly funny as he discussed what one should do about bad critics: the Chinese torture of a thousand cuts was suggested, or roasting them slowly. (As several prominent English and American critics were involved in these hilarious midnight discussions I will give no names, recalling only the solemnity with which he passed over one on whom we disagreed: 'He's yours, of course.') But the deeper concerns were always there: he was intrigued by the last poems of Yeats, and specifically wanted me to explicate 'Cuchulain Comforted' for him.

So Ireland and Yeats were no accidental choice, as became clear when I tried to arrange a reading for him at University College, Dublin, where the professor was a well known pundit on American literature. All he could offer Berryman, however, was £5 for a performance, which seemed to me ridiculous and ungenerous. Instead I hired a hall and, with the help of Liam Miller and Basil Payne who had been assisting me with a series of readings in the Lantern Theatre, made sure that it would be filled. For the programme he gave us his lovely Yeats poem. 'I have moved to Dublin to have it out with you,/majestic shade. . . .' But as the hall was filling up with a motley army of poetry admirers, recruited from every pub and college we could think of, we were told that Berryman had disappeared.

This habit of disappearance was also part of the pattern of the year. I often ate in a pub on the quays which had once been known affectionately as the Whore's Rest. I called him from there one evening and he said he would come and join me. Closing time came, and no Berryman, so I dropped around to see what had happened. Some time after I arrived he too came back in a taxi having left to find me a long time before. He did not seem to have the least idea of where he had been, or where he had left for, so after a few questions his wife and I dropped the subject. But when the rumours began to filter in that he was fortifying himself for his first and last public appearance in Dublin, and might even not make it, all our preparations seemed in danger.

Appear he did, and one of the strangest poetry readings I have ever attended took place. With great difficulty Patrick Kavanagh had been persuaded to come, on the condition that the name of a certain Irishman was not pronounced in public. Kavanagh lurked in the back with his troops, coughing as he waited, while I tried to create an atmosphere for the reading with an introduction where I said that this was the most important occasion of its kind since Robert Frost had read in Dublin. Unfortunately, I mentioned our first meeting at Iowa: protests from Berryman behind, who disliked all mention of that state, which he regarded as a minor region of Limbo. Then he began to greet old friends in the audience, like the composer Brian Boydell whom he had known at Cambridge. The sight of the domed Boydell being warmly embraced by Berryman fascinated the audience, so that I was able to weave to the end of my introduction without further interruption. But when Berryman consented to come forward, he began his reading very graciously with a vote of thanks to those responsible for the recent recognition of Irish poetry abroad, in particular the man whose name Mr Kavanagh did not wish to hear (Liam Miller of the Dolmen Press).

Uproar, and exit Kavanagh. But many of his associates remained, including one critic who could not restrain his admiration for Berryman's more intense works, but kept publicly declaring his admiration when a line or word struck him. Another unexpected but very loyal supporter, Ronnie Drew of the Dubliners, who had been a Majestic drinking pal of Berryman's, took exception to this as an unprofessional intrusion, and kept calling on the critic, 'Shut up, John.' Since the genial offender bore the same name as both of us, Berryman kept glancing up in a puzzled way, and once stopped to look over at me: 'Am I doing alright, John?' He was not so much drunk as splendidly oblivious, and soon himself and the audience were talking away as if he were reciting in some bar, as he sometimes did. 'Do you really like that poem?' he asked, after one woman had insisted that he re-read that terrifying poem on his father's suicide: 'The marker slants, flowerless, day's almost done....' It was a great success, though a nerve-wracking one, the apotheosis of his Dublin stay.

A final glimpse of that glorious year. I had arranged to bring Berryman into the Dublin hills to meet Garech Browne, hoping to record John for Claddagh Records. It was a great excursion, one of those May days which make Ireland seem paradisal, a pet of a day. Anthony Kerrigan drove us up in his battered Mercedes and we sat in the garden at Woodtown Manor, laughing and drinking under the stare of the strange, squat stone lion that the previous owner, Morris Graves, had rescued from some ruined house. Berryman spoke a lot about Lowell, who would later marry Garech's great-eyed cousin, Caroline Blackwood. I remembered our first conversation over a decade before. Now, to use Berryman's expression, we were pals.

Then a small incident occurred which showed his essential innocence. John Hurt had joined us after a hard day's filming with John Huston in the Wicklow hills. When he saw him, Berryman went silent. After a while he nudged me. 'That's John Hurt,' he said incredulously. I agreed and went to get Hurt a glass. But Berryman was still agog as any schoolboy; himself and his wife had seen *A Man for all Seasons* only a few days before. 'But how can he be here,' insisted John, 'he's really famous, he's a star.' Later, when he was warmed up, John began to recite and roar his *Dream Songs* and Hurt unconsciously returned the compliment. He had never read Berryman then, but he was sure of what he heard, as Berryman dipped and dived through falsetto, innuendo, jive talk, blackface coonery, all the startling range of his new work. 'That man has genius,' said Hurt, listening in astonishment, 'And it's burning him up,' he added, prophetically.

Indeed it was. Now that his job was over, John seemed to be drinking at random. There was a tray on the lawn, for instance, and instead of keeping to one drink, he just poured whatever was nearest to him into his glass, whiskey, gin, vodka, white wine, an impossible mixture. In all my experience of Dublin drunks, even Fintona alcoholics, I had never seen the like. Some months later he called on me in Paris with his wife and daughter. It was a more subdued evening, but again he paid no attention to what he was drinking, as long as it was alcoholic. By the kind of coincidence that seems to characterize a real destiny, there was another American there who had been the tenant after Berryman in the New York flat where he wrote 'The Imaginary Jew'. John's daughter sat on his knee and laughed and pulled his beard, but when I remarked on that afterwards my wife's reaction was classically swift and French.

205

'She'd better enjoy him now,' she said grimly, 'she won't have him long.'

A tense, bespectacled intellectual against the background of a draughty Nissen hut in Iowa, a shaggy benevolent prophet holding forth in Jack Ryan's pub in Beggar's Bush; those were the two opposing faces of John Berryman for me, as though, under the pressure of experience, he had followed Yeats's prescription and found his own opposite. There was a final face, or absence, after the conflagration of achievement.

Twice when I was reading at the University of Minnesota I called to see him. On the first occasion he was drying out in a local hospital, the famous Golden Valley which Bellow memorably describes in his preface to *Recovery*. He shuffled out of an Alcoholics Anonymous lecture, hands twitching, face pale and uneasy as he greeted me. We talked a while in his room while he squatted on his yoga mat, but there was little heart to it. The contrast between our previous meetings in Dublin when he would roar out his latest dream songs, good, bad or indifferent, lovely or awful or 'delicious' (his own phrase for praise), was too abrupt. He had recognized his alcoholism now, and he was fighting valiantly against it, although he was clearly ill at ease in such a restrained life. For not only his habits but his habits of work were linked with drink; the ramshackle structure of *The Dream Songs* is based as much upon the ups and downs of the chronic drunk as anything else, the *longueurs* and sudden revelations, the licence to bore and blaze,which are part of any *Long Day's Journey into Night*.

Our last meeting was for dinner at his house a month before he died in 1972. A new baby swung from a cot suspended from the middle of the room. He was still quiet, but more talkative, in directions that surprised me. He emphasized, for example, that he had been going to both the Catholic church and the synagogue, which seemed to me a novel version of Pascal's wager. We had rarely discussed religion before and since there was only water to drink I found it hard to match the intensity of his new quest. But if I was taken aback by the purity of such a regime, he was thrown by the ardour of the young lady who was acting as my guide. It turned out that she and Kate Berryman had been to the same Catholic girls' school and John was eager to know how she managed to reconcile religion and sex, since she was still a practising Catholic. 'Oh,' she said, her young brow shining, 'every time I make love with a man, I go to the altar rails, to thank God for having sent him.' John's brow bulged with theological wonder; clearly he felt that if such prelapsarian ardour had been more common in the Catholicism of his youth, his path might have been easier.

[1974]

A BALLAD FOR BERRYMAN

John, a letter or a song
to celebrate our heady hours together;
memories to warm this filthy Irish weather,
of that long dreepy Dublin winter
we both had to suffer.

Hot toddies in Beggar's Bush
while you decanted another rush
or run of your fermenting *Dream Songs*.
I was still young, aghast at genius,
concerned about your happiness,

Finding a place, pals for the evening,
a practical hero-worshipper, only half understanding
your long turmoil or *hegira*
from our first meeting in Iowa
to Jack Ryan's barn-like bar.

Soon after, you came through Paris,
blundered your way up the rue Daguerre.
To Esteban, working under his cameo of Baudelaire,
you slowly pronounced, in stentorian French:
'*Où est le poète Irlandais ?*'

And Claude soft-footed across the way:
'*Il y a un Moïse Américain
qui te demande!*' Behold, behind him
then your great beard appeared; Henry,
grinning from ear to ear.

20

THE IMPACT OF INTERNATIONAL
MODERN POETRY ON IRISH WRITING

> . . . *portes ouvertes sur l'exil,* doors open on exile.
> St John Perse, translated by Denis Devlin

Let us begin with a simple geographical fact. Ireland is an island off
the coast of England, facing, across three thousand miles of ocean,
towards America. Anything grown there, whether animal, vege-
table, or mental, is bound to be affected by its geographical position
and consequent climate. An Irishman may travel, but the memory
of his maternal landscape persists. So Denis Devlin, the most
resolutely cosmopolitan of recent Irish poets, and the one whose
name will be most invoked in this essay, can begin one of his finest
love poems – 'Renewal by Her Element' – with an image of

> The hawthorn morning moving
> Above the battlements

and end with a cadence like Austin Clarke's 'Pilgrimage':

> My landscape is grey rain
> Aslant on bent seas.

Although the poem between owes more to modern French love
poetry, Aragon or Éluard, than to anything in the English or Irish
traditions, it curves back to these primal, very Irish images.

But while accepting that they are marked by Ireland, our countrymen have a long habit of exile, most often through necessity, but
also through curiosity. It seems to me significant that the first two
poets whose names are recorded in our literary history (after the

mythical Amergin, the bard of the Milesians) were both exiles. Columcille's only real subject matter was his native country but he might not have described it with such longing if he had been able to return.

> Clamour of the wind making music
> in the elms:
> gurgle of the startled blackbird
> clapping its wings.

> I have lost the three settled places
> I loved best:
> Durrow, Derry's ledge of angels,
> my native parish.

And then we have Sedulius Scottus, who was in charge of the cathedral school at Liège in the middle of the ninth century, together with four other 'charioteers of the Lord, lights of the Irish race'. I am not competent to judge his position in medieval Latin poetry, but what strikes one in the poem on his patron Bishop Hartgar's palace – 'Vestri tecta nitent luce serena' – is the ease with which he moved against this international background. And why not, when the most original philosopher of the period was an Irishman, John Scotus Erigena, and a scholar-poet like Sedulius could establish himself, as Professor James Carney, his translator, says, as 'a social personality, the friend of emperors and high ecclesiastics':

> Your halls are gleaming with a light serene
> and latest style in art adorns the scene
> with beauteous forms to populate your home
> And many merry colours in your dome. . .

All this may seem far removed from the problems of contemporary poetry but what I am trying to show is that while Irishmen often have to leave Ireland to learn, there was a period when they went to teach as well, when they formed a natural part of European civilization. The decline of the Irish Church, and successive invasions, may have obscured this relationship, but it could be of relevance again today. For in the first half of the twentieth century, Joyce in prose, and Synge and O'Casey in the theatre, re-estab-

lished Ireland as a presence in world literature, a proud tradition
still maintained by Beckett. The only literary art in which we have
not made our presence felt is the one in which we are supposed to
excel; this is, poetry. Yeats apart, few Irish poets have been
accepted as international figures in the way that Pablo Neruda is,
or Octavio Paz, or Ungaretti.

I place Yeats apart because his position is, as always, a richly
ambiguous one. In my only conversation with Auden, I remember
wondering how Yeats had managed to live and work in Dublin,
enduring 'the daily spite of this unmannerly town'. Auden dryly
remarked that, if one looked at the career of Yeats, it was extraordinary how often he was out of Ireland. The years in Woburn
buildings we know of, and his association with the Rhymers' Club.
But we should also remember that, despite his poor French, Yeats
had not only read Mallarmé (from whom he got the title 'The
Trembling of the Veil') but visited Verlaine, and attended, however reluctantly, the first night of Jarry's *Ubu Roi*.

Now Yeats may have learnt from the symbolist movement, but
even his long friendship with Ezra Pound did not make him part of
the international movement in modern poetry. He might learn
from his juniors how to make his language more active but he
remained faithful to what he regarded as the great traditional
themes of poetry. 'We were the last romantics', he said grandilo-
quently. This is part of the ambiguity I spoke of; there is also the
significant fact that he is very little read in Europe; Eliot, and more
recently, Pound, are much better known. This is partly due to the
absence of good translations, a situation which is being remedied,
but also the seeming archaism of his subjects. It may well be that
the later Yeats, the great meditations on politics and history, will
enter the European consciousness only as the great wheel dips
down towards the end of the century. I met a Yugoslav poet
recently who explained how his translation of the Byzantium
poems had created a whole new school of poetry in Serbo-Croat.
As we are sadly learning again, few writers have given better
expression to post-revolutionary disillusion:

> Hurrah for revolution and more cannon-shot!
> A beggar upon horseback lashes a beggar on foot.
> Hurrah for revolution and cannon come again!
> The beggars have changed places, but the lash goes on.

Louis MacNeice is the only Irish poet to form a natural part of the English literary scene; after Auden he was the most gifted poet of the thirties. Their collaboration in *Letters from Iceland* is an example of poetry confronting the problems of a period as they arise. The precedent of Byron is capital for both of them (MacNeice pays homage to him in 'Cock of the North') with his wide-ranging, almost novelistic gift. But Byron was much more of a European phenomenon than MacNeice, or even Auden, ever succeeded in being, and those who present MacNeice as a corrective example to more locally based Irish poets tend to forget this. So far as I know, Louis MacNeice has rarely been translated into another language, and even in America his reputation has never been high.

I am not denying his sensibility, nor the obsession with transience and death which is his most moving central theme. I am just saying that his work is very much in the non-experimental tradition of English modern poetry, and, as such, nearly unexportable. Paradoxically though, the one aspect of his influence which seems to me particularly healthy is his diversity of landscape: the ease with which northern poets, like Seamus Heaney and Derek Mahon, seem to move in the outside world may well derive from MacNeice's restless photographic eye. Few American poets, for instance, could equal his description of New York in 'Refugees' where the skyscrapers

> . . heave up in steel and concrete
> Powerful but delicate as a swan's neck

and the trains leave 'from stations haughty as cathedrals'.

To sightsee, though, is not necessarily to accept the influence of another culture: for MacNeice, Spain, Greece, India are backgrounds against which he defines his personal problems.

> This year, last year, one time, ever,
> Different, indifferent, careless, kind,
> Ireland, England, New England, Greece –
> The plumstones blossom in my mind.

It is interesting to compare his Indian poems with one by another Irish poet of the same generation describing a great

Buddha head at the Cambodian temple of Ank'hor Vat:

> No Western god or saint
> Ever smiled with the lissom fury of this god
> Who holds in doubt
> The wooden stare of Apollo
> Our Christian crown of thorns:
>
> There is no mystery in the luminous lines
> Of that high, animal face
> The smile, sad, humoring and equal
> Blesses without obliging
> Loves without condescension;
> The god, clear as spring-water,
> Sees through everything, while everything
> Flows through him. . .

The great interest of Denis Devlin is that he is the first poet of Irish Catholic background to take the world as his province. The initial influence on his work was French and in his first volume the aesthetic is a blend of *poesie pure* and surrealism, with the poem as a sequence of images, without reference to anything outside itself, without an obvious plot or story. This passage, for example, joins the spray of a fountain with the memory of someone playing the spinet, the connection being not so much in the mind as in the senses of a hidden observer, perhaps the poet:

> The tendrils of fountain water thread that silk music
> From the hollow of scented shutters
> Crimson and blind
> Crimson and blind
> As though it were my sister
> Fireflies on the rosewood
> Spinet playing
> With barely escaping voice
> With arched fastidious wrists
> to be so gentle.

Samuel Beckett compared this passage to a late poem by Hölderlin, which was heady praise for a young poet. And Devlin had studied German romanticism, from Goethe through Novalis to Hölderlin, as well as a good deal of Italian and Spanish poetry. The plangent opening of 'Meditation at Avila' shows the influence of both St Teresa and St John of the Cross:

> Magnificence, this terse-lit, star-quartz universe,
> Woe, waste and magnificence, my soul.
> Stand in the window. Fountain waters
> Bloom on invisible stems.

What makes the poems in his second volume more accessible is their increasing ease both in line and language, something he certainly learnt from his American contemporaries. During his period as first secretary in Washington he made friends with Allen Tate and Robert Penn Warren, who subsequently edited the American edition of his *Selected Poems*, and he could hardly help but be familiar with the great generation that preceded them, poets like Stevens, Eliot, Hart Crane (whose dense style resembles Devlin's), and Cummings. The result is this new kind of colloquial vigour:

> 'No, we can't get a licence for liquor, being too near the church,'
> Said the waiter. The church looked friends enough
> On its humble, grassy hillock. So I said: 'Excuse me,
> I must have a drink.' And I rambled on down West Street,
> To eat and drink at Socrates the Greek's.

It is when this ease is matched by an important theme, often a religious one, that Denis Devlin nears greatness. We may not have produced a Catholic novelist in Ireland, but in certain poems of Austin Clarke and Denis Devlin our racial drama of conscience smoulders with intellectual passion:

> All is simple and symbol in their world,
> The incomprehended rendered fabulous.
> Sin teases life whose natural fruits withheld
> Sour the deprived nor bloom for timely loss:
> Clan Jansen!
>
> ('Lough Derg')

I have preferred to concentrate on Denis Devlin as the most dedicated poet of his generation, and one whose work suggests possibilities for the future. In ways that are difficult to define (perhaps because the imperial habit dies hard, and the British Council is a more subtle version of the *Pax Britannica*) an Irish writer has a better chance of being a European than has an Englishman.

213

Samuel Beckett's first poem, for example, was a monologue on Descartes, and we know where that led him. And his friend Brian Coffey's translation of Mallarmé's greatest poem has never received the attention it deserves, as a possible example of non-iambic structure, of the use of the page in a kind of musical notation, all this before Charles Olson:

> waking
> > doubting
> > > rolling
> > > > shining and musing
> > > > > before halting
> > > > > at some latest point which crowns it

Because of the potent example of James Joyce, the Dublin poets of the early thirties tended to be French-influenced and apolitical. The long career of Ewart Milne, who in old age turned to anti-Communism, seems only to illustrate the savage epigram of Robert Frost:

> I never dared to be radical when young
> For fear it would make me conservative when old.

But he was one of the few Irish poets to assume a revolutionary Marxist position, and to strive for a kind of popular poetry, derived perhaps from the example of Lorca. He has travelled widely and his vision of 'The Martyred Earth' is a moving piece of rhetoric:

> Rivers empty chemical wastes into the seas,
> On their ocean feeding grounds the fish cannot feed,
> The herrings die and the herring fleet is disbanded. . .

The apocalyptic vision is carried even further in 'A Place of Testament':

> When mountains were oceans I sat down to warn
> For I couldn't believe all our tribe was gone. . . .

And his rebuke of his contemporaries in 'Deirdre and the Poets' could be a light-hearted version of my present theme:

> Though they leap for the lights of the great continents
> And cry from afar like the lapwing guarding his nest,
> Though they talk to the wall in their towns and villages
> And strive to clothe my bones in the ivy of the arch;
> Yet their voices are not heard among the halls of the
> > nations –
> It's time I got me a new set of poets;
> There's never one of all the lot I'd pardon,
> *Said the sore-tried woman of the roads.*

The most genuine political poet of the thirties was Charles Donnelly, who died in Spain at the age of twenty-three. Clearly he owes a lot to Auden's clinical style, but he was not playing with the idea of 'the inevitable increase in the chances of death', just preparing for it, in case it should be his own. I must confess that I find his last poem, which was posted up for the Lincoln Battalion on what they called *The Lincoln Wall Newspaper*, after he was killed on 27 February 1937, exceedingly moving, the most mature expression we have of that martyr's urge which lies at the heart of revolutionary action. Especially Irish revolutionary action; it is the kind of poem Padraig Pearse should have written –

> Between rebellion as a private study and the public
> Defiance, is simple action only which will flicker
> Catlike, for spring. Whether at nerve-roots is secret
> Iron, there's no diviner can tell, only the moment can show.
> Simple and unclear moment, on a morning utterly different
> And under circumstances different from what you'd expected.
>
> Your flag is public over granite. Gulls fly above it.
> Whatever the issue of the battle is, your memory
> Is public, for them to pull awry with crooked hands,
> Moist eyes. And villages' reputations will be built on
> Inaccurate accounts of your campaign. You're name for orators,
> Figure stone-struck beneath damp Dublin sky.

Donagh MacDonagh, who knew Charles Donnelly at the university, wrote an elegy for him. He also wrote poems on modern European history, like 'Fontainebleau':

> The surging power of war and of words
> Springs out of some dark fissure
> Varnish of culture cannot touch. . .

215

But that was when he was young, and here we strike against a dismaying aspect of our literature, our tendency to regress from an advanced position. Thus MacDonagh's early work was intellectual and urban (he wrote his MA thesis on Eliot) but he gradually retreated to a simplified version of the Irish tradition. Again I am not saying that Ezra Pound is necessarily more important than Aodhagan O'Rathaille for an Irish poet (one has to study both) but the complexity and pain of *The Pisan Cantos* are certainly more relevant than another version of 'Preab san Ól'.

Another false trail, from the point of view of this essay, is the work of W. R. Rodgers, the parson poet from County Armagh. His *Awake! And Other Poems* appeared in 1941 and its cascade of language might almost have been a warning to other Irish poets, caught in a neutral backwater:

> Always the arriving winds of words
> Pour like the Atlantic gales over these ears. . .

And sure enough, there were poems with Audenesque titles like 'Directions to a Rebel', 'War-Time', and even 'End of a World'. According to those close to him, however, Rodgers had not read Auden, or even Hopkins, which is astonishing: can one imagine a physicist, however remote, who had never heard of Neils Bohr or Schroedinger?

The scientific analogy is always partly false, but does illustrate my point: if one is going to be influenced by contemporary poetry outside Ireland, it should be at first hand and not by hearsay, years after the event. Having participated in one of the early readings of *Howl*, I found it depressing when the Ginsberg wave broke over Ireland a decade later, drowning many potential young poets. There are always those writers, like Dylan Thomas or even Patrick Kavanagh, who are so possessed by a private vision that their only real task is to protect it. But we move in a world which is increasingly both local *and* international, and in poetry, as in science, there is nothing so irrelevant as repeating someone else's experiments.

The best work of W. R. Rodgers, therefore, seems to me to be in his second book, a handful of religious and love lyrics which are colloquial in diction, but traditional in imagery. But the necessary task of providing Ireland with a contemporary poetry still had to be continued. After Austin Clarke had blossomed in his seventies, one tended to forget how reactionary his critical position was in those years, anything experimental being gloomily described as 'modernism'. Yet his later work, from *Pilgrimage* onwards, parallels modern experiment elsewhere and reveals a talent as considerable as that of Tate, Ransom or Muir. The main opposition to the neo-Gaelic lobby during and after the War years was Valentin Iremonger, whose jazzy rhythms and use of urban slang can be seen in 'Icarus'.

> But star-chaser, big-time-going, chancer Icarus
> Like a dog on the sea lay and the girls forgot him,
> And Daedalus, too busy hammering another job,
> Remembered him only in pubs. . .

More effective, because less programmatically modern, was his beautiful adaptation of John Crowe Ransom's 'Bells for John Whiteside's Daughter' to record another, very Irish, death:

> Elizabeth, frigidly stretched,
> On a spring day, surprised us
> With her starched dignity and the quietness
> Of her hands clasping a black cross.

If I say that Auden was the liberating example for Irish poets in the late fifties, I may seem to be contradicting myself, but by then he was no longer a contemporary, but an established phenomenon, looming over the English scene like a latter-day Dryden. Besides, the subject matter was so different: when Thomas Kinsella adapted one of his master's most typical stanza forms for his love poem, 'A Lady of Quality', it became both a homage and a comparison:

> 'Ended and done with' never ceases,
> Constantly the heart releases
>   Wild geese to the past.
> Look, how they circle poignant places,
> Falling to sorrow's fowling-pieces,
>   With soft plumage aghast.

The wider an Irishman's experience, the more likely he is to

understand his native country. So Pearse Hutchinson's translations from the Catalan, as well as being good poetry, directly
illustrate the problems of a minority culture. And in the image of
'The Dying Gaul', Desmond O'Grady, who lives in Rome, finds a
point of entry into our racial history. I have already mentioned the
naturalness with which northern poets respond to the outside
world. I am thinking of Derek Mahon's Canadian poems, Seamus
Heaney's lovely poem about driving through France:

> Signposts whitened relentlessly.
> Montreuil, Abbéville, Beauvais
> Were promised, promised, came and went,
> Each place granting its name's fulfilment.

And in 'Conversations in Hungary, August 1969', John Hewitt
finds himself discussing the problems of Belfast in a modern
context:

> Our friends at Balaton, at Budapest
> days later also, puzzled, queried why,
> when the time's vibrant with technology,
> such violence should still be manifest
> between two factions, in religion's name. . .

The attentive reader will have noticed that, with the best will
in the world, I have begun to equate international travel and
international poetry; it is a measure of ambivalence about my
subject. Although Irish poetry seems to me in a more healthy state
than at any time since the beginning of the century, it is still in
many ways a conventional, non-experimental poetry. Ironically
enough, our freest metrist was Austin Clarke, but his high spirits
showed more in his mastery of forgotten stanza forms, than in any
creation of new ones. The majority of Irish poets write as though
Pound, Lawrence, Williams, had not brought a new music into
English poetry, as though the iambic line still registered the curve
of modern speech. Thus the powerful mid-section of Thomas Kinsella's *Nightwalker* is muffled by the old-fashionedness of its form,
and what should have been a cautionary parable for all emerging
nations (for nothing resembles one post-revolutionary civil war
more than another) remains too heavy in movement and refer-

ence; he has discovered a new subject, but not, I feel, a new metric to energize it.

And this is where the example of Denis Devlin seems to me important. He was not completely successful in his efforts (because he did not publish enough his language lacks ease, and there is a vein of sentimentality in poems like *The Heavenly Foreigner*) but he wanted to write a poetry that would be as good as the best anywhere in the world. Like a composer or a painter, an Irish poet should be familiar with the finest work of his contemporaries, not just the increasingly narrow English version of modern poetry, or the more extensive American one, but in other languages as well. In his *Envoy* Diary Patrick Kavanagh declared that, as far as he was concerned, Auden was an Irishman. Less extravagantly, I would say that my contemporaries are not just the Irish poets I admire, but those with whom I feel an affinity elsewhere, Ponge in France, Octavio Paz in Mexico, Gary Snyder and Robert Duncan in San Francisco. I seem to be advocating a deliberate programme of denationalization, but all true experiments and exchanges only serve to illuminate the self, a rediscovery of the oldest laws of the psyche. For years I had been trying to find the rhythm in which to write a public poem, something that I could place beside Robert Duncan's great meditations on contemporary America, and not feel ashamed. When it finally came, it took the shape of a broken line, with two beats on either side of the caesura. Like the explorers of the North-West Passage, I had gone round the world in order to discover the oldest metric in English, the only public one, the Anglo-Saxon line. And the poem contained one of the most personal passages I had ever written; I will end with it now because it is about exile and return, and my earliest awareness of the relationship between the outside world and Ireland:

> Lines of leaving
>   lines of returning
> the long estuary
>   of Lough Foyle, a
> ship motionless
>   in wet darkness
> mournfully hooting
>   as a tender creeps
> to carry passengers

        back to Ireland
a child of four
        this sad sea city
my landing place
        the loneliness of
Lir's white daughters'
        ice crusted wings
forever spread
        at the harbour mouth.

[1973]

BIOGRAPHICAL NOTES

1929 (28 February) Born at St Catherine's Hospital, Bushwick Avenue, Brooklyn, New York, third son of James Montague and Mary ('Molly') Carney. His father had gone to New York in 1925 to join his brother John, after involvement in local republican activities in Co. Tyrone, selling his farm for unsuccessful business ventures, and failing to find employment. Mother and two elder brothers joined father in Brooklyn in 1928. His uncle Tom Carney also comes to live with them later.

1933 John and his brothers are sent back to live with relations in Ireland, sailing on the Cunard White Star Line. He has the measles during the crossing and remembers the attention of nurses and other members of the crew. The boys are met at Moville, Co. Donegal, by relatives from both sides of the family; they lunch in Derry before going on to the Carney home in Fintona, Co. Tyrone, where the older boys remain with their maternal grandmother and other Carney relations. John is taken (at his father's insistence) to the Montague home in Garvaghey, Co. Tyrone, where he is to live with his aunts, Brigid and Freda Montague. The house is situated on the remaining farm and is also the local post office. It is part of the legacy of his grandfather, John Montague, who had been a Justice of the Peace and a successful farmer and businessman. The house is filled wth mementoes (pictures, Bibles, etc.) of the Montague family, and John explores the unoccupied rooms. He enjoys the life on the farm and takes his part in the various chores.

1935-8 Enters Garvaghey Primary School; he enjoys his junior school experiences, teacher and classmates. He is considered a good student and is singled out for his ability to read aloud.

1936 John's mother returns to live in the Carney home, Fintona, Co. Tyrone. She makes yearly visits to Garvaghey, and he spends some holidays with his family (mother and brothers).

1937 Transferred to the senior side of Garvaghey school. On the first day in his new surroundings he is made to stand in front of the school and read aloud, reports of his ability having preceded him to the new teacher. Frightened and intimidated, a stammer breaks out for the first time.

1938-41 Transferred to Glencull Primary School, two miles away, where he is encouraged and admired by his new master, Harry McGurren. A priest instructs the children in the Irish language after school.

1941-6 Wins a County and College scholarship to board at St Patrick's College, Armagh. He enjoys his studies but finds the emphasis on sport in the school excessive; there is no foreign language study, for example, though he remembers with fondness his Irish master, Sean O'Boyle. He is aware of the effects of the Second World War on life in Northen Ireland: food rationing, blackouts, bombing raids, and the presence of American soldiers. He also sees German prisoners-of-war in a camp in Dungannon as he travels between home and school. Spends summer holidays during the War with his O'Meara cousins in County Longford, in the South.

1946-9 Wins a Tyrone County Scholarship to attend University College, Dublin, where he studies English and History. He finds life in Dublin after 'The Emergency' both exciting and claustrophobic; he feels himself to be an outsider (coming from the North) in an atmosphere of disillusion and isolation. Attends Roger McHugh's evening classes in Anglo-Irish literature. (Autumn) Cycles through France with a Derry friend. Publishes poems for the first time in a student magazine; wins a poetry competition organized by Austin Clarke on Radio Éireann, and the winning poems are published in The Dublin Magazine. BA with a double First in History and English.

1949 (Autumn)–1950 Begins work toward the MA in English at UCD. Succeeds Patrick Kavanagh as film critic for The Standard, a Catholic weekly newspaper. (Summer) Attends the American Seminar at Schloss Leopoldskron, Salzburg. Becomes friendly there with Saul Bellow. Travels through Austria, Italy and France.

1951 Contributes to the 'Young Writers' Symposium' in The Bell; the essay is well received but also provokes strong reaction. Sacked by The Standard.

1952 Receives prize (£100) as runner-up to John Jordan in Oxford Studentship. MA in Anglo-Irish Literature for articles on George Moore and William Carleton published in The Bell and for work on Austin Clarke. Offered a USA government- sponsored scholarship to study in the United States. Part of his intention in going to America is to visit his father in New York, but his father returns in 1952 to Tyrone where they are able to meet and spend time together.

1953 (Autumn)–1954 (Spring) Attends the Graduate School, Yale University, where he is aware of the pervasiveness of 'The New Criticism'. Robert Penn Warren is one of his teachers; he meets W. H. Auden and Robert Lowell during the year. Explores New York, staying with Eileen and Tom Carney (his uncle) in Brooklyn. Has a partial breakdown.

1954 (Summer) Attends the Indiana Summer School at the University of Indiana; works as a busboy to pay his way. Among the visitors and teachers are Richard Blackmur, William Empson, John Crowe Ransom, Richard Wilbur and Leslie Fiedler.

1954 (Autumn)–1955 (Spring) On the recommendation of John Crowe Ransom he is accepted at the Iowa Writers Workshop and given a part-time teaching position at the University of Iowa. Other students in the workshop include W. D. Snodgrass, Robert Bly, Peter Everwine, Donal Justice and William Dickey. Louis MacNeice and William Carlos Williams attend during the year to read and conduct seminars, while John Berryman leaves after being jailed. John enjoys the cosy discussion format of the workshop. He meets his future first wife, Madeleine, who is attending from France on a Fulbright. During the year they hitch- hike to New Orleans, stopping at Oxford, Mississippi. MFA from the University of Iowa for a collection of poems some of which are later included in *Forms of Exile*.

1955 (Summer) Travels extensively in Mexico visiting pre- Columbian archaeological sites, like Mitla and Monte Alban, settling for a time in Tehuantepec. Travels up the Pacific coast through Los Angeles to San Francisco and Berkeley.

1955 (Autumn)–1956 (Spring) Attends graduate school at the University of California, Berkeley, with the intention of doing a Ph.D. Through his friend Tom Parkinson, meets Gary Snyder (just returned from China and Japan) and Allen Ginsberg. Enjoys the student and 'beat' life where poetry is read, talked about, and 'lived' at parties and happenings at which Kenneth Rexroth often acts as 'compere'. Is present at the first reading of *Howl*.

1956 (October) Marries Madeleine de Brauer in Normandy, France, and sails back to Ireland, to a job recommended by Roger McHugh.

1956-9 Settles in 6 Herbert Street, Dublin, where Brendan Behan is a neighbour. Works at Bord Fáilte Éireann proof-reading, arranging publications, and writing speeches for various officials. Finds Dublin more open and interesting than before, with Austin Clarke and Patrick Kavanagh actively publishing, and new young writers beginning to emerge with the encouragement of Liam Miller of the Dolmen Press. Begins work on a collection, revising some early poems and writing new ones which appear in *The Irish Times*, *Threshold* and *Studies*. Begins work on a dissertation at UCD taking Oliver Goldsmith for his subject. Meets painter Morris Graves, who restores Woodtown Manor.

1958 (Christmas) *Forms of Exile* published by the Dolmen Press. Corresponds with Theodore Roethke and Robert Graves.

1959 Resigns from Bord Fáilte when his wife begins work at the French embassy. At work on an expanded collection of poems and a book of short stories for which he receives a commission from MacGibbon & Kee, London. The first-written of these stories, 'That Dark Accomplice', had been accepted for publication in *The Bell* in 1951 but subsequently rejected because the editor did not like the portrayal of the priest in the story. (8 November) Father dies in Tyrone after seven years back.

1960 Wins the May Morton Memorial Competition (£50) for 'Like Dolmens Round My Childhood, the Old People' and goes to Belfast to receive the award in the Assembly Rooms of the Presbyterian Church. Later the poem is read on the BBC (NI) 'Arts in Ulster' radio programme, but the 'Wild Billy Harbinson' stanza is excised. Travelling down home to Garvaghey from Belfast he plans the sonnets which open *The Rough Field*. Meets Theodore Roethke in Dublin and takes him to meet Mrs W. B. Yeats. Helps to found Claddagh Records with Garech Browne.

1961 Takes part in a poetry reading at the Hibernian Hotel Dublin with Richard Murphy and Thomas Kinsella. Moves to Paris and settles at 11 rue Daguerre, Montparnasse. He is Paris correspondent for *The Irish Times* (attends President de Gaulle's press conferences) during the final months of the Algerian War and until late 1963. He very much enjoys life in Paris at this time, especially the life of the 'quartier'. He describes himself as 'a little fish in a big pond' because around him are such world figures as Beckett, Ionesco, Sartre, Giacometti and others, whom he sees and meets on the streets. *Poisoned Lands* published in London. Edits *The Dolmen Miscellany of Irish Writing*.

1963 Essay entitled 'The Rough Field' appears in the *Spectator*. Works at editing *Collected Poems* of Patrick Kavanagh for MacGibbon & Kee.

1964 (Spring) Teaches the Poetry Workshop at the University of California, Berkeley. *Death of a Chieftain and Other Stories* published in London. Meets Robert Duncan, Louis Simpson, Thom Gunn and other poets in the Bay Area. Writes 'All Legendary Obstacles'.

1965 (Spring) Again teaches at Berkeley. Actively working on the various sections of *The Rough Field*. Witnesses the beginnings of the Free Speech Movement at Berkeley and the opposition to the war in south-east Asia; visits students in jail on political and drug charges. Decides not to stay.

1966 *Patriotic Suite* is the first section of *The Rough Field* to be published as a Dolmen Chapbook after rejection by *Studies*. Continues to work as literary director of Claddagh Records, Dublin (since 1960), arranging recordings during the years from 1962 to 1975 of Austin Clarke, Patrick Kavanagh, Thomas Kinsella, Robert Graves, Seamus Heaney, Hugh MacDiarmid and others reading their own works.

1967 (Spring-Summer)–1968 (Spring) Teaches Anglo-Irish Literature at University College, Dublin and lives in Anglesea Street. *A Chosen Light* published in London. Engaged in work on *The Rough Field*, translations from the Irish, and, when Valentin Iremonger is unable to carry on because of illness, begins work as editor of *The Faber Book of Irish Verse*.

1968-71 Lives in Woodtown Manor now owned by Garech Browne and teaches at UCD. *Hymn to the New Omagh Road* and *The Bread God* sections published by Dolmen Press. Living off and on in Paris, but for lengthy periods in Ireland as his first marriage breaks up. Is in Paris during the Spring 1968 student/worker demonstrations, where he meets his future second wife. Reads *A New Siege* outside Armagh Jail.

1970 (Spring) Teaches at the Experimental University of Vincennes. *Tides* published in Dublin, Autumn Recommendation of the Poetry Book Society, London. (Autumn) Tours with John Hewitt as 'The Planter and the Gael', giving poetry readings in Northern Ireland sponsored by the Arts Council.

1971 (April) Second reading tour with John Hewitt in Northern Ireland. Receives a bursary (£250) from the Arts Council of Northern Ireland to help complete *The Rough Field*. (October) Attends the funeral of his friend Sean O'Riada, in St Gobnat's, West Cork.

1972 *A Fair House: Versions of Irish Poetry* published by the Cuala Press, Dublin. *The Rough Field* published in Dublin. Liam Miller arranges a reading in the Peacock Theatre, Dublin, on 11 December 1972, with music by the Chieftains. The performance is broadcast in two parts by Radio Éireann. Marries Evelyn Robson in Gloucester, Mass., and they begin to set up house in Cork, first at Roche's Point then on Grattan Hill in the city. John had been encouraged earlier by Sean O'Riada to come, and this is now made possible when he is offered an assistant lectureship in the English Department at University

College, Cork. Represents Ireland at a Poetry Festival in Yugoslavia. Begins his association as contributing editor of the magazine *Exile* in Toronto where he publishes work in progress and translations from the French.

1973 Represents Ireland at 'Fanfare for Europe' in London and Edinburgh. A performance of *The Rough Field* is presented by the British Irish Association at the Roundhouse, London, on 8 July 1973. (August) First child, Oonagh, born in Cork. (11 November) His mother dies in Enniskillen.

1974 Brings Hugh MacDiarmid to University College, Cork. *The Faber Book of Irish Verse* published. Represents Ireland at a Poetry Festival in Rotterdam. (Summer) Teaches at the State University of New York at Buffalo. (Autumn) Begins work on *The Dead Kingdom* while on the Dublin-Cork train.

1975 A *Slow Dance* published in Dublin, Christmas Recommendation of the Poetry Book Society, London. Helps to arrange return of Robert Graves to Ireland in his eightieth year: the events are filmed by RTE. (Summer) Teaches at the University of Toronto. (Autumn) Lives on Vancouver Island.

1976 Receives the Irish American Cultural Institute Award ($4000) at a presentation in Dublin. Says he can now 'put new slates on the house or take a trip to Greece'. Continues *The Dead Kingdom* and puts slates on the roof.

1977 A new and extensively revised edition of *Poisoned Lands* published in Dublin. Contributing editor of *Poesie* (Paris). He and his wife publish *November*, a choice of translations from the French, for the visit of André Frenaud to Ireland in April. (Summer) Teaches at the University of Vermont.

1978 *The Great Cloak* published; it will receive the bi-annual Alice Hunt Bartlett Award (£200) from the Poetry Society of Great Britain. Brings Michel Deguy (editor of *Poesie*) to Ireland.

1979 Travels in northen India. *The Leap* published in Dublin and Massachusetts. Founding member and first president of Poetry Ireland. (5 December) Second daughter, Sibylle, born.

1980 Receives a Guggenheim Fellowship. Second performance of *The Rough Field* at the Roundhouse, London, on 17 February during the 'Sense of Ireland' Festival. His mother's home in Fintona, Co. Tyrone, known locally as 'The Poet's Pub', is wrecked by a 100lb bomb set off in the centre of town.

1979-81 Attends Rudloph Steiner reading group in Cork. At work on *The Dead Kingdom* and *Selected Poems*. Attends the International Poetry Festival, Toronto, May 1981. Encourages new generation of poets at Cork.

1982 Visiting Professor at the Sorbonne. Delivers 'The Unpartitioned Intellect' at American Conference of Irish Studies (ACIS) in Vermont. Suffers arthritic attack and convalesces in Greece. Summer at La Montagne Noire. (September) Park Atwood Clinic near Birmingham, England. *Selected Poems* appears.

1983 Directs the Galway Writers Workshop. His wife's first show in Triskel Gallery, Cork. First summer in Mauriac near St Emilion, where he starts *The Lost Notebook*, and other stories.

1984 Second trip to India as guest of India government. Summer in Mauriac. *The Dead Kingdom* published.

1985 Writer in residence at Albany, New York, and (Autumn) Berkeley, California. Summer in Mauriac. Starts gathering *Bitter Harvest*.

1986 Attends Poetry Conference, Florence. His elder brother Turlough dies, as will his friend and publisher Liam Miller, and his cousin Brendan, all in their early sixties, and all from cancer, within the year. Is finally made an Associate Professor at UCC.

1987 Arranges the transfer of his papers to the Buffalo Poetry Collection, where he first saw Joyce's papers in 1956. Third trip to India for a conference on Spirituality. (May) Awarded D.Litt. by State University of New York (SUNY) and is received by both Houses of New York State Legislature. *The Lost Notebook* published.

1988 Resigns from University College, Cork, after sixteen years, to become a full-time writer again. First Hughes Award presented for *The Lost Notebook*. Spends half the year in Mauriac. *Amours, marees* published by William Blake in Bordeaux. *La Langue Greffée*, translations by Deguy, Esteban, Marteau and others, published by Belin in Paris. *Mount Eagle* appears in Ireland.

1989 Sixtieth birthday celebrations. American and English editions of *Mount Eagle, Hill Field*, a Montague festschrift, the anthology *Bitter Harvest, The Figure in the Cave and Other Essays*, and *New Selected Poems* published in Ireland and America.

ACKNOWLEDGMENTS

Thanks and acknowledgments are due to the editors and publishers of the books, periodicals and newspapers in which the following chapters of this volume originally appeared.

1 'Tyrone: The Rough Field': *The Spectator*, 26 April 1963 and *Conor Cruise O'Brien Introduces Ireland*, André Deutsch, 1969.
2 'The War Years in Ulster': *The Honest Ulsterman*, 64, Sept. 1979–Jan. 1980.
3 'The Unpartitioned Intellect': *Irish Writers and Society at Large*, ed. Masaru Sekine, Irish Literary Studies, No. 22, 1985.
4 'A Primal Gaeltacht': *The Irish Times*, 30 July 1970 (under title 'An Gaeltacht Inniu').
   'I Also Had Music': originally written for publication in *Hibernia*, 1971.
   'A Note on Rhythm': *Agenda*, 10, Autumn-Winter 1972-73.
   'Tides': *The Poetry Book Society Bulletin*, Autumn 1970.
   'On Translating Irish without Speaking It': Preface to *A Fair House*, Versions of Irish Poetry, The Cuala Press, 1972.
   'A Slow Dance': *The Poetry Book Society Bulletin*, Winter 1975.
   'Poisoned Lands': Introduction to 2nd Edition, *Poisoned Lands*, Dolmen Press and Oxford University Press, 1977.
   'The Rough Field': Preface to 3rd Edition, *The Rough Field*, The Dolmen Press, Blackstaff Press and Wake Forest University Press, 1979.
   'The Dead Kingdom': *The Poetry Book Society Bulletin*, Spring 1984.
5 'Oliver Goldsmith: The Sentimental Prophecy': *The Dolmen Miscellany of Irish Writing*, eds John Montague and Thomas Kinsella, Dolmen Press, 1962; and a shortened version in *The Art of Oliver Goldsmith*, ed. Andrew Swarbrick, Vision and Barnes & Nobel, 1984.
6 'William Carleton: The Fiery Gift': *The Bell*, April 1952.
7 'George Moore: The Tyranny of Memory': *The Bell*, August 1951.
8 'James Joyce: Work Your Progress': *Irish University Review*, Vol. 12, No. 1, Spring 1982.
9 Based on a speech delivered on 9 December 1986 in Trinity College, Dublin, at the launch of *Hermathena*, Winter 1986, a special issue for Samuel Beckett's eightieth birthday.
10 'In the Irish Grain': Preface to *The Faber Book of Irish Verse*, 1974.

11 'Louis MacNeice: Despair and Delight': *Time Was Away: The World of Louis MacNeice*, eds Terence Brown and Alec Reid, Dolmen Press, 1974.
12 'Kinsella's Clarke': *The Irish Times*, 17 July 1976.
13 'Patrick Kavanagh: A Speech from the Dock': *The Irish Times*, 5 and 8 July 1980 (under title 'Collecting Kavanagh').
14 'John Hewitt: Regionalism into Reconciliation': *Poetry Ireland*, 3, Spring 1964.
15 'Hugh MacDiarmid: The Seamless Garment and the Muse': *Agenda*, 5, 1967-68.
16 'The Young Writer and *The Bell*': *The Bell*, October 1951 (under title 'Contribution to the Young Writers' Symposium').
17 'Fellow Travelling with America': *The Bell*, June 1951.
18 'American Pegasus': *Studies*, Summer 1959.
19 'John Berryman: Henry in Dublin': *Hibernia*, 24 May 1974 (under title 'John Berryman's Exile: Memoir of the American Poet in Dublin').
20 'The Impact of International Modern Poetry on Irish Writing': *Irish Poets in English*, ed. Sean Lucy, The Mercier Press, 1973.

Most of the above essays and reviews have been modified or amended for this volume. The poems 'Scotia' and 'A Ballad for Berryman' were published in *Mount Eagle*, The Gallery Press, 1988. The texts used here include some variants.

Mark Waelder's assistance in the compilation of the 'Biographical Notes' is gratefully acknowledged, also that of his wife Karen Waelder, who typed 'the lost manuscript'.

This book is published with the assistance of The Arts Council / An Chomhairle Ealaíon, Ireland.

In *Benets Readers Enc.*

INDEXED IN *EGLI 1990*

DATE DUE

R0127831579 humca   S 824
                     M759

Montague, John
The figure in the cave and
       other essays

R0127831579 humca   S 824
                     M759

Houston Public Library
Humanities